BUFFALO BILL

and the

MORMONS

BRENT M. ROGERS

University of Nebraska Press
Lincoln

Portions of this book previously appeared in Brent M. Rogers, "When Buffalo Bill Came to Utah," *Utah Historical Quarterly* 87, no. 2 (Spring 2019): 116–31.

The University of Nebraska Press is part of a land-grant institution with campuses and programs on the past, present, and future homelands of the Pawnee, Ponca, Otoe-Missouria, Omaha, Dakota, Lakota, Kaw, Cheyenne, and Arapaho Peoples, as well as those of the relocated Ho-Chunk, Sac and Fox, and Iowa Peoples.

Library of Congress Cataloging-in-Publication Data
Names: Rogers, Brent M., author.
Title: Buffalo Bill and the Mormons / Brent M. Rogers.
Description: Lincoln: University of Nebraska Press, [2024] | Includes bibliographical references and index.
Identifiers: LCCN 2023016565
ISBN 9781496213181 (paperback)
ISBN 9781496238689 (epub)
ISBN 9781496238696 (pdf)
Subjects: LCSH: Buffalo Bill, 1846–1917. | Latter Day Saints—West (U.S.)—History—19th century. | Pioneers—West (U.S.)—History—19th century. | Buffalo Bill's Wild West Show. | Bighorn Basin (Mont. and Wyo.)—History—19th century. | West (U.S.)—History—19th century. | BISAC: HISTORY / United States / State & Local / West (AK, CA, CO, HI, ID, MT, NV, UT, WY) | RELIGION / Christianity / Church of Jesus Christ of Latter-day Saints (Mormon)
Classification: LCC F594.B94 R64 2024 | DDC 978/.02088289332—dc23/eng/20230912
LC record available at https://lccn.loc.gov/2023016565

Set in Minion Pro by A. Shahan

Once again for Ashley, Keagan, Makinsey, and Braxton

Contents

Illustrations

Acknowledgments

This project has been a part of my life for a long time. I'm not even sure how far back it goes. Maybe it started during childhood road trips from California to visit relatives in Nebraska and Kansas and passing by Buffalo Bill's Scout's Rest Ranch in North Platte, Nebraska. Maybe it began in the historic Sutter Creek Theatre, where, as a nineteen-year-old, I went to the performances of my good friend Lanae Rhodes in *Annie Get Your Gun*. It can certainly be traced to opportunities I had in graduate school at the University of Nebraska–Lincoln, where I had the good fortune to work with Doug Seefeldt. Among other projects, Doug included me in the Papers of William F. Cody and introduced me to Kurt Graham and Jeremy Johnston, both of whom have supported me and my research along the way. Working with the Cody Papers took me from a latent to an invested interest in understanding Buffalo Bill and his world. That opportunity put me on a trajectory that has shaped my career. Working on the Cody Papers positioned me to land a job with the Joseph Smith Papers Project, which has given me untold experiences and has supported my family for more than a decade.

Wherever it began, the momentum for this project coalesced in the mid-2010s. While I was finishing my first book on Utah Territory's place in national discourse on popular sovereignty, a question about Buffalo Bill kept troubling me. Why, in his autobiography, did William F. Cody claim to have gone to Utah as an eleven-year-old boy during the 1857–58 Utah War? Was he really there? If not, what did that manufactured memory mean to him and his celebrity? What did it mean to contemporary readers and admirers of his day? I became determined to find out more about Buffalo Bill's Utah connections and what they meant.

Soon after my first book came out in 2017, a senior scholar asked me what I was working on next. I mentioned these questions about Buffalo Bill and his ties to Utah and the Latter-day Saints. This person curtly queried, "Well, who the hell would care about that?" I cannot recall how I answered in the moment, but my answer is that I care. The anxiety that moment generated did not deter me from the research and has calmed over time as I have compiled findings and interacted with a host of individuals about this project. This book is the result of my journey and my best effort to find out more.

Buffalo Bill has taken me all over. I have had the privilege to travel throughout Wyoming, Nebraska, Kansas, Utah, and Arizona. I have gone to Chicago, Denver, and New York City in search of answers. And I have been able to experience Las Vegas, New Mexico, and Glasgow, Scotland, in search of Buffalo Bill and his influence. I am glad for the experiences that have come because of these historical adventures.

The research travel for this book was made possible, in large part, by a Resident Fellowship of the Buffalo Bill Center of the West, in Cody, Wyoming. I am most thankful to that institution and its excellent staff. In particular, I thank Deborah Adams, Linda S. Clark, Sam Hanna, and Jeremy Johnston. These individuals opened their archival treasure trove and were generous with their time and knowledge. The Buffalo Bill Center of the West also funded my travel to the Newberry Library in Chicago. The Charles Redd Center for Western Studies at Brigham Young University awarded me a Charles Redd Fellowship Award in Western American History, which funded my research on Abraham O. Woodruff and the Latter-day Saints who moved to Wyoming's Big Horn Basin. The Church History Department of The Church of Jesus Christ of Latter-day Saints provided me a publication grant to help complete the book. I am humbled by the generous support of these individuals and institutions.

In addition to the help of the aforementioned people and institutions, several individuals have shared or directed me to research material. I am especially grateful to David and Grant Barnes, Kathryn Burnside, Steve Friesen, Janiece Johnson, Jake Olmstead, and Mike Seegmiller for opening new avenues of research. Several others have read parts of the book along the way, including Brett Dowdle, Holly George, Matthew Godfrey, David Grua, Matthew McBride, and Jed Rogers. Darcee Barnes deserves a special recognition. Not only did she share her expert knowledge on Wyoming's Big Horn Basin, but she also read early drafts and commented on the entire manuscript. I am indebted to her for the wisdom she shared with me. My friends Spencer McBride and Brenden Rensink also read and provided insights on the whole manuscript. Just as Kurt Graham was there at the beginning of my scholarly journey with Buffalo Bill, he was there at the end, reading the whole book and giving encouragement along the way. I also want to thank Brian Cannon, Matt Grow, Jason Heppler, Mike Homer, Terrance Rucker, Brian Sarnacki, Michelle Tiedje, Emily Utt, Brad Westwood, and Rebecca Wingo. The staff at the University of Nebraska Press is top-notch, especially Bridget Barry, an extraordinary editor and a better person. Her enthusiasm and support for this project have never wavered. Thank you, Bridget! I am also grateful for the excellent editorial eye of Susan J. Silver. Her substantive questions and copyedits brought a fine polish to the text; anything that is amiss is solely my responsibility. Many other colleagues, friends, family, and acquaintances have indulged me as I have talked about this project. I thank all for their warmth and support.

My family has been right by my side through this whole journey. Ashley, Keagan, Makinsey, and Braxton, my words cannot adequately express my love for each of you. We have already written so many stories together. I am excited for the next chapters of the new stories that we will write together and that you will write on your own. To the rest of my family: thank you for your love and support. It is felt and appreciated.

I also want to acknowledge sleepless nights and carpooling to different children's activities. The uninterrupted quiet of the early morning hours and later dropping children off at basketball practice or acting class, then heading to the closest fast-food establishment, usually a McDonald's or Del Taco, to write for forty-five minutes to an hour, propelled the production of this book. That's how this book was written, in fits and starts, an hour here and an hour there (usually in a restaurant)—that and with a lot of Coca-Cola. Portions of every chapter were worked on over lunches at Sticky Bird Red Barn Farms in Farmington, Utah. I am grateful to the staff for their kindness and their overall mission to support addiction recovery.

And finally, thank you for reading this book. I hope you enjoy it!

A Note on Style

The church founded by Joseph Smith in 1830 was called the Church of Christ. In 1834 the name changed to the Church of the Latter Day Saints. Then, in 1838, the church adopted the name The Church of Jesus Christ of Latter-day Saints. While this has remained the church's official name since 1838, throughout its history the church has been alternately referred to as the Mormon Church or the LDS Church. Other individuals, institutions, and practices trace their religious origins to Joseph Smith and exist under the umbrella terms of Mormon and Mormonism. This book is specifically about William F. "Buffalo Bill" Cody and his history, interactions, and relationship with The Church of Jesus Christ of Latter-day Saints, its history, and its adherents. This book uses the official name of the church as appropriate and uses "the church" as shorthand. When referring to church members, this book uses "Latter-day Saints," "Saints," and "Mormons" interchangeably.

This book relies heavily on nineteenth- and early twentieth-century historical documents, in which the spelling and grammar is often erratic. In quotations from these documents, the original spelling and grammar are preserved, unless they impede understanding and are then silently corrected.

This book also engages with the history of a region in northwest Wyoming defined by a mountain basin. That area, in modern and governmental usage, is often referred to as the Bighorn Basin. The single-word usage of "Bighorn" refers to natural geographic features. The variant spelling for those features and the area is Big Horn Basin. The two-word usage of "Big Horn" has typically been connected with human establishments such as towns and counties. "Buffalo Bill" Cody and the Latter-day Saints did not differentiate between natural geographic features or human establishments. In their advertisements and writings, both Buffalo Bill and the Saints called the region, its features, and human establishments by the two words "Big Horn." Therefore, this book will use the two-word variant for consistency and to match historical use, except for rare instances when naming the natural geographic features requires the single-word usage.

BUFFALO BILL

and the

MORMONS

ACT I

Introduction

Buffalo Bill Greets the Saints

At his home in the Big Horn Basin town of Cody, Wyoming, the town he had founded four years earlier, on a frigid cold evening in mid-February 1900, William F. "Buffalo Bill" Cody readied himself for an important meeting.[1] The nearly fifty-four-year-old Cody sported his signature goatee and long, pulled-back hair, now with a salt-and-pepper coloring that was growing more salt than pepper under his cowboy hat. His handsome face had become puffier with age, but he remained the ideal white western American man in the hearts and minds of an adoring international fanbase.[2] Over the past thirty years, first as a stage actor and then as the figurehead of arguably the world's most popular outdoor exhibition, Buffalo Bill had built a brand as the exemplar of white American conquest of the West.

Buffalo Bill was not content sitting atop the entertainment world. The ever-ambitious Cody branched out into other ventures, including the founding of the town that bore his name. He hoped the town, nestled in the Big Horn Basin, would become not only a western metropolis but also a launching point for the exploration of western America. The wealthy and famous Buffalo Bill had, however, struggled to attract permanent settlers and the infrastructural investment needed to make his dream town a reality. As he prepared to brave freezing temperatures and travel about fifteen miles from his home to the stage station at Eagle's Nest to meet a group of potential settlers, the showman assumed the role of land agent and booster. The group that he hoped to sell on the region consisted of fourteen members of The Church of Jesus Christ of Latter-day Saints, commonly called Mormons. It included Abraham O. Woodruff, a member of the church's second-highest ecclesiastical body, the Quorum

3

1. Profile of William F. "Buffalo Bill" Cody, circa late 1890s.
Buffalo Bill Center of the West, Cody, Wyoming, Buffalo Bill
Museum, MS006 William F. Cody Collection, P.6.0870.06.

of the Twelve Apostles, and a son of former church president Wilford
Woodruff. Yet, if the Mormons had become the settlers that Buffalo Bill
so earnestly sought, it would require a dramatic plot twist in the entrepreneur's storied life.

William Cody's adventures had brought occasional contact with the
Mormons, but usually in antagonistic ways. As an eleven-year-old boy,
Cody claimed to have joined the wagon train of Russell, Majors, and

Waddell, the company supplying the U.S. Army traveling west to Utah in 1857 to suppress an alleged Mormon rebellion.[3] During the next fifteen years, Cody experienced life on the plains of Kansas and Nebraska as a U.S. Army scout (for which he earned a congressional Medal of Honor in 1872) and as a buffalo hunter. Cody's life and exploits caught the attention of dime-novelist Ned Buntline, who introduced Cody to show business. Embracing the naturalist movement in theater and literature, plays written for Cody featured the plainsman acting onstage as himself. His first performance was in an 1872 play titled *The Scouts of the Prairie*, which Buntline had written expressly for Cody. It featured a heroic Cody rescuing a woman taken captive by a lascivious, polygamous Mormon man and his American Indian allies. That first play was a commercial success and helped launch Buffalo Bill's acting career. Cody soon formed a traveling variety show, taking that act, and eventually others, to stages across the United States.

As much as Mormons played villainous foils in some of Cody's earliest plays, it was the performance of *May Cody, or Lost and Won*, from 1877 to 1879, that cemented the anti-Mormon reputation of Buffalo Bill's early stage career. This play reenacted the "sensational, startling, [and] intensely interesting" Mountain Meadows Massacre, the real-life killings of a California-bound train of emigrants by Mormons in southern Utah Territory in 1857.[4] Playing out publicly just prior to the premiere of this stage performance was the 1876 trial for and 1877 execution of John D. Lee, a longtime Latter-day Saint, adopted son of powerful Mormon leader Brigham Young, and the only person held legally responsible for his role in the massacre.

Buffalo Bill's timely anti-Mormon stage performances gave a face, voice, and visual portrayal to the most negative tenets of Mormonism. At a time when both American politics and culture targeted Mormons, popular audiences craved an "authentic" view of the religious sect that Cody's shows displayed. Those performances depicted Latter-day Saints largely through the lens of violence, lustful depravity, and the presentation of the polygamous home as imagined in popular culture.[5] American audiences witnessed on the stage the difference in the home dynamics and lifeways of the defamed religious group. Buffalo Bill, on the other hand, emerged as the symbolic champion and defender of the proper, monogamous American home and family.

While *May Cody* brought in large crowds and considerable profits, it was notoriety gained from his service as an army scout and taking "the first scalp for Custer" in the Indian Wars that catapulted Cody into stardom. His re-creation of a duel with a Cheyenne soldier onstage was wildly popular. He soon outgrew the stage and in 1883 introduced Buffalo Bill's Wild West show, an outdoor exhibition of horsemanship, historical reenactments, and gun shooting. Ten years later, following overseas travel and performances for European royalty, Buffalo Bill Cody introduced a new, improved, and more diverse Buffalo Bill's Wild West and Congress of Rough Riders of the World during the 1893 World's Columbian Exposition in Chicago.[6] Buffalo Bill's celebrity increased. By the time of the February 1900 meeting in the Big Horn Basin with Abraham Woodruff and his Latter-day Saint contingent, Cody was perhaps the most famous, or at least recognizable, American of his time. With his visibility Cody helped shape the social and cultural currents of the day, giving credibility to popular conceptions and misconceptions.

With fame came fortune. Buffalo Bill was generous, especially with loved ones and friends. He bought his sister a house and newspaper press and put his former boss, Alexander Majors, on an annual retainer. Cody invested in a dizzying number of ventures, but it was his town in the Big Horn Basin of Wyoming that captured his attention—and a great deal of his funds. The picturesque oval basin in northwest Wyoming is cradled by the Big Horn, Owl Creek, Bridger, and Absaroka Mountains. The powerful Shoshone River cuts through its center to form, what Cody deemed, a natural paradise. The effort to build up the town of Cody specifically, and the basin generally, demanded water. This was true of all the arid West: irrigation was a fundamental prerequisite for success. But by the 1890s the Shoshone River had not yet been harnessed for the region to realize its agricultural and urban potential. To prove that the basin was a paradise found, Buffalo Bill needed to construct an irrigation empire, but his efforts to do so had floundered quickly.

Buffalo Bill knew where to look to solve his irrigation issues, and it was 450 miles to the southwest. In an April 1898 letter to the land agent C. B. Jones in Galesburg, Illinois, Cody wrote of the possibilities of the Big Horn Basin and the blueprint to realize the promise. "We have only to look at what the Mormons have done in the great Salt Lake Valley," he explained, "which at the time of its settlement was the most desolate of deserts . . . and today there is no more prosperous and wealthy state on the continent . . . than Utah." Cody concluded that greater results could be accomplished in the Big Horn Basin by following the example of Latter-day Saints.[7]

Mormon Utah had indeed set an example for making arid lands productive. Through religious devotion, sacrifice, industrious enterprise, community cohesiveness, and centralized planning, the Latter-day Saints developed an archetype for irrigation and reclamation in the inhospitable West.[8] Early observers took note of the crystalline streams, bountiful gardens, impeccable order, and diligent productivity in Salt Lake City.[9] Though scorned for decades as religious, even racial, others, Mormons increasingly embraced and marketed themselves as prime examples of American economic and agricultural civilization. By the 1890s Latter-day Saints had claimed their place as hardy pioneers in a nation increasingly infatuated with the symbolic pioneer. The physical transformation of their environment contributed to their economic capabilities and growth within the region. Reclaiming the land through labor may have been a devotional act, but it had a worldly outcome.

⁓⁓⁓

William F. Cody's views on Mormons before the 1890s are largely inferred from his stage performances, autobiography, and other writings. Though his plays were authored by others, and some writings attributed to him were ghostwritten, Cody lent his increasingly popular name to them and approved their messages. It seems clear that he, like most Americans, had an overwhelmingly negative view of the religious group in Utah. That opinion started to change for both Cody individually and Americans collectively following the church's end to the practice of polygamy in 1890.

Buffalo Bill observed Mormons in a new light when he visited Utah in late 1892 on a hunting trip to the Grand Canyon and in search of a place to establish a big-game preserve. Just after his trip through southern Utah and north to Salt Lake City, according to a *Washington Post* report of the expedition, Cody described the Latter-day Saints as "law-abiding, energetic, and hard-working people" and, as far as he could judge, "good American citizens."[10] The famous plainsman extolled the Mormons' work to develop irrigation infrastructure and technology to reclaim the Salt Lake Valley. "Out of a desert they have made a garden spot," Buffalo Bill declared after witnessing the fruits of Latter-day Saint labor.[11] Cody respected what he observed from the Saints. That personal experience added a new layer to his understanding of the untapped potential of the intermountain region of the U.S. West. It also helped him see the long maligned religious group as an American exemplar in its own right.

The Utah Mormon example was on display the next year at the Chicago World's Fair. Crowds gathered at the Utah Agricultural Pavilion through-out the fair's six-month operation to view and understand the scientific results of irrigation that brought to a place, "where once the verdure of Nature was unknown, fields of growing grain, bounteous orchards and vineyards." Mormons were becoming a model in the physical alteration of the region from a barren and desolate landscape to one of productive and useful lands, at a time of increasing importance for the politics of irrigation and reclamation of arid lands as the nation's growth shifted west-ward. The agricultural displays, irrigation maps, and statistics attested that Utah yielded "more wealth from the soil per capita, than any other State," all of which created a favorable impression of the industrious Latter-day Saints.[12] Meanwhile, Buffalo Bill exhibited his Wild West and Congress of Rough Riders in front of packed grandstands just outside the world's fair grounds. While in Chicago Cody invited Wilford Woodruff, then president of The Church of Jesus Christ of Latter-day Saints, and other leaders into his tent for a friendly visit, renewing the niceties established in Salt Lake City the year before.

The relationship between Cody and the Mormons had thus been formed when Buffalo Bill set out for Eagle's Nest station that freezing night in

February 1900 to meet Wilford Woodruff's son, Abraham, and his company. But Cody was not the only one courting the help of the Mormons. By 1900 many western speculators, town builders, and state officials had made overtures to recruit Mormon settlers for labor to irrigate the Intermountain West. Investment brokers, real estate agents, and irrigation companies in Montana, Idaho, Colorado, and Wyoming all reached out to bring in Mormon settlements.[13] They understood what Buffalo Bill did when he labeled Latter-day Saints as "the greatest irrigators on earth." As the visit with the Mormon group approached, Buffalo Bill spoke with high praise about the Latter-day Saints. In an interview with a midwestern newspaper in January 1900, he exclaimed, "Look what they did with the Salt Lake country! Well, I expect them to do the same thing in the way of irrigation in the Big Horn basin."[14] This popular national and international figure, an influential man who helped create a shared representation of and vision for the American West, had accepted the Saints.[15]

What was in it for the Mormons? For Abraham O. Woodruff, the twenty-seven-year-old apostle in charge of church colonization efforts, interest in northwest Wyoming had its roots in the economic climate of Utah. Though celebrated at the Chicago World's Fair, Utah's agricultural base was not immune from national economic trends, and the state suffered financially following the depression of 1893. By 1900 Utah and its residents faced an inadequate number of jobs and amount of available farmable land. As one southern Utahn said, "About 1900 it was apparent the country was too small for everyone to make a good living."[16] Woodruff and church officials ever anxious to place their people in a position to succeed became highly interested in the economic opportunity of the Big Horn Basin settlement. Buffalo Bill Cody and his company held most of the valuable land and water rights alongside the Shoshone River in the Big Horn Basin.[17] Securing his support and assistance for Mormon colonization to the area, Latter-day Saint leaders hoped, would be of mutual interest and provide a new prospect for financially beleaguered church members in the Intermountain West. This opportunity brought the young apostle and thirteen other Latter-day Saints to Eagle's Nest that cold February night.

Buffalo Bill greeted his guests warmly and regaled them with stories of his life. Listening with rapt attention to their genial host, the Saints enjoyed Cody's tales, even those from his supposed time with an army charged with subduing their people in 1857. Buffalo Bill had metaphorically fought against the Mormons during the second half of the nineteenth century. But Cody changed his stance toward the religious minority with the dawning of a new century. He now spoke in reverential tones about the religious group as American pioneers. The futures of Buffalo Bill, the Mormons, and the Big Horn Basin now seemed inextricably linked.[18]

The famous entertainer invited the Mormon group to visit his home, but they had other plans to visit a different part of the basin on their trip. Before parting ways Cody embraced the opportunity to advertise the economic potential of the region. According to Latter-day Saint settler James Wasden, Cody was undeniably a promoter who "had vision of the possibilities of this country."[19] The dream rested in the availability of land and the ability to harness water from the Shoshone River.

Before the meeting ended, Cody presented his religious visitors with a bold, if desperate, proposition. He told Abraham Woodruff and his party, "I have secured a permit to irrigate nearly all of the lands on the north side of the Shoshone River, from Eaglesnest to the Big Horn River, but if the Mormons want to build a canal and irrigate the land down lower on the river I will relinquish both land and water to them, for if they will do this I know they are the kind of people who will do what they agree to do."[20] What an offer! Free land and water rights to a substantial tract of land showed Buffalo Bill's desperation and business acumen—and a bit of his signature generosity.[21] The famous scout saw tremendous value in his liberal offering. It had the potential to bring hundreds of settlers willing to fund and construct their own canals that would in turn create essential infrastructure and encourage more settlement and business opportunities in Cody's basin paradise. Their shared past reconciled and reinterpreted, Cody and his Mormon guests parted ways with an eye toward their shared future.

Like a play in two acts, this book illuminates the fascinating story of Buffalo Bill and the Mormons. The first act starts from Cody's birth in 1846 and examines his alleged participation in the Utah War, his anti-Mormon stage performances and their context in the 1870s and 1880s, and his visit to Utah and interactions with Utahns in the 1890s. The second act further investigates the events leading to the meeting at Eagle's Nest, the settlement of Latter-day Saints in the Big Horn Basin, and the sometimes-contentious relationship that emerged between Cody and the Saints thereafter. The second act unveils the changing aspects of Cody's personal feelings toward the Saints juxtaposed against his public representation of that group.

Buffalo Bill Cody and the Mormons play dynamic protagonists in this history. For Cody the Latter-day Saints first represented a threat to the home and American society, a concept he, his writers, and other cultural influencers exploited for personal profit. That threat became neutralized for Cody and others as the religious group publicly abandoned its practice of plural marriage, utilized its whiteness to align with mainstream culture, and demonstrated the economic potential of the arid West.[22] For the Latter-day Saints, Cody represented first prejudice and then the personification of American acceptance. He became the means of a business opportunity and finally someone the Saints called a friend.

Like two parallel tracks of a railroad that meet at occasional junction points, the interlocking histories of these two pillars of the American West, Buffalo Bill and the Mormons, provide insights into more than sixty years of U.S. political, cultural, economic, and environmental history. Their shared history is a story of the complexities of perception and self-interest. Theirs is a history about creating narratives, those that were true and those that they wanted to be true. And it is a reminder that the stories we tell one another matter and the stories we tell about others matter even more.

— *1* —

Setting the Stage

On the outskirts of Le Claire, Iowa, near the west bank of the Mississippi River, sat the modest log cabin and farm of Isaac and Mary Ann Laycock Cody. The two had met and married in Cincinnati, Ohio, in 1840 before moving to Iowa Territory later that year. Together they worked the land surrounding their cabin, and Isaac drove a passenger stagecoach to provide for their growing family. In that cabin, on February 26, 1846, Mary Ann Cody delivered the couple's third child, a son they named William Frederick.[1]

Earlier the same month and approximately 120 miles southwest from William Cody's birthplace and on the opposite bank of a curve in the Mississippi River, members of The Church of Jesus Christ of Latter-day Saints, better known historically and colloquially as Mormons, or Latter-day Saints, began their flight from Nauvoo, Illinois. Living near a river town, especially one so close to the information and transportation hub of Davenport, Iowa, Mary Ann and Isaac Cody had likely heard about the Mormons—and not just about their religion but about the years of troubles they had with their neighbors that led to their westward exodus in February 1846.[2]

⁓⁓⁓⁓

The first Latter-day Saint wagons crossed a frozen Mississippi River into Iowa Territory on February 4, 1846. Thousands more left Nauvoo over the coming months. A newspaper commented on the mass departure but expressed concern that the religionists had begun their journey too early in the season "before the winter has terminated, and long before grass shall appear, upon which to subsist their cattle and horses." These conditions portended a journey that would be "hazardous, and likely to be attended with severe trials and much suffering."[3]

The Saints, though, were anxious to leave an increasingly untenable position.[4] In late June 1844 Joseph Smith, the founder of the Latter-day Saint faith, and his brother, Hyrum Smith, were murdered by a mob while being held in a jail in Carthage, Illinois, on charges of treason. Their deaths were the culmination of more than fifteen years of violent persecution at the hands of the church's critics in Illinois and Missouri before that. Prejudice and discrimination toward the Mormons only increased in the months that followed, and the Saints' prospects to remain peacefully in Illinois diminished quickly.

As president of the Quorum of the Twelve Apostles, the second-highest governing body in The Church of Jesus Christ of Latter-day Saints, Brigham Young, a man unflinchingly devoted to Joseph Smith and his faith, filled the leadership void left in the wake of the murders. He was a strong leader who could still teach a master class on organization and order. He presided over the church in a tumultuous time. The tensions between the Saints and their neighbors fluctuated between verbal threats and physical violence. The strain came to a head in early 1846. Illinois governor Thomas Ford led Young to believe that a federal army was en route to Nauvoo to arrest him and the faith's other leaders. Young readied the citizenry of Nauvoo to leave their homes at a moment's notice; the Saints organized in companies with hundreds of horses, oxen, cows, and wagons, ready to start westward.[5]

Brigham Young, however, wanted to ensure that the Saints had the opportunity to attend special religious ceremonies and ordinances in the temple, an edifice sacred to Latter-day Saints, before they left Nauvoo. After nearly five years of work, the Nauvoo Temple was ready for religious services in December 1845. So great was the anxiety among church members to receive their religious rites in the temple that Young was worried they would have to remain in Nauvoo longer and face capture, or worse, from their enemies. During the first weeks of 1846, Young spent most of his days and nights tirelessly administering ordinances to the Saints. Having suffered for more than a decade and receiving no assistance from any level of government, the time had come to move to a place where they could govern themselves. On February 3, 1846, Brigham Young said it was time to "be away from this place immediately."[6] The next day the Saints began their trek toward the Rocky Mountains.

Thousands trudged, painfully slow, through mud across Iowa before reaching the west bank of the Missouri River in the summer of 1846. There, just north of present-day Omaha, Nebraska, the Latter-day Saints established a temporary headquarters. The following spring Brigham Young and a vanguard company of 143 men (including enslaved Black men Green Flake, Hark Lay, and Oscar Crosby), three women, and two children departed their winter refuge. Traveling in wagons and blazing a new trail across the plains on the north side of the North Platte River, Young and the Saints ventured into the Rocky Mountains.

The company rejoiced as it reached a point that overlooked the Salt Lake Valley in late July 1847. One of the Saints, Orson Pratt, enthusiastically wrote in his journal, "[We] ascended this hill, from the top of which [was] a broad valley. . . . We could not refrain from a shout of joy which almost involuntarily escaped from our lips the moment this grand and lovely scenery was within our view."[7] Brigham Young, sick with fever, sat up in a wagon and purportedly pronounced, "This is the right place; drive on!"[8] The Latter-day Saints had found a site for a city of refuge more than one thousand miles west of American settlements, at an intersection of Great Basin Indigenous peoples' homelands, which they named Great Salt Lake City.

By the end of 1847, two thousand settlers had arrived, and over the next decade immigration swelled the number of white residents in the Salt Lake Valley and surrounding settlements to more than forty thousand. The Latter-day Saints flocked to this Great Basin valley in such large numbers that they could control the politics, economy, culture, and social structure. There were almost no other white settlers. They had found the place they had longed for: a place apart, a new sacred space where they could practice their religion and protect themselves. Their choice of location, however, was in an arid region with limited natural resources. Access to water was a major concern. The lack of rainfall and groundwater in the area made an irrigation system essential for growing crops to sustain themselves. One Latter-day Saint, Samuel Rogers, reported in his journal, "In this country the settlers occupy the valleys near the streams so that they can lead the water upon their fields and gardens as irrigating the land."[9]

From their earliest settlement in the Salt Lake Valley, church leaders and members instituted a program of community control over water resources. Church members dug canals for the good of the community, providing access to water for all even during times of drought. Digging a canal or constructing a water ditch was as important an act of religious dedication as Sabbath worship.[10] This cooperative system, overseen by church leaders, was markedly different from water rights in other parts of the United States. Cooperation and cohesion helped the Saints' settlement flourish in the Great Basin. Over the next few years, Mormon immigration poured in, and by 1852 Latter-day Saints had established hundreds of colonies or settlements, from southern California to northern Utah and everywhere in between.[11]

During the time the Saints struggled to move west and began to establish an empire in the Great Basin, the Cody family was also on the move. In 1849 the Codys left the log cabin of William's birth and moved to a two-story frame home overlooking the Mississippi River in nearby Le Claire, Iowa. The move was a step up for the Cody family, and they now lived in what they considered a good, proper American home. William spent the next four years of his childhood in that house. He had his first equestrian experience, received a basic education at the village school, and spent much of his time swimming, sailing, and stealing fruit from neighboring orchards.[12] But it was also in Le Claire that the family faced its first tragedy: William's older brother, Sam, died at the age of twelve after being crushed by a bucking mare.

In 1854, looking for new opportunities and knowing that immense tracts of land to the west and south were on the cusp of opening to large-scale white settlement, the Cody family moved again. This time they settled in Kansas Territory in the Salt Creek Valley west of Fort Leavenworth and north of Topeka. The Iowa transplants now lived at a crossroads of overland travel. The excitement and wonder left an indelible imprint on young William. Never one to sit still very long, William yearned to be out on the move and often was, despite his mother's best efforts. His mother was a devout reader of scripture and encouraged Bible study in their Protestant Christian household. Mary Ann had presented her son with a Bible, which he spent some time reading while injured as a youth. But William was apparently ambivalent about religion, an uncertainty he carried through most of his life.[13] Instead, the young man observed with great interest the movement of the plains.

William was impressed by the considerable number of wagons that passed by bound for Utah and California. He marveled at the droves of travelers, cattle, and white-covered wagons congregating around the streams near his home. The curious boy questioned his father about this westward flow. Isaac taught his son about the trails and the people. He educated young William to distinguish between California-bound emigrants, government freighters, and Mormon wagons. He warned his son to steer clear of the latter, especially for fear of catching "the cholera." Latter-day Saints and other overland travelers suffered from this waterborne infection, though Isaac's admonition may have been a subtle insult as well. Mormons were viewed as people to avoid. Equating Mormons with diseased peoples or disease carriers would have only reinforced the view of the religious group as undesirable. During one father-and-son outing, Isaac and William watched as the Mormons held a funeral service for companions who had died on the trail. William heeded his father's cautions to be wary. He later said that he would hold his breath when passing a Mormon burial site to keep from catching a disease. Learning about the movements of peoples and goods from his father, as well as breaking horses, encountering Native Americans, hunting and scouting, and living on the plains generally, left a great impression on the boy.[14]

As many children do, William revered his father. Isaac Cody had been a local politician and a justice of the peace in Iowa. He was an abolitionist who did not shy away from stating his opinions on controversial issues. He swore he would exert all his power to prevent slavery from taking root

in his new homeland. Proslavery advocates attacked Isaac for his sentiments and harassed his family, but the Cody patriarch continued to give
speeches espousing a Free-Soil ideology, which opposed slavery and its
expansion as a threat to white men's free labor and economic potential.
Isaac worked hard to prevent slavery's expansion into Kansas. During
one speech, amid jeers and threats, a man with a bowie knife pounced
on Isaac, stabbing him twice before bystanders interfered. Isaac barely
escaped with his life. His wounds continued to trouble him but did not
prevent him from promoting his Free-Soil platform. Territorial politics
influenced the Cody home, which became the site of Free Kansas rallies.
Free-Soil voters eventually elected Isaac to the Topeka legislature, the free-
state government formed to compete against the proslavery legislature
that had already been established.[15]

Violence erupted between the state's proslavery and antislavery pro-
ponents. Raids, theft, destruction, and even murder were commonplace
in the territory in the mid-1850s. In late May 1856 proslavery warriors
ransacked Lawrence, Kansas, burning down a Free-Soil meeting place and
destroying affiliated newspapers. Such attacks were met with retaliatory
guerilla responses from antislavery forces. As the struggle intensified
during the 1856 summer of "Bleeding Kansas," Mary Ann Cody protected
her children and their home while Isaac attended to political matters in
Topeka.[16] The Cody home was constantly under siege from proslavery
partisans looking to silence Isaac. Always on edge, Mary Ann, William,
and the rest of the family managed to evade the ever-present danger that
summer. Isaac and the Cody home remained safe, but Isaac soon grew
ill and died in early 1857. He was just forty-five years old. Mary Ann and
her now six children were left in "poor circumstances."[17]

William, as the oldest living male in the Cody household, would have
to help provide for and protect the home fractured by the death of his
father. Mary Ann would eventually rent out rooms in the family home to
help keep the family financially afloat, but the family would rely on William's wages to survive. In this condition, living near Fort Leavenworth,
an epicenter of trade and travel, had its economic advantages. William
had herded cattle for the freighting firm of Russell, Majors, and Waddell

as a nine-year-old boy. Now, at eleven years of age, he returned to his old employer for more work.[18]

⁕⁕⁕⁕⁕

The Saints had moved into a region fraught with political and cultural conflicts. As the United States expanded its territory westward, conflicts over and in Texas sparked war with Mexico. Just after the Saints began settling in the Salt Lake Valley in 1847, the United States declared victory over Mexico. The Mexican government made a major land cession to the United States that included coveted territory on the Pacific Coast and the expanses of the Great Basin, where the Saints were establishing their new home. Accordingly, the Mormons became a major stumbling block to the incorporation of the West into the growing United States.[19]

The Latter-day Saints, from their experiences in Illinois, understood the power of local autonomy. They formed their own provisional government structured similarly to the church, with Brigham Young at the head and other ecclesiastical leading men in civil governing positions. The Latter-day Saints believed these men of God could run Christ's church. They also considered them capable men to run a civil government.[20] They did not want their society governed by strangers who opposed their will and their desire to protect their religious rights and practices.

Unfortunately for the Saints, the U.S. Congress did not grant them self-governing statehood but instead created a new territory named Utah in the Great Basin. The U.S. president appointed federal officials to govern the Latter-day Saints. Their reports, coupled with public perception, helped spark greater suspicion about the remote Saints. For example, fears of a Mormon-Indian alliance in the Intermountain West spread and intensified in the 1850s. Although the Saints' colonization of Native lands had displaced some and created competition for scarce resources that sparked conflict between the colonists and the Indigenous, reports to federal authorities and columns in newspapers painted a different portrait about their relationship. Federal officials informed authorities in Washington DC that Latter-day Saints taught the American Indians of the Great Basin, particularly Utes and Paiutes, that the Saints "were a superior

people to the Americans, and that the Americans were the natural enemies of the Indians, while the Mormons were their friends and allies."[21]
Such activities, these men believed, were subversive and violated federal
laws. Furthermore, fears that persuasive white people or groups could
turn Native peoples into enemies to be unleashed against the nation had
been embedded into the American psyche since at least the Revolutionary
War. Cultural rhetoric as depicted in newspapers, political cartoons, and
later plays and dime novels positioned Mormons and Indians as allies
dangerous to the American family in the West. They were therefore subject to ridicule, revile, and reform.

More important, officials and commentators reported on the Latter-day
Saint religious practice of plural marriage, or the marriage of one man to
more than one woman. That practice markedly plagued the perception of
the faith group. The plural marriage system had been suspected by those
outside the religious group years earlier and was a factor in the Saints'
exodus to the Great Basin. It became openly acknowledged in 1852 and
was quickly drawn into territorial politics of the era. Mormon polygamy
in Utah was intertwined with slavery in Kansas during the presidential
election of 1856, when the Republican Party introduced the proposition
to outlaw in the territories the "Twin Relics of Barbarism: slavery and
polygamy."[22] America was a heavily Protestant-leaning nation dedicated
to monogamy and Jacksonian democracy, while the Latter-day Saint
system promoted plural wives and unity of power.[23] Plural marriage and
its perceived negative effect on society in the expanding West made Mormons public enemies. The Mormons had fled one set of problems on the
banks of the Mississippi River in 1846 only to be engulfed in new crises
in the West.

Shortly after his inauguration in 1857, U.S. president James Buchanan,
the Democratic victor of the contentious 1856 election, and his cabinet
had already concluded that Latter-day Saints in Utah did not uphold
federal laws, particularly those concerning Indian affairs, or operate a
republican form of government. In a move to better manage the vast western territory, in May 1857 the Buchanan administration ordered a large
contingent of the standing federal army, ultimately led by Gen. Albert

Sidney Johnston, to Utah with the stated goal to restore and maintain "the sovereignty of the Constitution and laws over the Territory of Utah."[24] The troops assembled at Fort Leavenworth in Kansas.

⁓⁓⁓

Needing work to help his beloved mother provide for their family, eleven-year-old William Cody went to nearby Fort Leavenworth. There he found employment with the prominent government freighting and transportation company Russell, Majors, and Waddell. Cody's first job with the company was herding cattle. While corralling some cows in July 1857, the boy became engaged in a fight with an unnamed group of Native Americans on Plum Creek, which Cody described as being "on the South Platte River, thirty-five miles west of Old Fort Kearney" in Nebraska Territory. The group had run off the cattle herd Cody's envoy was driving. During the skirmish William shot and killed one of the Indians. According to Cody's later autobiography, from that time forward he "became a hero and an Indian killer." The freighters turned back to Leavenworth in July, where a newspaper interviewed William about the fight. For the first time William saw his actions glorified in print.[25]

At Leavenworth the freighting firm was busy fitting out wagons. The firm had a major government contract to supply the U.S. Army troops leaving Fort Leavenworth in the summer of 1857. They were headed to Utah Territory "to fight the Mormons," who were supposed to be in rebellion against the federal government.[26] Following his Indian fight, William Cody was apparently ready to take a new assignment from his employer. Now taken with life traversing the plains, William, against his mother's wishes, joined a supply train led by wagon master Lew Simpson, en route to Utah Territory to support the troops.

Of this time of transition, William Cody's sister Helen remembered, "Will was not long at home. The Mormons, who were settled in Utah, rebelled when the government, objecting to the quality of justice meted out by Brigham Young, sent a federal judge to the territory. Troops, under the command of General Albert Sidney Johnson, were dispatched to quell the insurrection, and Russell, Majors and Waddell contracted to transport stores and beef cattle to the army massing against the Mormons in the fall of 1857."[27] William's father had spoken out and fought against slavery in Kansas. Now the boy was ready to aid in the fight against polygamy, the other relic of barbarism. Young William certainly remembered his father's teachings about the Mormons and perhaps heard even more about the religious group from wagoners in and around Fort Leavenworth. The Mormons and their supposed rebellion were well documented in the press, and the entire nation, it seemed, wanted to bring them to heel. William must have imagined himself a great hero about to embark on a thousand-mile journey to fight a reviled foe. The trajectory of William Cody's life now seemed set to bring him into direct conflict with the Mormons.

The U.S. Army's advance infantry left Fort Leavenworth on July 18, 1857, with Simpson's train closely on its heels. On the trip west, Cody claimed to have become acquainted with James B. Hickok, the man who became "Wild Bill" and whom Cody later described as a "tall, handsome, magnificently built and powerful young fellow." Cody later described many remarkable incidents that occurred while traveling with the army wagon train along the westward trails, including his observation that the "country was alive with buffaloes."[28]

When the company arrived near Green River, in what was then northeast Utah Territory, Cody claimed that approximately twenty armed horsemen approached them. William's tale mirrored the events of October 4–5, 1857, when Latter-day Saint Lot Smith led a group of more than forty men to raid a government supply train. Smith, a veteran of the Mormon Battalion during the U.S.-Mexico War, was an experienced leader and an excellent horseman. He commanded a group of Latter-day Saint rangers during the Utah War. Since word of James Buchanan's decision to send the federal army to the Great Basin territory had reached Latter-day Saint leaders, they instructed militia units to prepare for a fight. Some were stationed in the mountain canyons to combat the invading force, while others ventured east onto the trails to burn forage grasses, stampede the army's mules and cattle, and otherwise harass the incoming troops. Smith and his group were among those going on the offensive.[29]

On the night in question the Lot Smith–led company captured and burned three Russell, Majors, and Waddell wagon trains, some seventy-five wagons in all, carrying, among other items, food, clothing, gunpowder, and whiskey for the army. One of the wagon trains that Smith's company destroyed was headed by Lew Simpson. That much is certain. Simpson gave an affidavit, or statement of facts, about the encounter shortly after it occurred. The wagon master stated that he had inspected the train and teamsters before going to gather the cattle from a nearby ravine. "We had got them up and were driving them down the ravine, when my assistant said that he saw a dust on the road west of the ravine. I had proceeded to within 50 yds. of the train, when I saw 28 men on horseback, around it, all armed with rifles and Colt's revolvers." Simpson then saw a dozen more armed horsemen on the surrounding bluffs when Lot Smith rode up to him and demanded his revolvers. Smith apparently told Simpson that he had "better give up [his] pistols by good means, or [Smith would] take them by other means." Simpson produced the weapons. The wagon master then asked Smith what he was going to do. He answered that by orders of Brigham Young he and his men were going to burn the wagon train. According to Simpson's affidavit, Smith and his crew destroyed twenty-four wagons, all loaded with government stores.[30] For his part Lot Smith later complimented the wagon master, avowing, "Captain Simpson was the bravest man I met during the campaign."[31]

Others also gave detailed affidavits of the encounter with the Latter-day Saint raiders. William Eads, a teamster, put the number of mounted Mormons in the attack at seventy-five to one hundred. "They charged on us," Eads said, "like a parcel of savages." Lot Smith gave the order to drive off the cattle, which amounted to more than seven hundred head, and to burn the wagons. Smith had his orders, according to Eads's affidavit, from Brigham Young "to burn grass, destroy all U.S. property, and scalp every soldier and officer that he could get hold of." Following the attack, Eads stated, the armed Mormons "ran the cattle over the hill, with a whoop like Indians." The teamster's retelling of events depicted Mormons and Indians as common enemies to the soldiers and the wider public.[32]

The Lot Smith–led attack was also heavily publicized in newspapers and periodicals reporting on the 1857–58 Utah War. Commentators considered the attack and burning of the government wagons seditious and as more proof of Mormon rebellion, steadfast obedience to Brigham Young, and the religious sect as a violent threat to the United States. Lot Smith became something of a hero to the Mormons for his actions. The act dealt a blow to the encroaching federal force and helped keep them in the mountains and out of Salt Lake City for the coming winter. The public exposure of Lot Smith's attack damaged army morale and placed the troops in a precarious position that winter, one that William Cody had the audacity to compare to the travails faced during the American Revolutionary War. With the loss of the goods and animals from Smith's attack, the army and teamsters were left camping in frigid temperatures near a burned-out Fort Bridger "amid privations no less severe than those endured at Valley Forge eighty-one years before."[33] The Lot Smith wagon-train burnings bolstered the perception of Latter-day Saints as dangerous enemies and provided fodder for mythmaking.[34]

William Cody's first recording of the Utah War experience was in his 1879 autobiography. His autobiography, which biographers have concluded was either written or dictated by Cody himself, indulges in a fictitious, melodramatic recounting of the Lot Smith raid. The strangers were white men armed with shotguns, rifles, and revolvers. They rapidly approached the wagon train on horseback. Before the wagon master or teamsters were aware of the danger, "three guns were leveled" at Lew Simpson. A fantastic dialogue between Simpson and one of the raiders occurred, wherein the armed stranger revealed his identity as "Joe Smith," the leader of the "Mormon Danites."[35]

The Danites, named after the tribe of Dan in the Old Testament and known popularly as both the "Destroying Angels" and "Avenging Angels," were an oath-bound military society organized among the Mormons to protect church members during their conflict with Missourians in 1838. Though they were disbanded shortly thereafter, stories of their continued existence permeated in popular thought well into the late nineteenth century and beyond.[36] Danites in these stories were the secret police of Brigham Young, armed with his approval to kidnap women into polygamy, kill apostates, and steal the property of innocent travelers, among other heinous acts. To be chased by the Danites, the marauding face of religious violence, evoked a sense of suspicion, fear, and dread about Mormons. Mid-nineteenth-century writers drummed up fictitious stories using formulaic narratives of their own creation full of titillating escapades involving Mormon polygamy and Danite pursuers. There was a lucrative market for such sensational stories about Mormons that gave writers and cultural influencers a financial boost. And because so many writers were saying the same thing, the credibility of the myth about Mormon Danites endured.[37]

Cody's inclusion of Danites in his story followed the rhetorical mode that positioned this group as a symbol of zealous adherence to Brigham Young and religious violence. In Cody's account these Mormons disarmed the whole of the wagon train and looted the supply wagons before setting them ablaze. Young William described it as "a very hot, fierce fire" that produced smoke in dense, dark clouds. With an added dramatic flair, William ended the scene in his autobiography noting that some "of the wagons were loaded with ammunition, and it was not long before loud explosions followed in rapid succession."[38] Hundreds of thousands of pounds of supplies intended for the U.S. Army had been laid to waste by Latter-day Saint avengers. The members of the wagon train were then stranded in the mountains at Fort Bridger that winter, along with the thousands of troops who had been unable to reach Salt Lake City that fall. The young Cody claimed to have suffered through the winter with the troops before returning east to Kansas the following spring.

Cody's survival of the Mormon raid and the brutal winter at Fort Bridger became part of his lore. It was prominent in the early pages of his autobiography. Others penned accounts supporting his tale, though these supporting accounts are reminiscences or histories written after the publication of Cody's own autobiography and after he had achieved international stardom. For example, in the mid-1880s the *Life of Buffalo*

AN ARMY TRAIN CROSSING THE PLAINS.

2. A wood engraving from *Harper's Weekly* depicting the U.S. Army crossing the plains during the Utah War, April 1858. Library of Congress, LC-USZ62-78976.

Bill was printed as part of a series that provided "Histories of Poor Boys who have become rich, and Other Famous People," published by the New York–based Knapp and Company. These tiny books were packed and distributed in Duke's cigarette boxes. The mini-history, which was full of inaccuracies, summed up Cody's boyhood exploits:

> In April 1857, the boy's father died, and a month afterward he started for Salt Lake City with a herd of beef cattle, in charge of Frank and Bill McCarthy, for General Albert Sidney Johnston's army. During this trip he killed his first Indian, and when he got into Leavenworth, he was interviewed for the first time in his life by a newspaper reporter, and next morning saw his name in print as "the youngest Indian slayer on the plains." He then became connected with Russell, Majors and Waddell's bull-train outfit, which then transported Government provisions, using 75,000 oxen and 8000 men for the purpose.[39]

Family members and others also provided narratives placing the young Cody in Utah Territory. Later writings of William Cody's sisters attest to his presence on the Simpson train at the time of the Lot Smith attack. Julia Cody Goodman, a sister nearly three years William's senior, stated that her brother headed to the Salt Lake Valley with Simpson's train but placed the events in the summer of 1859, two years later than the actual events. She stated that her brother and the freighting crew had "lots of trouble with the Mormons and they had their whole train taken from them," forcing William to start back to Leavenworth on foot.[40]

William's younger sister, Helen, wrote about his travails in Utah in similar tones. She noted the "double danger of Mormons and Indians," which increased her brother's pay. Helen wrote of the setback suffered near the Green River, when her brother and the Simpson train were "surrounded and overcome by a large force of Danites, the 'Avenging Angels' of the Mormon Church, who had 'stolen the livery of the court of heaven to serve the devil in.'" These tools of Brigham Young and the Latter-day Saint faith, Helen described, were "responsible for the atrocious Mountain Meadow Massacre, in June of this same year, though the wily 'Saints' had planned to place the odium of an unprovoked murder of innocent women and children upon the Indians."[41] Helen proceeded to provide her thoughts on the outcome of the trial of John D. Lee, the only Latter-day Saint brought to justice for the Mountain Meadows Massacre, whom she said "deserved his fate, but Brigham Young was none the less a coward," before she returned to the train burning and the "irksome winter" that followed.[42]

Private Robert Morris Peck, a member of the U.S. Army contingent dispatched to Utah in 1858, described his experiences from that campaign. In 1901 Peck, looking back more than forty years, stated that young William "only impressed me as a rather fresh, smart-elleck sort of a kid. The bull whackers had made quite a pet of him and one of them informed me that Billy was already developing wonderful skill at riding wild horses or mules, shooting and throwing a rope, etc." He continued, "I had almost forgotten that I had ever seen the little dirty-faced bull-whacker when . . . asking an old comrade who had been with me in Utah, 'Who is this Buffalo Bill I hear so much about?' he answered 'Why don't you remember Bill Cody, that smart little fellow that was with Lou Simpson's bull-train as an extra hand?' my recollection of him was revived."[43] Peck's account, though, is suspect, as he told it decades later after Cody had earned international notoriety and had admitted that someone else told him to remember Cody's presence in Utah.

Cody demonstrated a deep commitment to telling his supposed adventures, whether fact or fiction, in the Utah War. Later in life, the stories William spun of his childhood days sounded convincing to his wife, Louisa Frederici Cody. In her "Memories of Buffalo Bill," Louisa wrote of first meeting William Cody and hearing his life story. "It all seemed inconceivable. And yet there was something about the quiet, modest seriousness of the tone that told me that every word he was speaking was the truth," Louisa remembered. She continued, "There were no frills about Will Cody's story as he told it to me that night on the porch, no embellishments—it was only the natural story of a young man who had faced hardships and who, no doubt, was forgetting more than he told." Sitting on the porch of her family's home in St. Louis that evening, Louisa took Cody at his word as he described herding beef cattle alongside the wagon train supporting Gen. Albert Sidney Johnston's army across the plains to fight the Mormons.[44] He apparently told his tale with conviction to his prospective wife in 1865.

When William Cody met with a Mormon contingent in Wyoming's Big Horn Basin in February 1900, he elaborated on his time with the army supply train in 1857–58. To his Mormon visitors Cody reportedly recounted "his career with General Albert Sydney Johnston, who led the army to Utah in 1857. Colonel Cody was a herdboy, and when asked if the army actually suffered much for food, laughingly replied: 'We had mule meat and it took one man on each side to hold the mule up while another killed him.'"[45] His time with the army's supply train had become an entrenched part of his identity. But were his stories true?

Ample evidence suggests that Cody invented these stories. While his autobiographical account corresponded with actual events, inconsistencies in the timeline of his events in the summer of 1857 make it improbable that Cody went to Utah. The timing of William's fight and killing of an Indian in July 1857 and the departure of the Simpson-led wagon train about the same time is particularly suspect.[46] The historian Louis S. Warren, in his biography of William Cody, wrote that Cody's "account of the Mormon War and the winter at Fort Bridger is remarkably similar to the one recounted by John Y. Nelson, an old trail guide, buffalo hunter, and teamster who also claimed to have been on the Utah Expedition and to have spent the same winter at Fort Bridger that Cody did." Nelson joined Cody's theatrical troupe in 1877, two years before the publication of Cody's autobiography and the same year that Cody starred in a major anti-Mormon drama. Cody may have heard and unapologetically borrowed Nelson's account to construct his own memory of the event.[47]

If Cody did not travel to Utah, why did he manufacture, peddle, and commit to this story? Current events, goals, and knowledge can influence the constructive process of one's storytelling. This can often mean that stories or constructed memories speak more to present circumstances than to an experience of the past.[48] Cody grew up in a culture saturated with a repulsion toward Mormons, and at the time he published his autobiography, that disdain was only swelling.

Mormons, as followers of Brigham Young, a man many viewed as a dictatorial prophet, were perceived as an antirepublican threat in a region crucial to the nation's future following the Civil War. As Northerners and Southerners reconciled after the war, calls to end the remaining twin relic of barbarism flouted by the Latter-day Saints intensified. Mormons, as practitioners of polygamous marriage, were perceived as a threat to the monogamous family, an institution Americans of Cody's day were generally concerned about in their rapidly changing country.

Cody was keenly aware of the importance of defending the family unit.[49] The battle of the home was a battle of perception, and Cody wanted to be on the right side of it. These perceptions and other factors allowed Cody to write himself into history as someone adamantly opposed to the Mormon threat. It allowed him to merchandise on the growing anti-Mormon animus in America in a way that would present him as heroic and authentic. Cody's persona could be represented then as a great American protector against the popular anxieties surrounding marriage and family in post–Civil War America. Therefore, the Utah War was something that Cody felt worth attaching himself to, building his image on, and committing to his persona. In the climate of the late 1870s, Cody conveniently exploited this history and inserted himself into it to profit on national anti-Mormon sentiment.

⁓⁓⁓⁓

William Cody was not the first, and certainly would not be the last, to capitalize on anti-Mormon rhetoric and performance. Two prominent New York theaters, Burton's and Wallack's, first took advantage of the Utah War in producing contemporary dramas about the Mormon problem. Burton's Theatre, a venue for dramatic plays and various theatrical entertainments, presented *The Mormons, or Life at Salt Lake City*, a melodrama in three acts, beginning in March 1858, a time at which the outcome of the Utah War remained undecided, and Cody claimed to be waylaid in the mountains. The play, written by Thomas Dunn English, established a model for the nineteenth-century anti-Mormon stage genre. It featured a white male hero, in this play named Eagle Eye, searching for the murderer of his sister; a damsel in distress, the orphan Mary, who was about to become the seventh wife of a rapacious Mormon elder; a couple, the Woodvilles, recent converts to the Latter-day Saint faith; a corrupt New York official who turned Mormon to escape the law, furthering the image of Mormons as lawbreaking bad guys; American Indians; units of the U.S. Army; Whiskey Jake, a scout of the plains who ultimately helped free the main hero from bondage; and "the grand arch-demon" Brigham Young.[50]

The play made use of the Danite trope with the Mormon elder seeking to use the "sword of the destroying angels" on the hero who courted Mary. Eagle Eye warned Mary of the "sensuality, hypocrisy, and murder, which form the base of the Mormon faith," telling her (and the audience) that common sensibilities will be shocked and wounded by the miseries of polygamy. Rather than see Mary doomed to a life of horror, Eagle Eye offered her protection and freedom from Mormon brutality. The Brigham Young character told him that if he remained more than forty-eight hours in Utah, he would be killed, referencing the violence of the faith and the belief that Young often ordered the death of outsiders and those who left the church. The play had a strong theme of Mormon violence. In the play the Young character provided a so-called revelation that the Mormon elder "must take another wife by the Church's command." Conjuring revelations to meet his desires, and those of his followers, exposed the prophet as a fraudulent con artist.

The play shifted in the second act to a scene in the Mormon temple. Though a sacred space for Latter-day Saint religious worship, the temple was viewed from the outside as a nefarious place where individuals were coerced into plural marriage. In Thomas Dunn English's play, the wickedness of the Latter-day Saint faith was highlighted in a temple endowment ceremony, wherein Mormons were dressed in black with hoods and torches to perform a plural marriage. When the man, Mr. Woodville, reversed course and refused to enter into the polygamous union, he declared, "I have recovered reason, self-respect, and honor." His statement alerted the audience that Mormons had none of these attributes and again highlighted violence when Brigham Young responded to the change of heart by sentencing him to death. This scene with its dark milieu revealed the strange ritualism others perceived among the Mormons. The play culminated as Eagle Eye, Mary, and the Woodvilles escaped the grasp of the Mormons, with the help of the scout Whiskey Jake and the U.S. Army.[51] The message provided hope that the country could be freed from Mormon ritual and influence.

The plot of the play claimed to present an "authentic" view of Mormonism to the Woodville family and by extension to the audience and observers. George Clinton Odell's *Annals of the New York Stage* provided an excellent summary, stating that the play "was written to exhibit a practical view of the actual and exciting doings of the Mormons in their own homes—the Policy of their Rulers, their connection with the Indians, Hostility to the Federal Government—the Workings of their peculiar institutions—Sufferings of the numerous wives and children—Public ceremonies and private habits and manners, with an interesting story of American emigrants, and the assassinations by the Danites."[52]

The play certainly spoke to contemporary concerns about the Mormons during the Utah War. But more than just the war atmosphere and the desire to see the U.S. Army, and by extension the federal government, bring the Mormons to heel, it sought to inform the public that Mormons were a threat and too different or suspicious to be embraced as good American citizens. Claims to authenticity about Mormonism and its tenets helped cement Mormon social and cultural difference. A *New York Times* reviewer who believed the play authentic and singularly free from exaggeration noted that English's play excited indignation about Mormons and their lifeways before claiming "any scene of the play is better than the last." The Burton's crowd gave the drama a good reception, and the *New York Times* reviewer believed the play was "destined to enjoy a long and prosperous career."[53]

The play at Burton's Theatre was popular, and another play, *Deseret Deserted, or The Last Days of Brigham Young,* which played at Wallack's Theatre beginning in May 1858, followed a similar storyline. The leading man in this performance, Lucifer Sparks, traveled to Utah to rescue Marian, a "Flower of the Prairie," and other women led away by a Mormon preacher. The play's program described Sparks as a "deliverer of persecuted young ladies and champion of oppressed but virtuous crinoline," a reference to a stiffened or hooped petticoat worn to make a long skirt stand out.[54] Sparks commented, "All we have to do, is to bring about an insurrection among the females, hoist the red petticoat of rebellion, erect barricades of crinoline, and make the defense of Salt Lake City" to destroy the Mormon cause.[55]

This approach had been alluded to years earlier, after a small contingent of U.S. troops stayed briefly in Salt Lake City from 1854 to 1855. The *Brooklyn Daily Eagle* reported, "Brigham Young, complains very bitterly of the troops who were quartered at Utah last winter. It appears that they created quite a rebellion among the women, and when they left for California, carried off a number with them. Brigham vows vengeance and death to all who shall in future make any such demonstration toward his female flock. The President had better send a regiment out there with instructions to court the women. It would very soon break up the nest.

Get the women away and the men would not stay long." If the army could infiltrate Mormon society through sexual conquest of their women, this newspaper report indicated, they could reduce "those Turks of the desert" to "the Christian standard of one wife apiece."[56] Other soldiers also wrote that they had convinced some women to leave with them. They had discovered the best method to divide and conquer the Mormons: through the seduction of Mormon women.[57]

Deseret Deserted presented this idea of American manhood that patriarchal control over women was not acceptable, but the seduction and even Lothario-like conquest of women was permissible. Beyond the more overt gendered and sexual aspect of this play, *Deseret Deserted* made a clearer connection between Mormonism and Islam with dialogue between the prophet Brigham Young and prophet Mahomet, the two getting drunk and commiserating together, and references to the religious sect in Utah as Turks. Mormons were presented in the play as culturally and socially different but also as racially suspect and insufficiently masculine. While *Deseret Deserted* was considered glibber and more comical than its predecessor production at Burton's Theatre, it still provided plenty of commentary on Mormon violence, with Sparks singing about "blood-thirsty Mormons" and the strangeness of Mormon religious rituals.[58]

These 1858 Broadway performances capitalized on a time of heightened anti-Mormonism in the United States. They were popular and entertaining in pitting despotic, lecherous Mormons as violent threats against respectable white American men for the affection of women as symbols of the home. The Utah War provided an early opportunity for theaters, playhouses, and playwrights to capitalize on anti-Mormonism through the stage. These plays helped to establish the anti-Mormon stage genre in New York City. It was a genre that proved exceedingly popular and would inspire similar narratives from later writers who helped build William Cody's acting brand as Buffalo Bill.

The Utah War ended in 1858, as U.S. Army troops completed the construction of two new federal forts in Utah Territory. The federal effort,

however, did nothing immediately to change the polygamous backbone of
Mormon society. Such change would wait until after the Civil War, which
began three years after the conclusion of the army's Utah expedition.

During the Civil War, the federal government began to address the "Twin
Relics of Barbarism" that plagued American society while it planned for
western expansion. In 1862 Republican leaders shepherded several bills
through Congress that had been stalled by the conflict over the expansion
of slavery, including the Homestead Act, the Morrill Anti-bigamy Act,
the Pacific Railroad Act, and a law outlawing slavery in the territories.
Each legislative action strengthened the government's design to better
develop the transcontinental country. In June 1862, as the U.S. Army was
being repeatedly attacked and defeated by Confederate forces in Virginia,
Congress enacted and President Abraham Lincoln authorized a statute
outlawing slavery and involuntary servitude in U.S. territories. On July
8, 1862, Lincoln signed the Morrill Anti-bigamy Act, introduced by Vermont Republican Justin Morrill, which outlawed plural marriage in the
territories. It was the first federal law regulating marriage in the United
States. The Republican promise of 1856 to prohibit the "Twin Relics of
Barbarism" in the western territories had been fulfilled.[59]

The Morrill Act and other legislation passed in 1862 further extended
congressional reach and signaled the staying power of national institutions
and authority in the West. These laws provided the foundation to fulfill
expansionist dreams of a transcontinental nation filled with free, loyal
American settlers. And with them the question of the federal government's
authority over the western territories was settled. With this new legislation Morrill and the Republicans put into motion the reconstruction of
what they saw as a debased society in Utah. However, the enforcement
of the Morrill Act and the implementation of the other major 1862 laws
did not come quickly or easily.

Two other landmark 1862 congressional acts set into motion major
events in William Cody's life. On July 1, 1862, President Lincoln approved
the Pacific Railroad Act, which further promoted western migration as
well as quicker transportation and communication from coast to coast.
That act supported the construction of a transcontinental railroad, giv-

ing the Union Pacific Railroad Company the right of way through an immense stretch of public lands from the Missouri River to California. It also provided the company the right to take from the adjacent lands of the roadway precisely two hundred feet on each side, earth, stone, timber, and other materials for constructing the road, which greatly disturbed the flora and fauna in and around Native American homelands. Section 9 of the act authorized the Leavenworth, Pawnee, and Western Railroad Company of Kansas to construct a railroad and telegraph line from the Missouri River at the mouth of the Kansas River, approximately at Leavenworth through Kansas west to the Rocky Mountains to connect the Intermountain West and Kansas with points east and west.[60]

Just a month and a half earlier, Congress passed and President Abraham Lincoln signed into law the Homestead Act. Through the act an applicant received 160 acres of free land, provided the applicant improved the land. While the free land was intended for farmers, land speculators and town builders snatched up lands to build and sell. As with the Pacific Railroad Act, the federal government would have to remove Native Americans from lands in the West to make way for homesteaders.[61] The two acts seemed to combine seamlessly. An early Kansas newspaper, the *Freedom's Champion*, lauded the two bills, declaring they presented "to our Kansas friends the most encouraging prospects for the future of their State." Kansas, the article boasted, reaped the benefit of the mighty traffic "that must roll through this great artery of trade, and branches from both North and South must pour their business into it," which assuredly would bring a substantial population and economic benefits to the state.[62] The railroads provided homesteaders easy transportation to the expansive lands of the Great Plains, while also luring new immigrants westward with exaggerated claims of farming prospects to sell off excess land at inflated prices. Railroads provided big business opportunities and could transform the economic potential of towns along the lines.[63]

Many people poured into the plains. Men flocked to Kansas to work for the railroad or to take up a homestead.[64] An era of fervent urbanization emerged in the plains, as many people tried to build or be part of the early growth of the next boomtown. Bold speculators claimed acreage through the Homestead Act in the believed path of the coming railroad. Rather than making agricultural improvements to the land, as the Homestead Act intended, the speculators laid out towns with streets and storefronts, promising settlers that the railroad would build a station in the city. Deeds for town properties sold and resold at increasingly exorbitant prices as the end of the tracks approached. Just as quickly as speculators could build up a town, the railroad could destroy its growth if it chose a different route.[65]

In the spring of 1867, William Cody had big dreams. During the intervening time from his alleged travels to Utah, he had served in the Civil War, first as a scout for the paramilitary group the Red Legged Scouts and then as a soldier in the Seventh Kansas Volunteer Cavalry. Cody and the cavalry marched through Missouri, Tennessee, and Mississippi, helping the Union secure victories over Confederate troops led by Nathan Bedford Forrest and Sterling Price. He had fought against slavery just as his father had.

During his travels at the end of the war, Cody obtained a post in St. Louis, where he met Louisa Frederici. After months of courting and William's discharge from the military, the two were married on Louisa's family's Missouri farm in March 1866. They returned to Cody's home in the Salt Creek Valley in Kansas, and nine months later the newlyweds welcomed the birth of their first daughter, Arta Lucille. Living in Kansas once again, William Cody saw an opportunity to make a name for himself and to better provide for his family. He wanted to establish a good home for Louisa and Arta.

In May 1867 the Kansas Pacific Railroad was complete to Ellsworth, in the middle of the state, and railroad contractors began grading and locating a route westward through neighboring Ellis County. Looking to establish a new town in the unsettled county along the route of the railroad, William Cody teamed with William Rose to establish the city of Rome, the first town founded in Ellis County. Railroad construction agents in Kansas City made Rome a clearing house for laborers, and it became a bustling settlement on a creek flowing through the open prairie. Cody put up the first building, then he and Rose built a two-room drugstore. Rose appointed himself postmaster, and Cody made his first foray into politics, serving as the town's first mayor and marshal.

For seven or eight months Rome howled with growth. Some twenty-five buildings went up, rapidly joining Cody and Rose's first structures. For that short period, it was the largest town in the western half of Kansas. Shortly after Cody and Rose founded Rome, the federal government announced that it would locate a new military post approximately one mile southeast of the new town. Fort Hays was officially established on June 21, 1867. As the railroad proceeded west, settlement followed it. Military forts also dotted the rail lines as a policing force against Native Americans and to assist in "American progress." The forts offered security for town building and railroad interests. They also provided protection for the expansion of the American home and family. With the railroad approaching and the establishment of the protective fort nearby, prospects looked good for Cody's city of Rome.

Cody lobbied for the recognition and the organization of municipal and county officers based in his growing city. On August 26, 1867, Cody and a dozen other Romans petitioned the governor for an appointment of a justice of the peace to introduce law to the area.[66] Kansas governor Samuel J. Crawford denied the petition in early September because Rome was not yet officially attached to a county. That same month Cody's town was dealt another blow. A competing urban developer started building a new town just one mile to the east. The *Denver News* received a telegram from Fort Hays reporting on the growing towns springing up around it. "One is being built by the Big Creek Land Company, of St. Louis," the *News* stated, "and is called Hays City. The Company are bringing 50 families from New York State to settle as farmers on their land. A large hotel is being built. The town will be a county seat. A large number of buildings are going up." While the article mentioned towns in plural, it did not mention Rome.[67]

Hays City, about a mile east of Rome, became the preferred location of the railroad because of its connection to the Big Creek Land Company. At the same time, the railroad raised its approaches to the Big Creek Bridge, creating a plateau, cutting off Rome from Fort Hays, and ensuring that a railroad station could not be built off the high embankment. On October 10, 1867, the tracks reached Hays City.[68] Little by little Rome's population melted away into the new settlement.

By 1870 there was little left of Rome, save the ruins.[69] The multidirectional vortex of urban development, military forts, and the railroad bypassed the young entrepreneur.[70] Cody failed in his venture at Rome, but it would not be his last attempt at town building. He had learned some hard lessons about the importance of the railroad for urban expansion, lessons that would help him navigate his future endeavors.

After Rome declined, William Cody, like many other Romans, moved to the rival Hays City. He tried, at first, to operate a hotel but was not successful. He then parlayed his skills as a plainsman scout and hunter into a contract with the Kansas Pacific Railroad as a buffalo hunter to provide meat for rail-construction workers. The area to which he was assigned, just outside of Hays City, was in the heart of buffalo country. Many thousands of the majestic creatures migrated through the plains constantly on the search for forage and water.[71] Large herds were seen constantly by army soldiers and railroad workers. Buffalo captured the imagination of those in Kansas and in the East alike.[72]

Before the railroad hired Cody as a contract buffalo hunter to provide meat for the construction workers, buffalo hunting became a popular American sport and a tourist enterprise in the West. Nearly every Kansas Pacific Railroad train leaving or arriving near Fort Hays in late 1867 had a race with herds of buffalo. The train then slowed to a rate of speed about equal to that of the herd; the passengers got out firearms, which were provided on the train for defense against Native Americans, and opened fire on the animals from the windows and platforms of the cars. In one newspaper report of a buffalo hunt on the Kansas Pacific, the train encountered a large herd, and the expected frenzy of gunfire began. They secured the kill in the baggage car, and everyone on board bragged about their kills. "Ladies who are passengers on the trains frequently enjoy the sport," according to the *Harper's Weekly* article on the subject, "and invariably claim all the game as the result of their prowess with the rifle."[73] People held church benefits and other social engagements on excursionist trains for the sole purpose of shooting buffaloes. William E. Webb, in a railroad advertising publication, considered Kansas the best buffalo-hunting spot on the continent.[74]

In Kansas the buffalo, associated with everything wild and daring, could now be hunted indolently, under the comforting auspices of business-eager railroads. The railroad announced weeklong excursions at low rates from Cincinnati, Chicago, and St. Louis. They boasted that passengers could kill dozens of buffaloes in less than six hours.[75] *Harper's Weekly* reported, "The Kansas Pacific Railway sends out 'sporting trains' for amateur hunters, who shoot from the car windows, and in this tame travesty of sport kill hundreds of thousands of buffaloes every season."[76]

Buffalo excursions on trains and the popularity of buffalo hunting continued in the decades that followed. Between 1870 and 1883, Euro-American hunters slaughtered millions of bison to make way for railroad construction and white settlement and to force Plains Indians—dependent on bison for their subsistence—onto government reservations. The widespread killing of the majestic buffalo generated great wastefulness.[77]

The railroad also hired buffalo hunters to provide sustenance for its laborers. While at the same time killing the bison and destroying their habitat, the crews depended on the buffalo for meat as construction extended far into the plains. The Kansas Pacific employed a construction gang of 1,200 men, and the commissariat relied largely on several buffalo hunters to provide meat for them all. In 1868 William Cody was employed as one of those buffalo hunters, earning a middle-class wage of $500 per month. In exchange for this wage, William's contract called on him to kill an average of twelve buffaloes daily, oversee the cutting and dressing of the meat and looking after its transportation. The pay was high because of the danger of the chase and the likelihood of an encounter with Native American hunters.[78]

Each day William Cody ventured out onto the plains in all directions from the railroad camp to hunt buffalo. Each day, as he rode back into camp with the hindquarters and humps of the bison he had slain, the road-hands cheered on the man responsible for providing their dinner. It was those laborers who initially bestowed on Cody "the very appropriate name of 'Buffalo Bill.'" It was an endearing appellation given in a particular context, but it was a moniker that nevertheless stuck and only grew in esteem as the eponymous figure grew in prominence.

Buffalo Bill was a prolific hunter. Over a period of eighteen months, Cody claimed to have killed 4,280 buffaloes.[79] In April 1868 Cody engaged in a hunting competition with Billy Comstock, a successful buffalo hunter and an army scout under George Armstrong Custer, twenty miles east of Sheridan, in western Kansas. Cody mounted his horse, a pony he said he obtained from a Ute in Utah and that he named "Brigham" after the Mormon prophet, and started off on the hunt.[80] The contest lasted eight hours, with Cody killing sixty-nine bison to Comstock's forty-six. Professional hunters claimed they could kill forty to fifty buffalo in a single day, and Cody proved them right.[81] The Kansas Pacific Railroad mounted, distributed, and advertised the heads of buffaloes slain in Cody's hunting competition with Billy Comstock, further popularizing the sport of and tourism around buffalo hunting on horseback with guns.[82]

Building the railroad and general westward expansion brought a constant threat to American Indians. In the names of "civilization" and "progress," the U.S. government fought to remove Indian nations from their lands and onto reservations, thereby clearing the corridors for white settlement and travel. White Americans also threatened resources, like the buffalo, critical to the survival of Plains Indian nations. White Americans felt justified in what became an utter extermination of Native culture and lifeways. The U.S. Army, though undermanned and overextended, served as a blunt, but effective, tool in the government's ongoing efforts to enable white families to settle the West after the Civil War. All told, more than nine hundred battles between whites and Native Americans occurred between 1865 and 1891. In this context men with military backgrounds and those who had worked on the railroad, like William Cody, were considered extremely valuable in the settlement of the West.[83]

Cody's experiences in Kansas were part of ongoing trends in transportation development, town building, buffalo hunting, and white American conflict with American Indians, all of which he later glorified in his stage performances and Wild West extravaganza. The Pacific Railroad Act and the Homestead Act encouraged white progress and settlement and environmental change through urban development, the killing of bison, and large-scale agriculture. They also encouraged armed conflicts with Native Americans.

William F. Cody lived side by side with the railroad in the middle of many of these changes as they occurred in the late 1860s. He attempted to build the next great town of the West. He saw the illimitable buffalo herds that covered the plains and killed thousands of them. Cody encountered Native Americans of many different tribes, and he scouted their movements and assisted the U.S. Army in fighting and displacing them.[84]

The federal government had established numerous military forts in the vast territory of the Great Plains and Intermountain West with this purpose in mind: to fight American Indian peoples, restrict their mobility, and remove them from the path of "American progress." The forts furnished to the railroads escorts of officers and men for the protection of railroad surveying and construction crews.[85] The forts also served as headquarters for military campaigns against American Indians. Military leaders such as William T. Sherman and Gen. Philip Sheridan were fixtures in the forts of the Kansas plains after the Civil War. They led men and devised plans to exterminate Cheyennes, Comanches, and Arapahos under the guise of protecting railroad men and settlers.[86]

In the fall of 1868, William Cody became chief of scouts for the U.S. Fifth Cavalry out of Fort Hays under Gen. Eugene A. Carr. With white American desire for commercial and cultural growth in the region, the presence of Native peoples brought many physical conflicts. Cody includes at least sixteen different fights or battles with Native Americans in his autobiography. He continued his service as an Indian scout for the Fifth Cavalry as the regiment transferred to Fort Lyon, in present-day Colorado, in the fall of 1868 and from there to Fort McPherson, Nebraska, in May 1869.

In July of that year, Cody's scouting outfit, led by Maj. Frank North, directed the Fifth U.S. Regiment of Cavalry trailing Tall Bull's band of Cheyenne Dog Soldiers to the northeastern corner of Colorado Territory. The U.S. soldiers attacked the camped Cheyennes in what would be known as the Battle of Summit Springs. During the fighting Cody shot a Cheyenne on horseback that he claimed was the chief, Tall Bull, though Capt. Luther North later disputed this claim.[87] The army cavalry, commanded by Col. Eugene A. Carr, killed approximately thirty-five Cheyennes and captured an additional fifteen. Carr, Cody, and the cavalry claimed victory for the United States, one of hundreds of battles fought in the Indian Wars of the West.

⁓⁓⁓⁓⁓

Shortly after the Battle of Summit Springs, Cody, the scouts, and the soldiers returned to Fort McPherson. Col. Edward Judson, known by his penname as Ned Buntline, a prominent journalist and novelist, was in the area on a temperance lecture circuit. He stopped at the fort, wanting to meet and write about Wild Bill Hickok, but had the fortune of being introduced to William Cody and joining him for a scouting expedition. Buntline, apparently enthralled with Cody, asked him many questions. The men rode horses side by side at breakneck speeds, crossed treacherous waterways, hunted game, and followed Indian trails. Buntline's time with Cody provided the enterprising writer with fodder for a new story titled "Buffalo Bill, the King of Border Men," which he published just months later in December 1869.[88] Buntline's drama became a definitive western, with a formula of villains, abductions, pursuit, and rescues. It catapulted Cody to fame and made "Buffalo Bill" the most recognizable name of his era.

Beginning on February 19, 1872, at the Bowery Theatre in New York City, the story about Buffalo Bill played live onstage. Having received an invitation to that city from some gentleman he had led on a hunt in 1871, Cody determined to visit New York City. While in the city, Cody tracked

3. Forbes lithograph prominently featuring Buffalo Bill, the scout, on his horse, leading a troop of soldiers, circa 1860s. Library of Congress, LC-USZC4-6424.

down Buntline. He also saw the sights of the city and received numerous dinner invitations. Curious to see how his character was portrayed on the stage in the Buntline drama, the real Buffalo Bill went to the Bowery Theatre. When the theater manager learned that Cody attended one of the showings, he insisted that the man who inspired the play get onstage to address the crowd between acts. Embarrassed, Cody gave a barely audible, awkward speech.[89] He did not make a great impression his first time on stage. But his character did.

While the Buffalo Bill play continued in New York, Cody returned to Nebraska, where he participated in buffalo-hunting tourism. He had led prominent individuals, including the Russian Grand Duke Alexei Alexandrovich, on hunts. He continued in that work on the Nebraska plains. Cody also reengaged in politics; he was elected as a representative for the Twenty-Sixth District in the Nebraska legislature in 1872. But it was his physical magnetism and western exploits that kept storytellers and audiences from allowing him to live quietly on the plains.

During the summer of 1872, Ned Buntline wrote incessantly to Cody, imploring him to return east to play himself on the stages of the nation's largest cities. The writer encouraged Buffalo Bill, assuring him that money and fame awaited him. "There's money in it," Buntline wrote, "and you will prove a big card, as your character is a novelty on the stage." Remembering his previous poor showing onstage, Cody feared he would be a total failure. In his autobiography he wrote, "That I, an old scout who had never seen more than twenty or thirty theatrical performances in my life, should think of going upon the stage, was ridiculous in the extreme—so they all said."[90] Nevertheless, he grew convinced to give acting a shot.

As the winter of 1872 approached, Ned Buntline secured an engagement at Nixon's Amphitheatre in Chicago. This time Buntline wrote a sensational drama specifically for Buffalo Bill and his emerging character, titled *Scouts of the Prairie*.[91] Cody's first stage performance featured a lascivious Mormon villain and his Indian allies, the capture of a lovely white woman, prairie fire, and a dramatic rescue, a plot not too distinct from the Utah War–era dramas. The play that launched Cody's stage career was built on anti-Mormon tropes and came at a time of heightening anti-Mormonism in America.

2

Buffalo Bill and the Mormons on the Stage

William F. "Buffalo Bill" Cody took the Nixon's Amphitheatre stage in Chicago on December 16, 1872. He was not a trained actor, but he made his acting debut playing himself in Ned Buntline's drama, *The Scouts of the Prairie*. Buntline also performed in the show as Cale Durg, a fictitious scout and trapper, and the narrator of the story, but it was Buffalo Bill who was the star. His performance was a novelty. As an actual western "hero" who had served in the military in the Civil War and the Indian Wars of the West, he seized the public's imagination on the stage. The show was a hit, attracting "more people than the house can hold" every night it played in Chicago.[1]

Those lucky enough to acquire a ticket jeered the main villain, Mormon Ben, as he tried to add a new wife to his harem of fifty others. It was a common antipolygamy trope of the day. Onstage Mormon Ben's band of renegade friends included a Native American leader and a drunken Irishman. Revitalizing fears of a Mormon-Indian alliance, Mormon Ben convinced his American Indian confidant, Wolf Slayer—dubbed the "treacherous Ute"—to abduct Durg's orphaned ward, the beautiful young woman Hazel Eye, and steal her away to Mormon Ben's ranch.[2] With Buntline's Durg tied to a torture post on the nefarious man's property, heroes Buffalo Bill and Texas Jack emerged on the scene to fight and run off the villains as the curtains fell on act 1.

Act 2 opened with the villains plotting their next steps. In one scene the renegade boss, Mormon Ben, picked up a bottle of alcohol to drown his sorrows for losing his female captive. The Irish character, also drunk in commiseration, declared to the audience that he was not a Mormon but loved the booze. Ned Buntline, a frequent temperance lecturer, inserted into the story several significant messages on the importance of sobriety, associating Mormons with drunkenness and using the Irish character to further demonstrate to the audience the need to control these unlicensed spirits in America. As act 2 continued, Mormon Ben's associates recaptured Hazel Eye and kidnapped an Indian girl named Dove Eye. Buntline's Durg was also recaptured and bound to a tree, where he gave a fiery temperance discourse to the audience before Buffalo Bill and Texas Jack once again came to the rescue, staging a fight with the villains. Durg was killed as act 2 closed.[3]

The third and final act saw Buffalo Bill avenge his friend's death as a prairie fire raged. After subduing the Indians in a bloody battle, the heroes Buffalo Bill and Texas Jack ended the illicit prospects of Mormon Ben and his fellow miscreants. Wiping out the Indians onstage and preventing the lustful Mormon Ben from enslaving another wife thrilled audiences in Chicago and at theaters throughout the eastern United States. The white western American hero had severed the symbolic Mormon-Indian alliance and dispatched the other foreign elements threatening to disrupt the American family. The plainsman scout proved triumphant and signaled to the audience that these malevolent constituents could not and would not thrive in western society.[4]

Despite its overwhelming popularity with audiences, critics gave *Scouts of the Prairie* a lukewarm reception. One newspaper reviewer opined, "It is literally a long drawn out duel between Buffalo Bill, Texas Jack, Cale Durg, Hazel Eye and Dove Eye, on the one side, and Mormon Ben, Wolf Slayer, Big Eagle and a lot of Indians and renegades on the other."[5] Critics also panned Buffalo Bill as an actor. Still, many reviews commented on his physical appearance, outdoor skill, and overall "powerful and energetic physical presence." One commentator wrote, "Buffalo Bill is a good-looking fellow, tall and straight as an arrow, but ridiculous as an actor." Of the whole performance this critic stated, "Everything was so wonderfully bad that it was almost good."[6] Others claimed Cody was one of the "finest looking men we have ever seen." He was a magnificent, captivating man.[7] Critics and audiences were enamored with the manly beauty of the dashing and daring scout of the prairie. Buffalo Bill's stage combination took *Scouts of the Prairie* to other cities in the midwestern and eastern United States during the following year, increasing Cody's reputation and giving large audiences the chance to swoon at the striking, handsome star.[8]

Those who attended the play or even just read about it in newspapers could quickly discern the moral of the story. Propagating a binary already established on the stage, in novels, and in the nation's culture, Mormons, Indians, and foreign-born peoples such as the Irish were deemed incompatible with and detrimental to the American nation in their current state of existence.

What *Scouts of the Prairie* presented were stereotypes already understood and popularized. For example, the allegory of rescuing distressed heroines from captors had long captivated American culture. Revolutionary-era propaganda surrounding the death of Jane McCrea, a young woman killed by Hurons allied with the British military during the American Revolutionary War, emphasized her beauty and created anti-Indian and anti-British outrage among the patriots. Later western adventure tales popularized the genre, perhaps most visibly in James Fenimore Cooper's Leatherstocking Tales novel *The Last of the Mohicans*, which dealt with Indian warfare and the rescue of women from their captors.[9] Captivity narratives such as these typically presented a white woman being captured by a fierce opponent, often portrayed by a man or group of people considered outside of the mainstream. Dime novelists and western dramatists, like Ned Buntline, produced formulaic and standardized stories drawing from the likes of Cooper. Buntline's western tales of ritualistic adventure were sensational and, by using Buffalo Bill as the main hero, a role typically reserved for an eastern gentleman, introduced the white western man as an exemplar or ideal type. Buffalo Bill became the prime hero.[10]

The Scouts of the Prairie offered moving, realistic visual images that vividly presented an idealized representation of good and evil and a vision for the American West. White American men of the West vanquishing villainous Mormons and their American Indian or foreign allies created markers of difference in group identity and justified action, including violence, by the "good guys" against the bad.[11]

The play provided a glimpse of the dangers of Mormon home life. The generic Mormon man caricatured by Mormon Ben in *Scouts* presented a salacious representation that all men in the faith presided over hypersexual harems with dozens of wives, even though a majority of male Latter-day Saints never practiced plural marriage.[12] This was just one scene in a large tapestry of American critiques that portrayed the Mormon home as a place to enslave women, abuse them, and use them for sexual gratification. In a country and culture just removed from a brutal Civil War over slavery, the image of slavery, and that of enslaving white women, held immense power. Americans seem to have had an almost insatiable appetite for lurid tales of the Mormon home, wherein lecherous men preyed on helpless women held in bondage. The rhetoric, imagery, and performance imbued the Mormon home with erotic, even pornographic, messaging. The extreme victimization of women in these situations served as a warning to America that true women could not exist in the bonds of polygamy.[13] The American family needed saving from the sexual brutality of Mormons.

Theatrical presentations such as *Scouts* reinforced the popular image of Latter-day Saints as deviants who needed to be vanquished along with their renegade friends. But the play offered a remedy. Buffalo Bill represented the ideal American man—one who protected white womanhood and who protected the home from barbarian threats.

Scouts presented Mormons and their practice of plural marriage as a most dangerous threat to the American home and to the perceived virtue of white womanhood.[14] This sentiment was a part of that era's growing popular and political cultural phenomenon in the eastern United States. The same month that *Scouts* premiered in Chicago, the citizens of the Second City were treated to a lecture from the actor Sara Alexander on Mormonism.[15] Alexander, a former member of The Church of Jesus Christ of Latter-day Saints, had traveled from Missouri to Nebraska and then to Utah for her faith. In Utah she lived in Brigham Young's Lion House, a home for many of Young's wives and children, for five years and performed regularly at the Salt Lake Theatre, but she grew disillusioned with the church and life in Salt Lake. In 1868 she fled to San Francisco with John McCullough's theater company to pursue a life on the big stage.[16] Now, in Chicago, Alexander intended to reveal her experiences in Salt Lake City and her truth about the Mormon home.

Speaking with earnestness and grace, Alexander captivated her audience with her stories of Mormon life. She claimed to have been admitted into the temple, where she observed religious rituals and plural marriages performed in secrecy. She spoke of her experiences living in Brigham Young's polygamous home. The women of Utah lived in the most abject bondage, she declared, and dared not act or speak contrary to the instruction of the leading men of the church. Mormons enslaved women, plain and simple, Alexander warned. She spoke about the general religious fanaticism she observed within the faith and the control high-ranking officials had over their co-religionists.[17] Finally, Alexander informed her audience of a most threatening component of Mormonism, that of authority. "No clause in the constitution of the United States, no American law," she said, "is paramount to the church obligations."[18] Sara Alexander experienced great monetary success with her lectures on the moral, domestic, and political consequences of polygamy. Many others also profited from a reinvigorated anti-Mormonism within the country.

Like Sara Alexander, Fanny Stenhouse, a former Latter-day Saint, wrote about her experiences as a polygamist wife over a twenty-year period in *Exposé of Polygamy in Utah: A Lady's Life among the Mormons.* Published in 1872, the bestseller stimulated eastern American readers with Stenhouse's disillusionment with the religious practice of plural marriage and her leaving the faith.[19]

Among other books published in 1872, including John Hanson Beadle's *Brigham's Destroying Angel*, a book on the "Danite chief of Utah," Bill Hickman, was Mark Twain's *Roughing It.* In this western travel narrative, Twain wrote about his visit to the "home of the Latter-day Saints." The young Twain labeled Mormons as "creatures" and "goblins." He referred

to women by number (according to the order of their marriage) and not
by name. The novelist stated that he felt a "curiosity to ask every child
how many mothers it had, and if it could tell them apart." To Twain
Mormons were subhuman, especially the women, whom he described
as "poor, ungainly, and pathetically 'homely' creatures." He wrote, with
biting sarcasm, "The man that marries one of them has done an act of
Christian charity which entitles him to the kindly applause of mankind,
not their harsh censure—and the man that marries sixty of them has done
a deed of open-handed generosity so sublime that the nations should
stand uncovered in his presence and worship in silence."[20] Such written
caricatures created a distorted picture of a different, maligned people.

Other travelers similarly penned their observations of Mormons in
the early 1870s. One published account focused on the blind obedience
that Mormons had to their prophet, Brigham Young.[21] Another traveler
from New York wrote to a friend of an encounter with Latter-day Saints
on his travels. This westbound New Yorker provided this summary: "I
am sorry to say that the Mormons make a very poor use of the people
that join them. Thay make them work for the benefit of the church and
its leaders. Thay keep them Poor all their lives."[22] These comments and
those of Twain, Stenhouse, and Alexander expressed the deep anxiety
Americans had over the unconventional religion and the ways that powerful leaders could manipulate their followers. These types of sentiments
illustrated a vivid portrait of the perceived top-down patriarchal control
in the faith and home of Latter-day Saints.

The home was the cultural and political center of late nineteenth-century
America, when the ideal American home was white, monogamous, and
Christian. This type of home and family, according to political commentator Francis Lieber, was the pillar of white civilization. The preservation
of monogamous marriage was considered vital to white progress and
the future success of American society.[23] Mormons were believed to be
the antithesis of the ideal American home. Though the overwhelming
majority of Latter-day Saints were physically white and U.S. citizens,

their religious teaching, cohesive community, and practice of polygamy did not qualify them to be considered as white or properly American.[24] Instead, they needed to be forced into acceptable homes.

Of the period the historian Richard White has stated, "The home became the beating heart of an expansive political program that would create black homes, impose 'proper' homes on Indian peoples, exclude Chinese (deemed both a threat to American homes and incapable of creating their own), and expand the white home into the West."[25] In the case of Mormons, polygamy was the primary problem. Plural wives were constantly portrayed in periodicals, pamphlets, and performances as downtrodden slaves, while monogamous married women were depicted as free and able to differentiate themselves as proper and positive contributors to American greatness. Additional dynamics were at play as well. As the historian Sarah M. S. Pearsall has deftly described, "These wife-slaves were Mormon, Indian, Asian, and African. To transform a gender-based critique into one which emphasized instead racial and religious difference was, implicitly, to valorize Christian monogamy as the only acceptable form of marriage, one that preserved whiteness and civility."[26] Plural marriage placed Latter-day Saint men alongside men of color, in particular Black and Native American men, as dangerous deviants and hypersexual beings that needed to be conquered or controlled.

Mormons were just one of several groups targeted for their difference in the Reconstruction era. Americans imagined polygamist men as lustful, despotic sexual deviants who could not be assimilated into the republic of white male voters.[27] Latter-day Saint men were especially irresistible targets for public condemnation. They coerced helpless women under the guise of religion and held them subordinate for sex and labor. Until Mormons could be reformed and forced into proper homes, the American family needed protection from them.

Buffalo Bill's early stage performances, including the plot and action in Scouts of the Prairie, reinforced a long-held American notion that justified violence to protect the home. Cody was among many performers and writers who placed the home and the values of the monogamous family at the center of popular culture. The home and family positioned in scenes of the West projected the importance of protecting the American ideal as the nation expanded west and rebuilt the South after the Civil War. Cultural forums, like Cody's stage plays and the Leatherstocking tradition, glorified conflict between white settlers and other minority groups. The white settlers, though beset by challenges and even the occasional death, ultimately emerged victorious and vindicated through violence, which they believed justified by threats to home and family. The rhetoric and imagery from these products presented the white home and its values as a central place, which manifested in both federal policies and unifying national visions of the region where white homes would flourish and reunify a once-fractured nation.[28]

Buffalo Bill's theater company performed *Scouts of the Prairie* through 1873. That same year Ann Eliza Young commenced a crusade against the faith to which she had belonged. She sued Brigham Young, to whom she was sealed as a plural wife in a religious ceremony, for divorce. As a part of the divorce, she sought $1,000 in monthly alimony (equivalent to approximately $25,000 in 2022); $20,000 in legal fees (equivalent to approximately $500,000 in 2022); and $200,000 from his future estate (equivalent to approximately $5 million in 2022). For his part Brigham Young and his attorneys argued that the marriage was religious and had no legal basis and therefore he owed nothing to Ann Eliza. She was initially awarded $500 per month alimony by the federal court. That settlement was later overturned because the federal ruling implicitly recognized Ann Eliza's divorce suit as legal, which would have meant that federal courts would need to recognize plural marriage as legal, which they most certainly did not want.[29]

While the legal and political ramifications of the divorce case were significant, it was the cultural impact of Ann Eliza's effort to divorce Brigham Young that captivated audiences. Newspapers across the country printed copious columns on Ann Eliza's charges against the Latter-day Saint leader.[30] As awareness about the divorce grew, Ann Eliza found her way, like Sara Alexander and others before her, to the lecture circuit in the eastern United States. She told crowded audiences about Latter-day Saint temple ceremonies, polygamous homes and families, and the religious tyrant Brigham Young. Droves of individuals, including U.S. president Ulysses S. Grant and First Lady Julia Grant, listened with rapt attention to the former Latter-day Saint woman's tales revealing the stark difference between the religious group and prevailing American notions of home and family.[31]

In 1875 Ann Eliza published an autobiography, calling the public's attention to the brutal, diabolical, and stifling religious system that she said dominated the Intermountain West.[32] In it she stated unequivocally, "While I have a hand or a voice, Mormonism and Polygamy shall find in me a relentless foe." The newfound crusader railed against the plural marriage system and the religious rites surrounding it. She stated that polygamy always brought "the curse of a wrecked home and a life's unhappiness."[33]

Speaking in summary about polygamy, Ann Eliza passionately penned these words: "I had felt its misery; I had known the abject wretchedness of the condition to which it reduced women, but I did not fully realize the extent of its depravity, the depths of the woes in which it plunged women, until I saw the contrasted lives of monogamic women." Plural marriage damaged not only women, she insisted, but also men. "Women are the greatest sufferers," Ann Eliza stated, but "the moral natures of the men must necessarily suffer also. . . . Their sensibilities are blunted; their spiritual natures deadened; their animal natures quickened; they lose manliness, and descend to the level of brutes; and these dull-witted, intellectually-dwarfed moral corpses, the women are told, are their only saviours."[34]

Born into the Latter-day Saint faith, Ann Eliza explained how she came to deny the religious teachings and traditions of her forebears. She embraced mainstream Christian belief. She wrote of her own reformation and her perilous escape from the clutches of the Mormons. In telling of her break, Ann Eliza revived the trope of religious violence and the role that Danites supposedly played. Fleeing from Salt Lake City, Ann Eliza wrote, "We were not sure how closely we had been watched, or whether we had succeeded in eluding Mormon vigilance. Even then, the 'Danites,' those terrible ministers of Mormon vengeance, might be upon our track, and I could not cast off the feeling that every moment brought us nearer and nearer to some dreadful death."[35] Like many writings and cultural productions about women and Mormonism, Ann Eliza's work featured a traditional victim and captivity narrative of escaping the lustful and heretical lechers, not unlike *Scouts of the Prairie*. She did not have a Buffalo Bill to come to her rescue, but her message was that women could be awakened to rescue themselves.[36]

In addition to her detailed personal account, Ann Eliza penned scenes of other momentous events in Mormon history, including a chapter on the Mountain Meadows Massacre and John D. Lee. The publication of Ann Eliza Young's exposé and her remarks on the massacre were timely, given the surge in publicity surrounding the 1875–76 trials of Lee's involvement in the cold-blooded slaughter of 120 men, women, and children in September 1857. Brigham Young had excommunicated Lee from the church in 1870 for extreme wickedness after he learned new details about the massacre and Lee's role in it. Lee went into hiding in northern Arizona Territory, where he operated a ferry across the Colorado River. He was arrested when visiting one of his polygamous wives in Panguitch, Utah Territory, in 1874.

As preparations were made for Lee's trial, details about the massacre were splashed throughout the nation's newspapers. A *Harper's Weekly* article labeled Lee "a peculiarly atrocious scoundrel" before commenting on a particularly brutal act he supposedly committed. "While the massacre was going on," the *Harper's* article claimed that Lee "dragged a lovely young girl from the scene; when she resisted and struck at him with a knife, he shot her."[37] These stories further inflamed a public already averse to Mormonism. Entrenched suspicions about Mormon violence, homes and family, assimilability, and even whiteness reemerged as the national spotlight again fixated on the Saints.[38]

The first trial of John D. Lee began in Beaver City, Utah Territory, on July 23, 1875. Public commentators believed that the evidence would convict Lee as the leader in the massacre, but they also believed that the responsibility for the whole bloody affair rested on Brigham Young's shoulders. Press around the trial fixated on the involvement of Young and the Latter-day Saint church hierarchy. One Virginia newspaper, for example, believed "there will be testimony enough before the trial is over to fasten the guilt where it belongs, and convince the people of the United States that Brigham Young and his leading captains and counselors should be hanged."[39] Though Lee had grown bitter toward Young as his trial approached, he repeatedly denied that Young ordered the massacre, a portrait prosecutors attempted to paint during that first trial.[40]

In mid-July Lee provided prosecutors with a statement of his knowledge of the massacre. The U.S. attorney rejected his statement because it did not implicate Young or any church leaders for the crime. Young had long condemned the massacre and offered help to government officials in its prosecution. Rather than incriminate Young or other church leaders, Lee would face the court and stand trial on his own for the actions of many involved in the massacre. He was arraigned on July 21, and thereafter the prosecution and the defense went to battle, hoping to convince the assembled jury of their respective cases. The U.S. attorney passionately presented the details of the horrific atrocity perpetrated in the Mountain Meadows nearly twenty years earlier. The defense analyzed and questioned the credibility of witnesses to shed doubt in the jurors' minds about the role Lee played in the massacre. The trial concluded and was turned over to the jury on August 5. After two excruciating days of deliberations and with the country eagerly awaiting the decision, the court reconvened on August 7. The jury foreperson reported to the judge that it was "impossible for us to agree" on a verdict. The trial ended in a deadlocked jury.[41]

A second trial commenced the following year on September 15, 1876. This time the prosecution placed the blame squarely on John D. Lee. Two men testified that they saw Lee murder specific individuals in the meadows that September day in 1857. One stated that he had heard a "gun fired and saw Lee holding a gun pointed at a woman's head."[42] Both the prosecution and defense presented their long-winded arguments until September 20, when the judge presented the jury with instructions. The jury met for less than four hours and convicted Lee of first-degree murder. Twenty days later, on October 10, 1876, the court sentenced Lee to death.[43] The Latter-day Saint scapegoat chose to die by firing squad in the same mountain meadows where he participated in the mass killings. On March 23, 1877, several soldiers cocked their rifles and fired simultaneously into John D. Lee, who fell backward into an open wooden casket. The execution, however, did not satisfy the public's demand for justice. The leader of the Saints, Brigham Young, received no punishment, and he continued to preside over a religious system that Americans feared.

The Lee trials generated considerable attention and grabbed headlines. The *New York Times* printed a front-page story on "The Great Mormon Crime" the day after Lee's death, and newspapers throughout the country were awash with coverage in all the lurid details, not just about the trial and execution but about the role of Brigham Young and religious violence.[44] Publicity of the trial and the execution titillated the reading public. The publication of John D. Lee's autobiography, confessions, and trial transcripts five months after his death only thrilled Americans further.[45]

William F. Cody, whose celebrity steadily grew from his acting career, was among the multitude of Americans fascinated by the Mountain Meadows Massacre and the Lee trials. His acting company, like many other cultural influencers in the late 1870s, capitalized on the skyrocketing interest in all things Mormon.

ıııııııı

Thanks in large part to the Lee trials and antipolygamy imagery plastered in the pages of the nation's periodicals, America saw a resurgent interest in Mormon Danites as violent symbols of the Latter-day Saint threat to the home and family. Portrayals of the Mormons often employed the Danites, sometimes called "Destroying Angels," as a special band of executioners used by Brigham Young and other church leaders to rid the flock of apostates, outsiders, and opponents. A *Harper's Weekly* article on the Latter-day Saints in Utah suggested that "several mysterious murders of Gentiles have been set down to this agency."[46] Mark Twain's *Roughing It* also contained a scene in which Twain dined "with a Mormon 'Destroying Angel.'" Though this Danite was not as murderous as he imagined, Twain did nothing to tone down the violent image of this religious body who abused, plundered, and murdered in the name of God.[47]

So popular was the imaginary Danite that many writers employed the violent band of religious zealots in their novels and plays. In 1876, for example, Joaquin Miller produced the book *First Fam'lies of the Sierras* and premiered its dramatic adaptation titled *The Danites, or The Heart of the Sierras* the next year on Broadway in New York City. *The Danites* contained elements of revenge and romance. Miners in the Sierra Nevadas rescued a young girl "half-dead with hunger and fright," who had endured a terrifying pursuit by the Mormon Danites seeking to enslave her into polygamy. Miller's play struck a raw sexual nerve. In saturating the play with preconceived ideas about Mormonism, the playwright presented a veneer of authenticity and dramatized the peril of polygamy for white American women and their families. The miners protected the young girl as the Danites and their Native American allies (a reference to the long-held fear of a Mormon-Indian alliance, especially as it was portrayed in the Mountain Meadows Massacre) attacked the camp. Mormons and Indians were both suspect groups in America at the time, so it was no surprise to the miners in the play, or the audience, that Indians would abet Mormons in their vicious plots.[48]

Miller's *Danites* became a commercially successful anti-Mormon, frontier melodrama. The play spoke to the fear of lascivious men stalking innocent women, revealing the deep distrust Americans felt toward religious nonconformity, whether the religious practices were alarming dances of heathen Indians or the promiscuous multiple marriages of the Mormons. White Christian audiences were enamored at watching the peculiar plight of the Mormons. The threat of polygamy and rampant sex and the perception of a violent faith made Mormons the consummate "rapacious, conspiratorial villains."[49] Their history, rituals, and lifeways provided (and still provide) ideal melodramatic material.

Bill Cody's stage combination also took advantage of the public's reinvigorated interest in Mormonism. The Buffalo Bill company premiered the play *May Cody, or Lost and Won* during the 1877 theatrical season. The sensational drama, which best represents Buffalo Bill's early portrayal of Latter-day Saint history, reenacted the Mountain Meadows Massacre. In his introduction to the play, Charles E. Blanchett, Buffalo Bill's stage manager at the time, described the performance as depicting "truthful incidents" of "horrible butchery" and even claimed that young Bill Cody was present in southern Utah at the time of the atrocious massacre, a storyline that would have captivated American audiences simultaneously fascinated with and repulsed by the Mormons. Buffalo Bill's character and persona had again been inserted into Utah history.[50]

Unlike his autobiography, which placed him on the northern route to Utah at the time of the massacre, the *May Cody* script placed him in southern Utah ahead of the army and the freighting train on which he supposedly worked. Blanchett went so far as to claim that the young Cody was "one of the few" who had defended the emigrant wagon train, barely escaping from the ruthless Mormons.[51] Blanchett made up the story of Cody's involvement to convince eastern American audiences of the authenticity of the play and its hero. The Washington DC *National Republican* opined that "the plot cannot be said to be a deep one, nor is the play perfect. It seems crude and lacking in refinement, which facts, however, do not detract from the genuineness of the scenes of life on the frontier."[52] For this reviewer the veneer of authenticity was key, and it was heightened by depictions of the well-known Mormon characters John D. Lee, Brigham Young, and Ann Eliza Young.

May Cody was written by Maj. Andrew S. Burt of the U.S. Army. The major had apparently met William Cody in 1876, a year before the play's premiere, during the Great Sioux War, just after the scout had fought in the Battle of Warbonnet Creek. During that clash between Cheyenne soldiers and the U.S. Army's Fifth Cavalry Regiment, which Cody guided as chief scout, Buffalo Bill and a Cheyenne soldier named Yellow Hair engaged in an epic duel on the battlefield in northwestern Nebraska. Buffalo Bill opened fire on Yellow Hair, mortally wounding his opponent. Cody approached the fallen Cheyenne man, took out his bowie knife, and scalped the soldier. Cody grabbed the scalp and the attached fifteen inches of black hair and thrust it into the air. He triumphantly exclaimed, "The first scalp for Custer," in tribute to George A. Custer, who had led more than 250 American soldiers to their death against Lakota, Northern Cheyenne, and Arapaho forces at the Battle of Little Bighorn a month earlier. Cody's scalping of Yellow Hair became a symbolic and celebrated act. Not only did Cody take Yellow Hair's scalp, but he also took his feather bonnet, horse bridle and saddle, and shield, all of which he displayed onstage when he later performed *The Red Right Hand, or Buffalo Bill's First Scalp for Custer*.

Major Burt was taken with Cody's physique, manliness, and battlefield exploits. To express his admiration for the celebrity scout, Burt took up his pen and crafted *May Cody, or Lost and Won*, a drama in four acts, starring the incomparable Buffalo Bill Cody.[53] It debuted at the Bowery Theatre in New York City on September 3, 1877, not quite six months removed from John D. Lee's execution and roughly the same time that Lee's *Mormonism Unveiled* started selling out in bookstores. *May Cody*, like the performance of his conquest of Yellow Hair in *The Red Right Hand* the previous fall, was a deliberately timed drama that rode the wave of current events and amplified Cody's celebrity and star power.

May Cody, the heroine of the play, who was named after William's real-life sister born in 1852, played Buffalo Bill's sister lost in New York City. She had just been turned into the streets by Mrs. Stoughton, in whose house she had been living and whose son had fallen in love with her. Buffalo Bill ventured to New York to find May. At the same time John D. Lee, the leader of Mormon Danites and one of the main villains of the play, looked for her, having formed a passion for her and wishing to abscond with her to Utah. Buffalo Bill reached May first, and they began traveling together with Mrs. Stoughton's son across the plains with the intention of moving to California. On the way Lee waylaid them and the Mountain Meadows Massacre ensued.

Brigham Young first entered the performance at this point to incite the massacre, reinforcing a commonly held belief that Young was indeed responsible for ordering the murders. During the massacre May Cody was carried off by Lee, who wished her for himself but was overruled by his ecclesiastical leader, who wished to appropriate her into his own harem. Buffalo Bill, disguised as a Ute warrior, rushed into the endowment house, or temple, and at the foot of the altar rescued his sister and fled with her, narrowly escaping from the Mormon threat. Lee followed in pursuit and

4. Buffalo Bill, as he may have appeared onstage, circa 1877.
Buffalo Bill Center of the West, Cody, Wyoming, Buffalo Bill
Museum, MS006 William F. Cody Collection, P.6.0870.01.

engaged in a hand-to-hand conflict with Buffalo Bill, in which Cody ultimately hurled him to the ground and stood over him with a revolver. The
hero got the best of the Mormons and before exclaiming, "Lee has lost
and I have won," as he emerged victorious and eventually able to see his
cherished sister happily married to a monogamous man.[54] In this caution-
ary tale of danger and captivity, Bill once again vanquished the Mormon
threat and freed his sister from forced incorporation into the religious
snare, allowing her to marry and establish a proper American family.

May Cody used a similar formula to earlier anti-Mormon performances—
with dashing heroes, "villainous Mormon elders," and young women
kidnapped into polygamy—and employed these common stereotypes in
the form of Danites, polygamy, and the Mountain Meadows Massacre.[55]
In Cody's plays, in dime novels, and in the popular imagination, the
Danites embodied the nefarious nature of Mormons and prompted a fear
of religious violence. A part of that fear was the controlling influence of
ecclesiastical leaders. Enter Brigham Young's role in May Cody. The play's
synopsis suggests that Lee's Danites took orders directly from Young to
capture the beautiful May.[56] With such a representation, audiences would
have viewed Mormons as simpleminded, violent, and unquestionably
obedient to the dictates of Young, making the leader and his followers a
particularly dangerous group.[57]

In the play's third act, set in the Mormon temple, Brigham Young
attempted to force the abducted May Cody into a polygamous marriage.[58]
The drama May Cody, then, offered a commentary on the Latter-day Saint
practice of polygamy and the perception that it was a vicious, lustful system that kept women in bondage. In this dramatic interpretation, Young
used his authority as a religious leader to lure men and force women into
lives of moral depravity and rampant sex.[59] Setting the act in the temple
made a spectacle of the most sacred space to Latter-day Saints. It put the
temple and its religious ceremonies on display. By focusing on Brigham
Young and Latter-day Saints as violent and the temple as a place for sexual
exploitation, Cody's play was designed to prejudice audiences' understanding of Latter-day Saints. As the National Republican commented in its
review of the play, "Mormon life is shown up in all of its repulsive details,

5. Poster showing vignettes of scenes, starting in the upper left with the abduction of May and ending in the lower right with Buffalo Bill holding Brigham Young at gunpoint in the Latter-day Saint temple, from the play *May Cody, or Lost and Won*, circa 1877. Library of Congress, LC-DIG-ppmsca-54797.

from the interior of the temple to the diabolical plots in the wilderness."[60] The harmful depiction certainly would have influenced the perception of spectators, who likely left the theater with less tolerance for Mormonism than they had before entering, if they had any at all.

May Cody offered viewers a voyeur's look into the Mormon home, sacred space, religious practice, and sexuality, portraying it as titillating, though strange and repugnant. Polygamy was the ongoing scandal that Americans loved to hate. It presented another variation on the captivity narrative of stealing or enslaving white women by others.[61] Buffalo Bill's play put in front of the audience's eyes the potential peril of trafficking women into the Mormon fold. The play invited audiences to feel the thrill and horror of abduction and incorporation into Mormon polygamy.

A year after it first premiered, *May Cody* continued to draw large crowds. Returning to the nation's capital in September 1878, the play enthralled a packed National Theatre audience. The *Washington Post's* review noted that the drama "never flags, but is kept up by hair-breadth escapes from Indians and Danites. The massacre of the emigrants by the Mormons is realistic. Bill, the hero scout, always conquers in his defence of the right, and stands out as a prominent feature."[62] Buffalo Bill's character in *May Cody* ultimately saved his sister, representing the white American woman, from the ominous fate of a forced polygamous marriage and the grips of the reviled Mormons. While Cody may not have been involved in the writing of *May Cody*, he lent his increasingly popular name and persona to a prevalent anti-Mormon narrative. His production reflected the public's entrenched perception of Mormon men as lecherous polygamists, especially Brigham Young (even though he had passed away in August 1877). It was what audiences wanted to see at a time rife with efforts to end polygamy in the West.

Spectators of *May Cody* came from a culture that feared the degradation of white women. The Reconstruction era in America, which was closing as Buffalo Bill performed this anti-Mormon play, brought about a culture of white male reconciliation and white supremacy in the decades following the Civil War. In the southern United States especially, Reconstruction produced and was defeated by a violent reaction to changes occurring in the nation's public life that ultimately destroyed much of the Civil War's accomplishments toward racial, social, and economic equality. Patterns of racial dominance won out.

Violent segregation arose as a southern response to widespread changes occurring as several forces placed races together in political, economic, and sexual situations and impelled whites in the direction of firm racial control. This direction and these patterns emerged in culture and politics. Black Americans, previously depicted as submissive, genial slaves, were rendered as fiercely violent, animalistic, menacing, hypersexual threats to white women. Black men, white men feared, would abduct, rape, and otherwise brutalize white women; they simultaneously feared Chinese or Asian men taking white women into opium dens, the abuse of opium and interracial sex being prevalent fears at this time.[63] The Mormons were just one of several active threats capable of destroying white womanhood and the white American family.

Here is where the use of Ann Eliza Young as a character in the play becomes especially noteworthy. The show's playbill lists Ann Eliza Young as one of the prophet's wives, though the real Ann Eliza Young had divorced Brigham Young in 1875. She condemned polygamy and had become a well-known advocate against it and the Latter-day Saint faith. That Buffalo Bill's play cast a character for Ann, given her public efforts to "impress upon the world what Mormonism really [was and] to show the pitiable condition of its women," suggests that the playwright and the famous showman wanted their audiences to understand the same.[64] Much like the real Ann Eliza Young, the representation of her in the show seems to have been intended to inform the public of the undesirability and unacceptability of Mormonism in placing women in bondage.

Acting out the horrific Mountain Meadows Massacre, one of the darkest and most critical moments in Mormon history, and placing Buffalo Bill as a witness and savior only added to the narrative. Indeed, Cody's claims of authenticity made his performances both crowd-pleasing and memorable. People were drawn to a genuine depiction of Mormons and the West. One eastern newspaper reviewer explained the message embedded in *May Cody*: "It is a vivid illustration of Mormon iniquity, villainy and crime, and is worth more by its thrilling portrayal of what Mormonism really is, towards awakening the sentiment of the people against the monstrous practices of these people than editorials or speeches could ever amount to.

We . . . will say in all earnestness that every scene of every act is thrilling and awakens every emotion of the heart."[65] Another praised the play as "fearfully realistic at times" and its star and company as superior.[66]

Playing on preconceived notions of Mormons in Utah, Cody's company, with him as the figurehead, apparently understood that anti-Mormonism was lucrative. The drama sold to the people a "genuine" view of the religious group and its history, while it advanced Cody's own image as a western hero. Buffalo Bill's performance exploited a people and their faith for gain. It was a public display of popular history; it interpreted Mormons in a way that cohered powerfully in the imaginations of the spectators. It re-created a horrific part of the Mormon past to underscore how that history informed the present and the version of and vision for the American social order Cody wanted to sell.[67]

While Cody's play dramatized the Mormons as a type, it did the same thing for the actor. He presented himself as the antithesis of Mormon men, demonstrating to audiences the expected behavior of American men in shaping the social order. The American man "was virile, yet restrained, willing to follow the spiritual example set by wives, but still firmly in economic and social control, and married for procreation, not sexual gratification."[68] Buffalo Bill was the model of American manhood and the protector of white womanhood.

Reviewers commented on Cody's physical appearance, manly beauty, and realistic portrayal. His performance in *May Cody* exhibited "a far higher type of manhood than any of the pieces in which he has heretofore appeared," one reviewer effused, while another commented, "He is a handsome fellow, with a dashing, military appearance, and seems to have a true conception of the part he plays."[69] The San Francisco *Daily Alta California* newspaper enthusiastically labeled Buffalo Bill the "best man now on the stage" due to his "graceful manliness, his natural and easy style."[70] Cody's acting reflected his real persona at time when "realism was beginning to influence dramatic arts," making his performances innovative and giving them an air of authenticity.[71] He grew more credible as an actor because of his realistic portrayal of professed actual, historic events.

With Cody's good looks as the epitome of American manhood and its timely content, *May Cody* was the best drama Buffalo Bill had yet produced and "proved a grand success both financially and artistically."[72] Large and boisterous audiences welcomed Buffalo Bill and "May Cody" from San Francisco's California Theatre to the National Theatre in Washington DC to Ford's Grand Opera House in Baltimore, Maryland.[73] The 1877–78 seasons, in which Cody's combination performed both *May Cody* and *The Red Right Hand*, proved to be his most profitable, with his receipts more than doubling his expenditures.[74]

As winter thawed into the spring of 1879, Buffalo Bill and his company began a new season. On April 19 they performed at the Metropolitan Theatre in Sacramento, California, with an afternoon showing of *May Cody, or Lost and Won* and a night debut of Cody's newest sensational drama, *The Knight of the Plains, or Buffalo Bill's Best Trail.* In this performance Cody appeared as four distinct characters. Scenes in which Buffalo Bill presented his sharpshooting abilities with rapid and fancy shooting and those that included American Indian dances drew the most attention from reviewers. The *Sacramento Daily Union* commented on the double-header of plays produced by Buffalo Bill: "They are characteristic of the man and his career of daring and service to his country as a scout and guide to the United States forces in troublous times on plains and frontier. Mr. Cody has greatly improved as an actor, and his methods now are of a high order and quite equal to the demands of the plots in which he is placed on the stage."[75] After departing from California on the railroad east through Nevada, Buffalo Bill focused his gaze on Salt Lake City, his first look at the capital city of the Latter-day Saints.

William F. Cody arrived in Utah in May 1879, more than twenty years after he had claimed to be there during the Utah War. He had a packed itinerary. The *Salt Lake Tribune* reported that Buffalo Bill and his acting company toured the city and visited with officers at Fort Douglas, the military installation on the mountain bench overlooking the capital.[76] Cody then prepared himself for a two-night stand at the Salt Lake Theatre.

Though home to an exoticized people, Salt Lake City, observers commented, was a well-designed and healthy city. One *Harper's Weekly* article said of the Mormon capital, "Viewed from the heights above, the town appears a little paradise, so refreshing does this oasis of civilization seem in contrast to the surrounding desert."[77] The Salt Lake Theatre was a key component of the city. It was a popular, even vital part of the cultural life of the city. By the mid-1860s the theater regularly hosted touring actors, dramatic performances, and musical productions.[78] The theater, described as modern and one of the largest in the United States, was built in a classical style, with Doric columns and a beautiful interior with balconies. It was not only designed after but could rival the finery of the best theaters of the eastern United States. It could seat more than three thousand patrons and, according to Sara Alexander, was built with a stage of great length and breadth and other conveniences to benefit the performers.[79]

In one season in the early 1870s, the Salt Lake Theatre showed more than one hundred plays, with seventy of them featuring guest performers. The theater's roster of shows included a diversity of genres: tragedies, comedies, romances, westerns, and minstrel shows.[80] The theater was the property of The Church of Jesus Christ of Latter-day Saints. Ann Eliza Young claimed the theater was a source of great wealth to church leader Brigham Young, who "appropriated it as private property, and he pockets every dollar that is made at the theatre, and devotes it exclusively to his own use."[81]

Not everyone had the same opinion of Brigham Young as Ann Eliza did. Young believed in the performing and dramatic arts as an important educational factor for the Saints. The stage, Young said, could impress on the "minds of a community an enlightened sense of a virtuous life, also a proper horror of the enormity of sin and a just dread of its consequences."[82] He lent his influence to encouraging the arts during his life and considered the dramatic profession "an honored, and elevated profession." Though she abhorred Young's "obnoxious and unpopular church theories and social ideas," Sara Alexander, the esteemed actor who lectured against polygamy and Mormonism earlier in the 1870s, claimed that "every actor who knew him, holds him in esteem, so far as his attitude to the drama was practically exhibited; and the establishing of one of the best theatres" in the country.[83] Young wanted uplifting performances for the Saints, but he did not want them to see themselves or be seen as villains.

When Buffalo Bill arrived in Salt Lake City for his 1879 performances at the Salt Lake Theatre, however, he did not present *May Cody*. Instead, the Salt Lake City crowds watched *Knight of the Plains*, a new drama complete with romance, a stagecoach robbery, and a demonstration of Cody's shooting prowess.[84] Reviewing the plot of this play, one commentator wrote, "There was much drawing of revolvers and general denunciation of scoundrels and sundry impressive tableaux of manliness triumphant. . . . The gambling house scene included robbery and all sorts of playing and cheating and terminated in a duel. In the last act the villain is disposed of in a bowie knife fight."[85] Trying to draw a large crowd, Cody apparently chose *Knight of the Plains* because it did not have content directly related to Latter-day Saints. The large Mormon population in Salt Lake City almost certainly would have frowned on the damaging depiction of its religious culture and the darkest event of its recent past.

Despite Cody's efforts to play to the local population, his show brought in only a "fair-sized crowd." In its review of *Knight of the Plains*, the Mormon-owned *Deseret Evening News* stated bluntly that it could not recommend the performance or actors "as first class," noting that the dialogue was often inaudible and that the play dragged considerably. Still, the Mormon-affiliated newspaper did enjoy the spectacle of the burning prairie, stage robbery, "Mr. Cody's fancy shooting," and Buffalo Bill's fine stage appearance.[86]

꙳꙳꙳꙳꙳꙳

Later the same year that Buffalo Bill first performed in front of Mormon audiences, Frank Bliss, son of American Publishing Company president Elisha Bliss, published William Cody's autobiography, *The Life of Hon. William F. Cody*. Bookstores across the country carried the thick volume. It was also available for order by subscription, and Cody's fans could purchase a copy at theaters after one of his performances. The book, a bestseller, promoted the actor and bolstered his growing celebrity status.[87] The late nineteenth century was inundated with autobiographies, biographies, and memoirs of Civil War soldiers and western heroes with dramatic personal stories of lived events.[88] How much individuals took license with their autobiographical accounts probably depended on the person and the purpose for producing their life's history. For Cody, then thirty-three years old, the desire to control his life's narrative and, as the scholar Joy S. Kasson has stated, "take full possession of his own frontier persona" seems to have been paramount.[89]

Realism, authenticity, and believability were all part of the formula for Cody's success as Buffalo Bill; his autobiography made the stage persona that he created a part of his real encounters, often in melodramatic and sensational language that mirrored his performances and the dime novels written about him. Cody's autobiography contained truth and myth combined to create the known history of this increasingly popular figure. He was a northern Free-Soiler, teamster, trapper, buffalo hunter, army scout, and Indian fighter. Cody's life as told in the autobiography is a succession of jobs, experiences, and events that led directly to the persona that he embodied for decades and presented to millions of people in the United States and Europe.[90]

As a part of his carefully crafted public image, and perhaps to bolster his performative claims to having fought against the dangerous religious group, Cody used his autobiography to place Mormons in the role of one of the many threats that he helped defeat in his eventful life on the frontier. The autobiography conveyed the sense of realism that Cody had long battled the Mormon menace, even as a young boy.

The publication of the autobiography coincided with a time when all branches of the federal government, including Congress, began to strengthen their antipolygamy stance and when general anti-Mormon sentiment was on the rise in American culture. In 1878 Mormon polygamist George Reynolds, who had broken federal marriage laws by being married to multiple women at the same time and had been convicted in lower courts, took his case to the U.S. Supreme Court. Reynolds argued that his religion required him to marry more than one woman.[91] The case tested the limits of religious liberty, the Bill of Rights' free exercise of religion, and federal power. Supreme Court chief justice Morrison R. Waite delivered the court's first ruling: freedom of religion did not protect local religious practice at the expense of the law.[92] Boiling it down to its essence, legal historian Sarah Barringer Gordon has stated that the *Reynolds v. United States* decision confirmed that "Mormon polygamists had no constitutional right to engage in a form of marriage directly prohibited by Congress."[93] National law prohibited a man from being married to more than one woman at a time, and religious belief could not be put into action to supersede that law. According to this definition, Mormons were not free to exercise or physically act on their religious belief in plural marriage but could still believe in it. The laws and the judicial branch's upholding of those laws made it clear that the government was more forcefully using its supremacy to exterminate the Mormons' religious marriage practice. The 1879 Supreme Court decision in *Reynolds v. United States* made the Latter-day Saint arguments that the Constitution protected the practice of plural marriage moot.[94]

In the wake of the *Reynolds* Supreme Court decision, President Rutherford B. Hayes urged Congress to amend antipolygamy legislation and to put more power into punishing plural marriage. On December 1, 1879, in his third annual message, Hayes stated that the nation would not approve of Utah advancing to sovereign statehood while the Latter-day Saint population upheld a marital practice condemned as a crime by the laws of the nation. To execute marriage laws firmly and effectively, the president advocated for the withdrawal or withholding of the rights and privileges of citizenship of those who violated or opposed the enforcement of the law. Moreover, Hayes's administration sought to prevent foreign Mormons from immigrating to the United States.[95] Hayes again called for severe measures against Mormon polygamy, telling Congress the following year that "the sanctity of marriage and the family relation are the corner stone of our American society and civilization" and that the nation needed to "reestablish the interests and principles which polygamy and Mormonism have imperiled." Finally, Hayes recommended that Congress move to withhold the right to vote, any government office, and the opportunity to sit on juries in Utah Territory from those who practiced or supported polygamy. The president's comment unveiled designs to disenfranchise the Mormons.[96]

At a time and in a culture saturated with negative, even threatening, images of Latter-day Saints, readers of Buffalo Bill's autobiography would have understood and appreciated the valiant efforts of the young Bill Cody struggling to combat Mormons. Fashioning his identity in part around conflicts with the Mormons would have further endeared Buffalo Bill to American audiences. His autobiographical account would have also cemented the perceived realism of his stage performances. Buffalo Bill had become a character who fought against Mormons and protected loved ones from them. He had emerged from the 1870s as a symbol of manhood to preserve the West as a place for the American family to grow.

3

A Scene Change

Buffalo Bill's stage combination opened a new decade with a new performance. *The Prairie Waif: A Story of the Far West*, written by John A. Stevens, a respected playwright and manager of the Windsor Theatre in New York City, premiered in 1880.[1] Stevens had the audacity to pin a $5,000 price tag on the play—ten times what Cody had paid for any of his previous plays. Cody was taken aback, but the playwright was convincing, and they eventually agreed on the sum of $4,000.[2] Though expensive, *Prairie Waif* proved successful and became one of Cody's longest-running stage dramas.

The plot offered a tried-and-true formula. Descriptions and reviews of *Prairie Waif* vary, but one newspaper remarked, "The plot is simple, yet very instructive, interesting, and laughable. Onita, a little prairie flower, is captured by the redskins and Mormons, and after ten years time, is discovered by Buffalo Bill, rescued and taken back to her father, after thrilling skirmishes and desperate encounters."[3] Stevens had found success with the classic damsel-in-distress trope, a centuries-long mainstay of storytelling, in his previous play *Unknown* and adjusted it only slightly in *Prairie Waif*. Perhaps because of the recent success of *May Cody*, Buffalo Bill was willing to pay a large sum for a new anti-Mormon play, knowing the lucrative genre would reward him and his troupe.

The new play also incorporated the themes and archetypes previously made popular in Buffalo Bill's stage performances. Villainous Mormon and Indian allies disrupted an American home and captured a beautiful young white woman, only to have their plans ultimately thwarted by the hero. The alluring scenes depicted exaggerated visual images of Mormon male libertines. Buffalo Bill countered the polygamist with a powerful, protective dose of American masculinity. The play once again reinforced American morality and forewarned audiences of the need to protect female virtue. Theatergoers would have left uneasy or even frightened about the possible ramifications of a Mormon-Indian alliance and the influence those Mormon religious zealots could have on Native peoples or other minority groups. As demonstrated in the play, where dozens of Mormons were killed during its course, American society needed to crush these threats.[4]

Prairie Waif was Buffalo Bill's third anti-Mormon blockbuster. Like its two predecessors, *Prairie Waif* was built on the foundation of decades of anti-Mormon thought, which was again in the crosshairs of American politics and culture when Stevens penned the play. A collision of politics, law, and culture occurred at the intersection of religion, home, and family in the early 1880s. Plural marriage had been a crime under U.S. federal law since 1862, and politicians moved to strengthen the statutes further. In his 1881 inaugural address, U.S. president James A. Garfield touched on the moral and cultural impact of Mormonism. On a cold, snowy inauguration day, to an audience packed around the East Portico of the U.S. Capitol, Garfield declared, "The Mormon Church not only offends the moral sense of manhood by sanctioning polygamy, but prevents the administration of justice through ordinary instrumentalities of law." No ecclesiastical organization, Garfield declared, could destroy "family relations and endanger social order" or be permitted in any form "to usurp in the smallest degree the functions and powers of the National Government."[5] Mormonism, in other words, threatened American manhood, and legislative action was needed to protect the American family.

In his first annual message to Congress, U.S. president Chester A. Arthur, who had taken the presidential chair after Garfield's assassination in July 1881, picked up the rhetorical mantle of his predecessor. He spoke out against polygamy and for the federal government to lead the way in regulating Latter-day Saint homes and sexual practices. He encouraged Congress to pass forceful, resolute legislation to create divisions in the Mormon home by requiring women to testify against men in polygamy cases and mandating that all individuals seeking to be married in Utah first file for and obtain a certificate from the government.[6] Many political groups, including the Women's Christian Temperance Union, participated in antipolygamy political activism while encouraging congressional action.[7] Political rhetoric and cultural displays reinforced the notion that any group hiding behind religion to uphold polygamy as a divine institution was nothing more than "a band of criminals."[8]

Within four months of Arthur's December 1881 annual message, Congress passed a series of amendments to federal marriage laws. These measures, introduced by George F. Edmunds, a senator from Vermont, prohibited plural marriage and unlawful cohabitation. The Edmunds legislation further disenfranchised convicted polygamists or cohabitants, making them ineligible to hold political office. Under this legislation Mormon polygamists could no longer serve on a jury in cases involving plural marriage or cohabitation. The 1882 legislation also created a new federal bureaucracy in Utah, known as the Utah Commission, which directed elections in the territory and ensured that polygamists would be disqualified from holding office. The Utah Commission prohibited polygamists from voting by requiring all voters to take an oath certifying that they did not practice polygamy (women in Utah Territory had gained the right to vote in 1870). Laws like the 1882 Edmunds Act not only bolstered earlier antipolygamy legislation but also strengthened popular narratives that Mormons were deviant offenders of American law and culture.[9]

By practicing plural marriage, Latter-day Saints failed to conform to a basic component of republican society. Protestant moralists, lawmakers, and the press all believed that monogamy offered liberty and happiness in such a society. This was a primary message embedded in Buffalo Bill's anti-Mormon plays: the monogamist, masculine hero liberated white women from the clutches of polygamy. Though he played the hero, Buffalo Bill was perhaps not the monogamist that he claimed to be. He was accused of being a womanizer and may have had several affairs even as early as 1877, the year he first performed *May Cody* and when his first separation from Louisa occurred. His good looks, manly physique, and growing fame and fortune certainly would have made him very attractive to women in the many cities in which he performed. Being away from Louisa for long periods and the regular conflict in their marriage likely would not have helped his fidelity. After years of arguing, separations, and discord, Buffalo Bill made his first attempt to divorce Louisa in 1883.[10] But for Cody, those were private matters. His public persona remained firm in protecting the monogamist American family from external threats.

During the 1870s Latter-day Saints continued to travel about the United States preaching their doctrine as missionaries. Those missionaries found themselves particularly undesirable in the American South during the Reconstruction era. Southerners warned that Mormon men were a danger to the home. The presence of the faith's proselytizing missionaries "could create a 'tumult' in an otherwise peaceful community and 'destroy the unity and happiness of families and communities,'" the Reverend Martin Luther Oswalt, a former Latter-day Saint turned Baptist who profited from his anti-Mormon tracts, proclaimed. These white Protestant Christians believed that Mormonism victimized women and children, the essence of the home. This perceived victimization had the potential to destabilize or otherwise create vulnerabilities in the American home. In sum, Mormons were considered "home wreckers."[11] Those indulging in respectability politics pointed a giant finger at the presence and growth of the Latter-day Saint faith in the Great Basin as an impediment to white families in that crucial region.

Latter-day Saints pointed the finger right back. Mormons had long sought to combat prevalent American rhetoric of the evils of plural marriage by arguing that large-scale prostitution and extramarital affairs occurred frequently among monogamous Americans.[12] American male sexuality, they claimed, was lustful, and extramarital sexual activity was dangerous to women and families. Contrary to the prevailing notion of Mormon men, polygamy, Latter-day Saints argued, was not about male lust. Mormons glorified procreation as the sole aim of sexuality, turning lust into responsibility and providing every woman the opportunity to marry and become a mother.[13] It simply produced a type of home that was different from the monogamous mainstream. Americans wanted to change the Mormon home, and like any group under attack, the Mormons fought back.

By the 1880s they thought one method to safeguard their way of life was to invite the world into their homes. In 1885 Junius Free Wells, the thirty-one-year-old organizer of the Latter-day Saints' Young Men's Mutual Improvement Association, charged to help boys develop intellectually, recreationally, and spiritually, gave a powerful discourse about the purity of the Mormon home. Wells, a slender but sturdy, dark, and handsome mustachioed man, was a son of Daniel H. Wells, a commander of Mormon militia forces during the Utah War and a longtime counselor to Brigham Young in the First Presidency. Junius had grown up in a Mormon home with a father who practiced plural marriage. As Junius grew older, he traveled abroad in Great Britain and Europe as a missionary for his faith.[14] Over the years, he had become a talented writer and orator.

In Junius Wells's address to Latter-day Saints in Salt Lake City in July 1885, he invited people to come to Utah and see for themselves how the Saints lived. He declared, "Let them go into our homes and what will we show them there? We will show them respect of husbands for wives, wives for husbands, parents for children, children for parents and for each other. We will show them faith; we will show them virtue, and we challenge them to deny the truth of our showing to the American people." "The homes of the 'Mormon' people are homes constructed upon the principles of purity and virtue," the church leader declared. Though Wells, like other Latter-day Saints, felt the hate of the world against their faith, he believed in the pure intentions and desires of church members. But he also understood the ways American politics and culture represented the Saints. To remedy the perceptions of the nation and potentially suppress the efforts to alter the Mormon home, Wells called on both Americans and those overseas to come to Utah and see for themselves that the religionists were upright people capable of self-government and were not criminals. "I would undertake to show that in our homes there is not the element of crime or sin or wrong, but that they will compare favorably with the homes of any," Wells asserted.[15]

Politicians, press, and writers, though, were not ready to condone the Latter-day Saint home or its practice of polygamy. They often lumped Mormonism together with foreign and exotic non-Christian belief systems, in particular Islam, to emphasize its otherness, peculiarity, suspi-

6. Junius F. Wells (*standing*) with his father, Daniel H. Wells,
1890. Courtesy of the Church History Library, The Church
of Jesus Christ of Latter-day Saints, Salt Lake City.

ciousness, and danger. Adding to the perception of the Mormon menace in the early 1880s was the ongoing concern over immigration to the
United States. In an article titled "The Mormon Situation," the prolific
writer and later inflammatory editor of the *Salt Lake Tribune*, Charles
C. Goodwin, labeled The Church of Jesus Christ of Latter-day Saints as

"an institution so absolutely un-American in all its requirements that it would die of its own infamies within twenty years, except for the yearly infusion of fresh serf blood from abroad."[16] American opinion makers argued that Mormon immigration brought downtrodden women into the tentacles of Mormondom. In one of his *Harper's Weekly* cartoons, Thomas Nast christened these souls "cheap help-mates for Mr. Polygamist." In his depiction a malevolent Mormon man watched gleefully as women disembarked a boat with signs labeling them chambermaid, cook, waitress, nurse, laundress, and seamstress. These signs hung like weights around the women's necks as the man looked on pleased to lead them into a life of drudgery, servitude, and abuse.[17] Other period cartoons, editorials, and prominent political figures offered similar commentary on Mormonism and polygamy.

American presidents and their administrations made anti-Mormon immigration part of their foreign-policy rhetoric. As early as 1859, President James Buchanan had sought to limit Mormon immigration to the United States. Shortly after sending the U.S. Army to install a new governor and federal officials in Utah Territory, Buchanan pled with an English diplomat to prevent Latter-day Saints from defecting. "I would thank you to keep your Mormons at home," the U.S. president appealed.[18] By 1879 Rutherford B. Hayes's secretary of state, William Evarts, complained that "the annual statistics of immigration into the United States show that large numbers of immigrants come to our shores every year from the various countries of Europe, for the avowed purpose of joining the Mormon community at Salt Lake, in the Territory of Utah." Each year, thousands, primarily from Great Britain and Scandinavian nations, poured out of the hulls of ships at American ports headed for Utah. "The ignorant classes" of Europe, Evarts argued, strengthened the Mormon polygamy structure. Calling the Mormons perpetual criminal offenders, the secretary of state requested that European governments "check the organization of these criminal enterprises . . . [and] prevent the departure of those proposing to come hither as violators of the law."[19] Evarts received responses from several nations, including Italy, England, France, and Norway. The response from England suggested that the government

I think one wife is enough.—*Gillam.*

I imagine it must be a perfect Paradise.—

A DESPERATE ATTEMPT TO SC

Four artists who differ in style and in mind
This cartoon on the Mormons have jointly designed.

7. Cartoons illustrating American perceptions of the Mormon Question, from *Puck* magazine, February 1884. Library of Congress, LC-DIG-ppmsca-28293.

on the island would take it under consideration and use its influence to notify and caution its citizens about the American law and "against being deceived by Mormonite emissaries."[20]

Grover Cleveland's 1885 annual presidential message made the foreign-policy connection more direct, combining it with other federal efforts to end the Mormon belief and practice of plural marriage. "Since the people upholding polygamy in our Territories are reenforced by immigration from other lands," Cleveland pronounced, "I recommend that a law be passed to prevent the importation of Mormons into the country."[21] The president stated that incoming Mormons were already lawless, danger-ous criminals who presented a significant risk because of their belief in polygamy.[22] Large-scale immigration generated widespread fear among American citizens who increasingly viewed immigrants as inferior peo-ples and criminals. Deep cultural chasms formed between those whites who considered themselves "native" Americans and immigrants and their supporters. European immigrants who also identified as Mormons only added fuel to the rhetorical fire.

The overall campaign to cease Mormon immigration from European countries to the United States was largely unsuccessful, however, and caused some debate in Washington and in the press over freedoms and rights.[23] States could not control immigration and turned to the federal government to legislate and enforce controls. The first federal immigration act, passed in 1882, spoke to a broad exclusion of poor and undesirable peoples. Longer-range immigration regulation focused on excluding poor people, and Mormons were seen as poor, both morally and in a literal financial sense.[24] President Cleveland's desire to seal America's borders from Mormons, in the same era that saw a solidification of white Protestant supremacy in the United States and the banning of Chinese peoples from immigrating to the country, demonstrates the disdain for Mormon plural marriage.[25] Like other perceived evils, Mormonism remained a retrograde element unwelcome in the national family. The rhetorical effort to stem Mormon immigration continued through the decade.

While the American family drama with Mormonism continued to unfold in political and cultural circles, William Cody embarked on a new adventure. He took leave of the stage in 1883 to play in a larger arena. Buffalo Bill presented his first Wild West show that year in Omaha, Nebraska. A variation on the circus and roundup genres of the era, his Wild West combined displays of horsemanship, exotic peoples, sharpshooting, roping, and events from white American frontier life. The limits of the stage could not accommodate a parade of cowboys, Indians, and animals; Indian horse and footraces; a reenactment of the Pony Express; or an attack on a stagecoach. Though the cowboy's life was not romantic in the least, the image of a self-reliant, brave, and tough western individual had begun to permeate American culture as Cody introduced his new show. Cody presented a narrative drama of American civilization and white westward progress in real speed to offer an exciting picture of the lived experience of the West.

Mark Twain remarked about the emotion-producing realism of the performance after attending the Wild West show for the first time. Twain wrote that he thoroughly enjoyed the spectacle and that "it brought vividly back the breezy wild life of the Great Plains and the Rocky Mountains, and stirred me like a war song." He further expressed his approval of the show's authenticity, even down to its smallest details. "It is wholly free from sham and insincerity; and the effects produced upon me by its spectacles were identical with those wrought upon me a long time ago by the same spectacles on the frontier," the eminent novelist wrote to Cody in a letter that was quickly published in the newspaper. Twain also remarked on the "painfully real" display of horsemanship he observed, before closing his letter applauding Cody for producing a "purely and distinctively American" exhibition.[26] Buffalo Bill had become a master at producing the illusion of realism, and his genre-defining Wild West earned the endorsement of and praise from newspapers nationwide. Before long it would win acclaim and validation from European royalty as well.

Everything in Buffalo Bill's Wild West was artfully symbolic. The show presented a narrative of the western American experience from a white male perspective. It was a story of competition, protection, and control. As the audience watched a frantic Indian footrace, they witnessed speed. That speed provided a narrative element that white settlers needed to exceed Indian swiftness (and by extension that of other races and immigrant groups) to outrace and outperform them. Wild West performers presented an attack on a stagecoach, wherein treacherous Indians pursued the coach as the symbol of progressing westward civilization, with Buffalo Bill and his cowboys coming to the rescue to defeat the assailants. The speed and the ultimate victory of the American white man thrilled audiences. The attack on the stagecoach reenacted the symbolic passage from darkness and savagery to the conquering and civilizing of the vast spaces of the West.[27] The whole show, whether the stagecoach, the gun competitions, or the horse riding and racing, displayed the continuous struggle white America had against people of color, immigrants, industrialization, and urbanization. Cody's story was designed to reinvigorate white men.

The setting of the West was imperative. Western landscapes were beautiful scenes of power and the region of the nation's future following the Civil War. The Wild West show emerged in a post-Reconstruction milieu of white supremacy and provided an arena for simulated but realistic performance of muscular, hardy white American men defeating other men in front of enthusiastic audiences.[28] In the narrative of continuous struggle, white Americans would have understood that their frontier virtues could be lost quickly among the many unmanly and un-American threats, especially in the West, a place considered the last bastion of white America.[29]

Cody's Wild West also reminded audiences that western settlers needed constant protection. Virile white men would offer that protection to women and the home. Buffalo Bill's Wild West embodied this even more with the addition of a climaxing tableau that married his stage career with his new venture. The "Attack on the Settler's Cabin" essentially repurposed the Indian attack on the stagecoach but replaced the symbol of progress with a more familiar symbol of a virtuous home and family. Audiences held their collective breath as real-life Native peoples, employed as actors in the Wild West show, descended on the dwelling of a white American family. Buffalo Bill and his cowboys once again came to the rescue and saved the family and home, symbolic of these virile white men preserving the nation's domestic spaces from the threat of captivity and destruction.

The Wild West performances of the 1880s promoted the cowboy as a heroic type. Buffalo Bill's show thrust the cowboy as western protector into the American cultural mainstream.[30]

Focusing on the home, the most foundational place for the American family, Buffalo Bill's exhibition tapped into cultural anxieties surrounding the home, womanhood, domesticity, and family. Bombarded by the era's variety of cultural, racial, and economic threats, this messaging resonated deeply with white middle-class families. The show was entertaining and provided enough realism that middle-class women wanted to attend the Wild West spectacle and in turn encourage the virility of their fathers, husbands, or brothers to protect the household order. The message in Cody's display catered to a particular demographic. Where his presentation of an Indian attack was about the white defense of the home in a rapidly progressing world, Indian activists and others saw the same story as one of white pillaging and devastation.[31] The voices and perspectives of minority activists and groups, however, went unheard.

In his Wild West show, as in his earlier stage performances, Buffalo Bill was the symbol of white manhood who stood for family and home preservation. While he presented this epic narrative illusion to growing audiences, his own family faltered. He and Louisa fought over money and property and the time William spent on his show business. William established a massive residence, a far cry from the modest settler's cabin he portrayed in the Wild West performance. His estate featured a large, marvelous Victorian-style home and barn on some four thousand acres to support cattle, horses, and fields with irrigation agriculture near North Platte, Nebraska, a thriving cattle town. Louisa refused to live there, preferring instead to reside in a stately home in the town with their children. While the Scout's Rest Ranch, as Cody's property was christened, revealed to passersby the financial success of the scout turned showman, the separate residences of William and Louisa revealed a fracturing family.

Adding to the marital challenges, the Codys welcomed a daughter, Irma, in February 1883 but lost their eleven-year-old daughter, Orra, in October of the same year to unknown causes. Orra was the second of the Cody children to pass; their only son, Kit Carson, died in 1876 at the age of five from scarlet fever. Both Orra and Kit were laid to rest at the Mount Hope Cemetery in Rochester, New York, where Louisa and the children were living for much of the 1870s. The challenge of having an infant, coupled with the untimely death of Orra, created another complication for William and Louisa to navigate. Further driving a wedge in their relationship was William's taxing performance schedule and travel. In the mid-1880s he spent the summers and falls performing the Wild West show, and during the off-season he returned to the stage with his traveling theater troupe. Louisa deeply despised her husband's absences. Despite the friction it caused, Buffalo Bill continued to tour from city to city, and soon he would take his entertainment overseas.

Before he set sail for England, Buffalo Bill wrapped up his stage career. In February 1886, at Boyd's Opera House in Omaha, Nebraska, Cody's troupe received a joyous reception from a packed house that enjoyed the performance of the sensational, romantic John Stevens border drama *Prairie Waif*. Cody, with his "tall form, familiar face and flowing locks," was praised for his smooth, easy, and graceful performance and especially applauded for his skillful and quick handling of his revolver. Cody's combination had not played Omaha for some time, according to one report of the performance, which brought a surging throng of fans to Boyd's for his shows.[32] From Omaha Cody and his crew traveled west.

In late February 1886, Cody and his company were in Wyoming Territory and traveled via rail from Evanston to Ogden, Utah Territory, to again perform *Prairie Waif* at the Union Opera House.[33] Cody's combination had performed in Utah Territory in front of largely Latter-day Saint crowds in 1879. That time his company performed *Knight of the Plains*, a play that had nothing to do with Utah's dominant religion. This time, at the pinnacle of national anti-Mormon sentiment, Buffalo Bill's company did not shy away from a performance that cast Latter-day Saints as villains. The *Salt Lake Herald*'s announcement of the coming production, however, did not include a description of its anti-Mormon content but simply declared, "'Prairie Waif' is one of those plays calculated to picture frontier life, with its various vicissitudes, and especially the thrilling adventures of a scout."[34] The *Ogden Herald* also dropped any mention of the content but mentioned that beautiful new scenery would be on display. Another advertisement in the newspaper simply stated, "The company are highly spoken of by the press of the country, and we may expect a magnificent performance."[35]

The hype did not disappoint the Ogden crowd. Performing on his fortieth birthday, Buffalo Bill delighted the throng of theatergoers. According to the *Herald*'s summary of the single performance on February 26, the audience applauded the drama wildly, and the reporter found "the acting throughout the entire play was all that could be desired. Mr. Cody ('Buffalo Bill') makes a grand hit as the rough, uncultured, but steel-hearted scout, and hero of the play. Miss Lydia Denier as the 'Waif,' played with exquisite taste the part of the long-lost daughter of General Brown."[36]

The next morning Buffalo Bill's stage company traveled nearly forty miles south to Salt Lake City on the Denver and Rio Grande Railroad. At about 11 a.m., the group of twenty individuals arrived at the Valley House, a commodious downtown hotel located on the southwest corner of South Temple and West Temple.[37] That afternoon a downtown street parade for the company preceded a matinee showing of *Prairie Waif*, which filled the Salt Lake Theatre "to excess."[38] The show's message of the heroic Buffalo Bill protecting the American family and home against the threat of a nefarious Mormon-Indian alliance was not commented on by the Salt Lake City press. Nearly a year later, however, the *Salt Lake Herald* printed a short article about the future of a former sharpshooting marshal. Mentioning that this lawman might join Buffalo Bill's Wild West, the *Herald* article stated, "Bill would doubtless pay handsomely for a man who could bring down a Mormon, off-hand, the first shot."[39] This reference could have been to the performance of *Prairie Waif*, in which many Mormons were shot and killed onstage, or to the general notion that Buffalo Bill would have supported the shooting of a Mormon because of his anti-Mormon reputation.

The day before Cody's arrival, the internationally respected Italian actor Tommaso Salvini had performed in the city.[40] Salvini impressed

8. The exterior of the Salt Lake Theatre about the time of Buffalo Bill's
performance there, circa 1885. Courtesy of the Church History Library,
The Church of Jesus Christ of Latter-day Saints, Salt Lake City.

the crowd and newspaper critics by displaying his marvelous talents in a
French tragedy titled *The Gladiator*. The opportunity to witness Salvini's
performance was considered a once-in-a-lifetime occasion. The Italian
great spoke in his native tongue, but even those who did not understand
Italian, one Salt Lake City newspaper declared, would enjoy the power
of this acting master.[41] The *Salt Lake Tribune* called Salvini "one of the
world's greatest actors," and an advertisement for *The Gladiator* labeled
it "the greatest dramatic event in the annals of the stage in Salt Lake."[42]

Though Buffalo Bill's entertainment won unqualified approbation of
the spectators, he did not measure up to the critical acclaim of the Italian
great. A *Salt Lake Herald*'s reporter could not help but compare the skill and
sophistication of Salvini with the players in Buffalo Bill's western drama.
The *Herald* critic wrote, "Mr. Buffalo Bill has secured a coterie of artists
whose merits might cause Salvini himself to blush—for his profession."
In contrast to the Ogden reporter's review, the Salt Lake newspaper writer
mocked Cody's acting abilities, suggesting that he was better suited to be
a streetcar driver than an actor. The writer further criticized the western
drama's dialogue: "Miss Lydia Denier, the Waif, herself who gave utterance

to all such thrilling chestnuts as 'unhand me, villain!', 'Your bride? Never. I'd rather be a corpse!' and 'Death rather than dishonor' in much the same tone. . . . It was a grand spectacle; one we hope, which we shall never be called upon to sit through again." The critic blamed the Salt Lake Theatre's management for scheduling Buffalo Bill immediately after Salvini. In the end the *Herald*'s critic scoffed at the inelegance and crudeness of the western scout, viewing him as an affront to the refined acting of a "highbrow" professional.[43] This assessment might suggest a deeper message. It points to a people in a time and place yearning for respectability after decades of prejudiced opinion about the Latter-day Saint faith and its practices. The message appears to be that Utahns, especially those residing in Salt Lake City, appreciated fine art and were refined in their cultural tastes, in contrast to the lasting negative portrayal of Mormonism that the popular performer, Buffalo Bill, brought to the stage. Cody's troupe played Salt Lake City for just one day and continued touring before returning to Park City, Utah, for a show on March 29, 1886. Cody then took leave of Utah for another six years.

/////////

Almost exactly one year after his performance in Utah, the ever-ambitious Buffalo Bill set his sights on Europe. On the last day of March 1887, alongside his company, Wild West performers, and hundreds of animals, Cody set sail for England, fulfilling his decades-long desire to take his act overseas. Departing from New York harbor, Cody and his crew endured a rough, monthlong journey, battling fierce storms as they rode across the rolling waves before they arrived in England. The ship docked at Gravesend, and a special train conveyed the Wild West contingent into the bustling, lively, and noisy West End of mighty London. Cody began rehearsals at the Earl's Court exhibition grounds, west of Buckingham Palace. The showman met and invited Albert Edward, then the Prince of Wales and later King Edward VII, and his family to an advance showing of the Wild West performance with its dramatic narrative of American settlement and conquest of the continent. It thrilled the prince so much so that he arranged a show for his mother.[44]

On May 11 Queen Victoria, the monarch of the United Kingdom, arrived for a performance at the exhibition grounds. It was her first public appearance since the death of her consort, Prince Albert, from typhoid fever on December 14, 1861.[45] Not only did the queen approve of the show and its presentation of the white settlement of the American West, but she also bowed "deeply and impressively toward" the American flag, symbolizing a peace and friendship between Britons and Americans not known since before the Declaration of Independence over one hundred years earlier. In her actions, then, Queen Victoria conceded to and validated the presentation of American conquest and the maturity of American culture and entertainment as embodied by Buffalo Bill's Wild West.[46] After the show the queen commanded that Cody be presented to her. She showered him with "compliments, deliberate and unmeasured," before meeting others in the cast.[47] London newspapers later extolled the Wild West show and Cody for doing so much to bring Europe and America together.[48]

Early in his stay in London, Buffalo Bill wrote a short letter to an old friend. Vincent "Vic" Bierbower had served as a district attorney for the Fifth Judicial District of Nebraska in the western part of the state. The district attorney, an 1866 graduate of Dickinson College in Pennsylvania, probably crossed paths with and befriended Buffalo Bill during the latter's time as a state legislator for the Twenty-Sixth District of Nebraska, which included Bierbower's home of Sidney in Cheyenne County. Vic was a hard-nosed prosecutor who fervently upheld the law. During his tenure as district attorney, from 1880 to 1882, Bierbower's tenacity led to successful convictions in forty-two out of the forty-five cases he prosecuted.[49] Like many westerners of the era, Bierbower looked for new opportunities. By early 1887 he had found one. Vic had moved to Idaho for a position in the territorial government—within a decade he would serve as the senate's president pro tempore. En route to his new home, Bierbower stopped in Ogden, Utah, and there jotted a letter to his entertainer friend, informing Cody of his move and whereabouts.

Buffalo Bill received the communication while in London and quickly penned a response. "So you are still on top of the earth Eh," he teased Vic. Then, referring to Mormon Danites, Cody playfully wrote, "I had hoped that the destroying angels had sent you to the Mormon heaven." Wondering if his friend would stay long in Utah, Buffalo Bill then wrote tongue in cheek, "How many wives have you got?" Buffalo Bill quickly transitioned from barbs and quips about Mormonism to his success in England. "I've captured this little country from the Queen down," Cody boasted.[50]

Buffalo Bill's letter to his old friend Vic Bierbower not only showcases the showman's repartee, spirited demeanor, and confidence but also provides a rare glimpse into his personal thoughts about Mormonism. Outside of his autobiography and the anti-Mormon plays he performed, this letter is the only known letter in which Cody commented about the dominant religious group of the Intermountain West prior to 1892. His jest about the Destroying Angels killing Bierbower referred to and reinforced long-standing stereotypes of Mormon religious violence. His questioning his friend's marital status and the adding of women to a harem certainly demonstrates a wide-held association of Utah with polygamy, though it might also suggest that anyone could be seduced into polygamy while in Utah. Referencing danger and sexual deviance in Utah demonstrates that Cody believed or at least internalized the character and narrative elements of the anti-Mormon plays he had performed onstage for the previous fifteen years, which featured dangerous Mormon villains and the titillating yet revolting practice of plural marriage. Cody's letter and his stage plays mirrored the strong prejudice of Americans toward the Latter-day Saint faith in the nineteenth century.

After a season in England, Cody toured through France, Spain, Germany, and Italy with his Wild West exhibition. During his European sojourn, Buffalo Bill not only grew his own brand to the heights of international fame but also exported an appealing American entertainment. European countries, particularly England and France, were the era's major cultural influencers. This distinctively American phenomenon, as Mark Twain had called the Wild West show when he saw it, raised the profile of Americans in the minds of European cultural influencers. Americans could also perceive the show as real culture, and the history of America (and of Cody's life) as one of triumphant political and social progress in large part because of the legitimacy it gained in England and in Europe.[51] In England alone the company gave three hundred performances to more than 2.5 million people. In short, Buffalo Bill's Wild West show was a smashing success.

⁕⁕⁕⁕⁕⁕

The cultural and political climate that produced virulent anti-Mormonism began to reach a climax in 1887. During the year that Cody impressed the queen of England with his shooting prowess and equestrian skills, a crowd in Wales, enraged by an anti-Mormon crusade, badly beat a group of Latter-day Saint preachers. The British author Arthur Conan Doyle published *A Study in Scarlet*, his first Sherlock Holmes novel, the same year. Riding a wave of anti-Mormonism that had informed cultural and social understandings of the faith group, Doyle's detective story laid bare the horrors of Mormonism and presented the men of that religious group as libidinous and vicious despots.[52] Readers flocked to Doyle's tale, launching the widespread popularity of the now-famous fictional investigator. The western world, it seemed, despised the Latter-day Saints.

Also in 1887 the U.S. Congress passed its most draconian antipolygamy legislation yet: the Edmunds-Tucker Act. Latter-day Saint Emmeline B. Wells called the Edmunds-Tucker Act the "most cruel and infamous measure and contrary to all sense of justice and right."[53] The act required plural wives to testify against their husbands in court and officially dissolved The Church of Jesus Christ of Latter-day Saints as a nonprofit corporation, a legal classification for groups organized exclusively for religious purposes. The dissolution of the church as a legal corporation meant that the federal government could confiscate and seize the church's property, thereby preventing the church from functioning in its ecclesiastical spaces.

The act also disenfranchised the territory's women; suffrage had been granted to Utah women in 1870, but their voting rights were quickly taken away. In addition, the Edmunds-Tucker Act placed control of territorial public education squarely in the hands of federal officials; abolished the Latter-day Saint militia known as the Nauvoo Legion; made all judges in the territory federal appointees; allowed the government to confiscate the

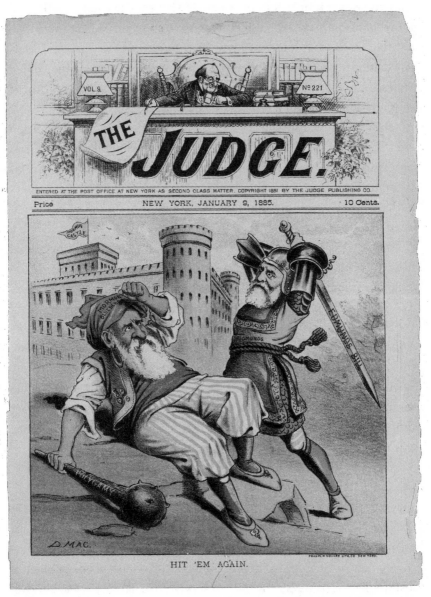

HIT 'EM AGAIN.

9. Cartoon illustrating the American hope that legislation in the form of the Edmunds Act would be the knight in shining armor that would finally slay the Mormon menace of polygamy, January 1885. Library of Congress, LC-DIG-ds-14610.

church's secular properties—considered to be real estate not directly used for religious purposes and valued over $50,000 (equivalent to more than $1.3 million in 2022)—and dissolved The Church of Jesus Christ of Latter-day Saints' fund to aid the immigration of its religionists to the United States.[54] Though direct presidential foreign policy to prevent Mormon immigration did not materialize, the provision of the Edmunds-Tucker Act forbidding the funding of immigration significantly halted Mormon efforts, slowing the immigration of people with "criminal character" and producing, in the short term, the results that earlier presidential administrations had sought. With presidential appointees running the entirety of the judicial system in Utah, Mormon violators of the law were imprisoned in greater numbers.[55]

Federal legislation and enforcement, judicial rulings, and presidential directives culminated in the imprisonment of church leaders, the confiscation of property holdings, and the slowing of Mormon immigration. The Supreme Court upheld the Edmunds-Tucker Act's provision to seize the church's property in a decision made in *The Late Corporation of The Church of Jesus Christ of Latter-day Saints v. United States.*[56] In upholding the constitutionality of the Edmunds-Tucker Act, the Supreme Court ruled that polygamy was "a crime against the laws, and abhorrent to the sentiments and feelings of the civilized world."[57] The Edmunds-Tucker Act threatened destruction of The Church of Jesus Christ of Latter-day Saints.

Considering the increasingly extreme legislation, George Q. Cannon, a church apostle, member of the faith's First Presidency, and former congressional delegate for Utah Territory, vocalized the need for community survival. "It would be a cruel waste of human effort," Cannon stated, "if, after having attained comfort in these valleys—established our schools of art and science—developed our country and founded our industries—we should now be destroyed as a community, and the value of our experience lost to the world. We have a *right* to survive. We have a *duty* to survive. It would be to the profit of the Nation that we *should* survive."[58] Cannon knew well the path the church would have to take to survive. The church and its members would need to abandon the practice of plural marriage. Following the laws of the land and "obeying, honoring, and sustaining the law" of the United States emerged as the greater principle. No longer were they willing to be perceived as criminals for the principle.[59]

Just over four months after the Supreme Court's ruling, Wilford Woodruff, the prophet and president of The Church of Jesus Christ of Latter-day Saints, decided he had to take a drastic stand to save the church. He issued a proclamation, which has become known as the manifesto, discontinuing the teaching and, eventually, practice of plural marriage among Latter-day Saints. "Inasmuch as laws have been enacted by Congress forbidding plural marriages, which laws have been pronounced constitutional by the court of last resort," Woodruff proclaimed, "I hereby declare my intention to submit to those laws, and to use my influence with the members of the Church over which I preside to have them do likewise."[60] Woodruff had arrived at this point only after decades of struggle and a final acknowledgment that it was the future destiny of the church "to aid in the maintenance and perpetuity" of American political, cultural, and economic institutions.[61] Woodruff's manifesto opened the door for the reconciliation of the Latter-day Saints with the American family.

After Woodruff issued his statement encouraging his church's members to obey federal marriage laws, news outlets reported on the monumental shift.[62] "The news from Utah is interesting," a *Harper's Weekly* article began. Because laws had been passed by the United States forbidding plural marriages, Woodruff made clear his intent to submit and to induce others to submit to the law, the article continued. The church president would no longer publicly encourage polygamy. "There is no further land of promise to which the Mormon law-breakers can flee," the *Harper's* article concluded, before offering a warning to the American nation that "the most constant watchfulness" was still required to truly abolish polygamy.[63]

⁂

Following his immense success with the Wild West show in Europe and approximately two years after Wilford Woodruff issued the polygamy manifesto, William Cody made a perception and relationship-altering visit to Utah and with members of The Church of Jesus Christ of Latter-day Saints. When Buffalo Bill returned to the Great Basin in 1892, he brought with him a new entourage. Instead of his traveling acting company or Wild West performers, Cody invited a coterie of military men, including Sir Henry St. John-Mildmay and Sir William Henry Mackinnon (both high-ranking British officers) and Robert "Pony Bob" Haslam, a Pony Express postal worker who made a famous ride of 120 miles in approximately eight hours to deliver Abraham Lincoln's inaugural address to the nearest telegraph station. Prentiss Ingraham, a Confederate colonel turned fiction writer who had written more than one hundred border novels (forty-five of them about Buffalo Bill) joined the party as a correspondent for the New York press.

In 1881 Ingraham, under the pen name Frank Powell, wrote an anti-Mormon dime novel, *The Doomed Dozen, or Dolores, the Danite's Daughter*, which featured Buffalo Bill Cody. Ingraham's novel presented anti-Mormon stereotypes and symbols common for the era: the kidnapping of women to become polygamous wives of lecherous Mormon men; secretive, violent Danites; a wagon-train massacre; and the chase and rescue of the women by the hero, Buffalo Bill.[64] Ingraham's writing echoed the cultural messaging of Buffalo Bill's anti-Mormon stage plays and the broader social understanding of Latter-day Saints. He was also an immensely popular writer whose stories were widely read.[65] In addition to other distinguished individuals, the expedition's participants included Latter-day Saints, including Junius F. Wells, Brig Young (a grandson of Brigham Young), and Daniel Seegmiller, an ecclesiastical leader in and former sheriff of Washington County in southern Utah.[66]

Latter-day Saints were particularly interested in Cody's expedition because of the potential to advertise their settled homelands. As mobility in the West increased and tourism became more prevalent in the last decades of the nineteenth century, the Saints were eager to seize an opportunity to display the natural beauty of the Intermountain West. The Saints in the areas of southern Utah and northern Arizona recognized the potential for natural tourism in the area, including hiking expeditions, explorations, game hunting, and grandiose scenery.

The possibilities of a tourist enterprise in that vicinity intrigued John W. Young, a businessman and son of Brigham Young who had lived in

10. Members of the expedition (*from left to right*): Junius F. Wells, Sir Henry St. John-Mildmay, William F. Cody, Sir William Henry Mackinnon, William H. Broach, and Prentiss Ingraham, November 1892. Courtesy of the Church History Library, The Church of Jesus Christ of Latter-day Saints, Salt Lake City.

London for ten years. During his interactions with English aristocracy, sportsmen, and other industrial titans, Young encouraged their travel to southern Utah, where they could hunt and find private recreation areas.[67] John Young also met William Cody in England in the late 1880s. Young propositioned Cody to investigate the "Arizona strip" north of the Grand Canyon. Young owned some cattle property in that area and told Cody of the landscape's beauty and economic potential as a tourist destination and big-game preserve. He sought to attract investors to the North Rim of the Grand Canyon. As John Young pursued many business opportunities, he persuaded Buffalo Bill to lead a group of English dignitaries to the region on a hunting expedition. Cody expressed interest, eager to see the region and its investment potential and to have some fun. He invited others interested in seeing "the Wild West of America, its game and wonderful scenery."[68]

John Young asked Junius F. Wells, the now thirty-eight-year-old talented writer and church leader who had, several years earlier, invited the world to come see the Mormon home, to act as his agent and point of contact to organize the logistics and work with Cody to ensure the success of the expedition.[69] According to John M. Burke, the general manager and press agent for Buffalo Bill's Wild West show, the trip came about in a slightly different way. Burke wrote, "When abroad Buffalo Bill heard so many officers of the army of France, England, and other countries ask about the Wild West of America, its game and wonderful scenery, that he extended an invitation to a number of gentlemen of rank and title to join him, with others from this country, on an extended expedition to the Grand Cañon of the Colorado, and thence on through Arizona and Utah to Salt Lake City on horseback."[70] Buffalo Bill also wanted to find a place to use as a game preserve with the idea to "establish a large park, stock it with all kinds of game, and use it as his private shooting grounds."[71]

Regardless of the motives or reasons for the trip, Junius Wells was instrumental in organizing the expedition. On October 19, 1892, Wells packed a bag and boarded a train at Salt Lake City's Union Station, headed east. He traveled to New York City, where a telegram from Col. William F. Cody awaited him. On October 25 Wells met with Cody and Prentiss Ingraham at the Hoffman House hotel, a favorite lodging place for Cody in New York City, where the three men "had good friendly chat and went over [the] general plan of the trip West." In early November the men departed New York City by rail. On November 4, they arrived at North Platte, Nebraska, and spent a few days at the commodious home of William F. Cody.[72] At Cody's Scout's Rest Ranch, Wells met Cody's son-in-law, Horton Sinclair Boal, and "a lot of Cowboys." Wells remarked that they "were entertained nicely by his daughter," a reference likely to Buffalo Bill's oldest daughter, the twenty-five-year-old Arta Cody Boal, although it is possible Cody's youngest daughter, nine-year-old Irma, could have been there as well. After their brief stay, Wells, Cody, Ingraham, and the rest of the party members boarded the train once again at the North Platte station and headed west.

The expedition reached Flagstaff, Arizona, on November 10, 1892. Daniel Seegmiller; Edwin D. Woolley, a man considered the father of tourism in the area; and "an escort of nearly half a hundred Mormon scouts, guides, and cowboys" met the party at the Flagstaff train station.[73] One report from Prentiss Ingraham provides insight into his perception of Seegmiller and Wells, two of the Latter-day Saints leading the expedition through the Grand Canyon. Ingraham wrote, "The escort was composed of cowboys, under the leadership of the chief of transportation, Daniel Seegmiller, an elder in the Mormon Church, and a man who understands the work he has to accomplish, and does it." "As we are invading Mormon-land," Ingraham continued, "we have also, as an honorary escort to Salt Lake City, Mr. Junius F. Wells, also a Mormon elder, a teacher, a preacher, and editor of the *Contributor*, published in Salt Lake City. Mr. Wells was a boy preacher of the Creed of Mormon. He is a genial gentleman and a man of learning and ability." Referencing the 1857–58 Utah War, Ingraham acknowledged Wells's heritage: "It was the father of Mr. Wells who was the chief councilor of Brigham Young, and who also was lieutenant-general of the Nauvoo Legion of Mormons, the army that faced the United States forces under Albert Sydney Johnston a way back in the Fifties."[74]

Taken together, Ingraham stated, "these gentlemen are a cavalier escort of Colonel Cody and his party through the land of the Mormon. All of them are most companionable to travel with, while they know the country perfectly and tell many good stories of their people. If there are any bad stories to tell we do not hear them, so take all they say on faith."[75] Labeling Seegmiller a cowboy leader (not unlike the image crafted for Cody) and Wells a genial, learned gentleman of ability, Ingraham demonstrated acceptance of these men, perhaps in spite of their faith. Far from the villainous lechers presented in Ingraham's dime novel or in Cody's stage performances, these men helped shift the paradigm and alter the narrative. Time and familiarity with these exemplary Latter-day Saints helped establish an atmosphere of trust and respect.

With fine weather attending them, the Cody party journeyed north toward the Grand Canyon. They hunted game as they rode across the desert "at great pace [on] charging horses."[76] Bear, mountain lions, elk, deer, antelope, and ducks were among the game the party pursued. Colonel Ingraham said of this stretch of the trip: "Every night we camped out without tents. The coyotes, knowing that we were a distinguished party, gave us nightly serenades."[77] As the men traversed through the majestic canyon, they enjoyed a visual feast of colors in the gorgeous horizontal layers of sandstone, limestone, and shale composing the canyon's steep vertical walls. It was "the grandest and most sublime scenery" they had ever seen. The beautiful fall weather conditions turned to wintry ones, quickly bringing snow and ice to the path as the party hiked unimproved trails and ascended heights of over eleven thousand feet on their treacherous journey through northern Arizona.[78] Despite the inclement weather and arduous travel, the men enjoyed the breathtaking scenery and convivial camp life.

The expedition was not simply a romantic jaunt through the mountains. Dangerous conditions lurked on the trail, and once the excursionists faced a frightening, narrow escape. While traversing a nearly perpendicular ascent in the San Francisco Mountains, two peaks near the North Rim of the Grand Canyon, British officer Maj. Sir Henry St. John-Mildmay's horse lost its footing, skating toward the edge of a cliff after misstepping on a piece of ice. The horse and its rider slipped, scrambled, and fell off the path, rolling down the trail several hundred yards.[79] Buffalo Bill rushed to his friend's rescue. He managed to throw a lasso to the major, who was clinging to a mountain precipice with one arm and to his horse with the other. Pulling the lasso over the horse's head, Cody led the charge in pulling the horse and its muscular rider back onto the path.[80] After that heart-pounding incident, Cody, the hero of the plains, looked at the novelist, Colonel Ingraham, and remarked at how a young boy's heart would thump when he pictured this thrilling incident.

Cody and Ingraham saw in that event the seeds of a dramatic story. Though the story had plenty of gripping details, Cody naturally wanted to embellish it. He dreamed of adding a beautiful maiden clinging to the horse's neck, while the brave English officer clung to the horse's tail. Still with energy after killing his "tenth Indian," Buffalo Bill would be there quick as a flash, he told Ingraham, to rescue the beautiful maiden.[81]

The men continued their journey, traveling north through the imposing Grand Canyon. It took the company eleven days to traverse the canyon before crossing the Colorado River at a calm, serene point on the mighty

11. Buffalo Bill and his party at the Grand Canyon, November 1892. Courtesy of the Church History Library, The Church of Jesus Christ of Latter-day Saints, Salt Lake City.

waterway known as Lee's Ferry, a location named for the infamous John D. Lee, in north-central Arizona near the Utah border. Cody and the members of his party apparently spoke about this place and its notorious namesake. In a public letter describing the journey, Cody reminded readers that Lee was a "Mormon Major" who led the attack during the Mountain Meadows Massacre and that this river crossing was the place to where Lee "escaped with his three wives in disguise." Lee became a ferry operator at this point, hiding in plain sight as he rowed across many individuals and officers who were looking to apprehend him for his role in the grisly massacre. Lee had been discovered, tried, and executed more than fifteen years before Buffalo Bill crossed the Colorado at his ferry point, but his name and his role in the massacre continued to hold the showman's interest.

Heading in a westerly direction around the brilliant red Vermillion Cliffs, the Cody expedition followed the same path trod by the Spanish friars Dominguez and Escalante in 1776. Moving west and north, they

12. Members of the expedition crossing the Colorado River at Lee's Ferry, November 1892. Courtesy of the Church History Library, The Church of Jesus Christ of Latter-day Saints, Salt Lake City.

climbed forested mountains and crossed the expansive Kaibab plateau and Arizona strip toward the crimson cliffs of southern Utah. The party passed through a few Mormon villages and spent a memorable evening at Buckskin Mountain, where Daniel Seegmiller and Edwin Woolley ran cattle for John Young.

While on the mountain ridge that spans from Coconino County in Arizona to Kane County in Utah, the expedition participants witnessed an awe-inspiring sight. According to Cody, "We saw the most remarkable display of falling meteors and stars that any party had ever seen." Neither Cody nor any of the other participants recorded their feelings about the meteor shower, but Cody did believe that this location would have made "the finest place in the world for an observatory" because it provided an "elevated location and clarity of atmosphere." After they

13. Buffalo Bill and his party pose for a photo on the Arizona strip, November 1892. Courtesy of the Church History Library, The Church of Jesus Christ of Latter-day Saints, Salt Lake City.

saw the stars, the Mormon guides warned the party that a severe storm was about to follow. Cody chose not to heed their advice and moved his party northward the next day, when a blizzard descended on them, bringing snow and dropping the temperature to thirty-one degrees below zero. The company survived the blizzard and proceeded on, where they endured the theft of "a number of" horses "by roving bands of Indians" and another significant accident. During a hunt Brig Young fell from his horse while leading the party and rolled down the side of the mountain. He was seriously injured and carried by the company to the next town to receive medical care.[82]

In late November Wells, Cody, and the rest of the party reached southern Utah and stopped at the border town of Kanab.[83] While there they met two Mormon ecclesiastical authorities from southern Utah and received lavish hospitality from the residents of Kanab.[84] Buffalo Bill and com-

14. Buffalo Bill and his party stop for rest at a ranch,
November 1892. Courtesy of the Church History Library, The
Church of Jesus Christ of Latter-day Saints, Salt Lake City.

pany stayed at the Woolley home for a few days to rest themselves and
their horses. Edwin Woolley's first wife, Emma, prepared a full meal,
including dessert, for the guests. Edwin asked Buffalo Bill to say grace
before they consumed their dinner. Though not a religious observer,
Cody obliged his host. With the sight of dessert and its smell wafting in
the dining area, Buffalo Bill bowed his head along with the others and
uttered this prayer: "God bless the hands that made them custard pies."[85]
Cody, his company, and the Woolleys enjoyed conversing as they ate
their supper and delicious dessert. One of the Woolleys' daughters, Mary
Elizabeth, was fascinated by the visitors, listening with rapt attention to
their plans and tales. While Cody and the others stayed at the Woolley
home, Mary observed, "During this time their conversation was almost
entirely devoted to an enthusiastic discussion of the wonderful canyon
and its potential future."[86] The scenery and the people impressed the visitors indeed. Prentiss Ingraham stated, "Starting northward for Salt Lake
we were entertained in all the pretty Mormon villages through which we

15. William F. Cody, standing in front of six Latter-day Saint cowboys in
Kanab, Utah, November 1892. Courtesy of the Church History Library,
The Church of Jesus Christ of Latter-day Saints, Salt Lake City.

passed with balls and banquets."[87] Ingraham spoke in the highest terms
of the many kindnesses they received at the hands of the Mormons in
the various settlements through which they passed.[88]

The party proceeded northward to Richfield, Utah, on December 5 and
took the rails to reach Salt Lake City the next day.[89] The Cody company
made their entry into the city on a six-horse coach. Crowds gathered as
the famous showman and his party in their frontier dress drove to the
Templeton Hotel, an impressive, luxurious six-story brick-and-stone
structure that had been completed just two years earlier. At the hotel
Buffalo Bill was immediately surrounded by old friends and new acquaintances, while his companions visited a nearby club. A *Salt Lake Tribune*
reporter took the opportunity to hold a thirty-minute conversation with
the famous visitor and published a hearty introduction to Cody in the
next day's issue by noting that his "exploits on the plains and recent exhibitions in Europe have made him familiar to almost every member of the
English-speaking race."[90]

While in Salt Lake City, Junius F. Wells introduced Buffalo Bill and the party to the First Presidency of The Church of Jesus Christ of Latter-day Saints, which then consisted of Wilford Woodruff, George Q. Cannon, and Joseph F. Smith. After visiting with Buffalo Bill and others, George Q. Cannon remarked, "Cody is a very fine looking man, and wears his hair full length."[91] Like many reviewers of Cody's stage plays and probably tens of thousands of others who had witnessed Buffalo Bill's performances, Cannon commented specifically on the great scout's physical appearance and manly beauty. Church president Wilford Woodruff also recorded in his journal that Buffalo Bill and company "were very much pleased with their visit to Salt Lake City."[92] Prentiss Ingraham and Buffalo Bill likewise praised the church leaders after the party paid their respects. Ingraham said, "President Woodruff was a wonderful man at 86," as he remarked to a newspaper reporter of the Latter-day Saint president's "geniality after passing through nearly half a century of utter and almost relentless agitation."[93] Following their meetings with the highest leaders of the Latter-day Saint faith, Cody and Ingraham expressed their appreciation that "every courtesy was shown them."[94]

Following that meeting Junius Wells shepherded Cody, Ingraham, and the hunting party up the hill to meet with U.S. Army officers at Fort Douglas on the eastern mountain bench overlooking the city.[95] Reporting on the day spent in Salt Lake City, the *Washington Post* stated, "At Fort Douglass, Gen. Penrose and his officers entertained Col. Cody and his party most royally, and the English officers were delighted with the drill of the Sioux soldiers and life in an American frontier post."[96] Colonel Mackinnon and Major Mildmay spoke highly of the Sioux, the first American Indian soldiers they had seen. Buffalo Bill also took advantage of the opportunity to meet with officers with whom he had shared the dangers of Indian warfare. There was a hearty interchange of reminiscences, reviving memories of the past.[97] Though Cody somewhat lamented the modern comforts of the soldier, thinking that they did not have it as rough as when he served, he nevertheless appreciated the opportunity to visit with old friends and show the British officers a U.S. Army base. Cody's party had an enjoyable and instructive visit at Fort Douglas, with the Latter-day Saint presidency, and in Utah's capital city. After spending nearly six weeks together, Wells bade Cody and the other men farewell as they boarded a train and departed the city on December 8.[98]

The timing of Cody's 1892 visit to the Great Basin and his meeting with Latter-day Saint authorities in Salt Lake City is worth noting. It came just two years after Wilford Woodruff issued the manifesto calling for the end of Mormons' practice of plural marriage. It also came amid the continued efforts of Utahns to attain statehood, which had evaded them for more than forty years. From at least the mid-1880s, Latter-day Saint officials had engaged in public-relations campaigns to neutralize and overturn the long-standing negative public image of the church and its people. Painfully cognizant of the ways the larger American public had perceived them, they sought to change their image. For example, they had made alliances with powerful political lobbyists and eastern newspaper editors, hoping to engender a more positive image.[99] While it is unknown precisely what was said during Cody's meeting with the church's First Presidency or in his many interactions with Junius F. Wells and others, it seems likely that the Latter-day Saint men wanted to persuade Buffalo Bill to publicly treat them more favorably than he had in his productions of *May Cody* and *Prairie Waif*. Mormons were desperate for national respectability, and Buffalo Bill, with his immense popularity, could help them attain it.

Following his 1892 adventure through Grand Canyon country and into Utah, Cody wrote two letters to Wells about the potential of a business venture that the men likely discussed during their time together.[100] Buffalo Bill had used the expedition as an opportunity to find a suitable tract of land to create a space for the conservation of western animals. Cody lamented, "Outside of the National Park at Yellowstone, America is wholly devoid of any place for the preservation of game."[101] On the journey through the Grand Canyon and into southern Utah, Cody's party saw "mountain sheep, elk, deer, antelope, mountain lion, wildcats, and coyotes," as well as plentiful numbers of quail, ducks, grouse, and turkeys.[102] Cody saw "the Grandest scenery in the world and the finest hunting."[103] He was interested in establishing an environmental conservation and gaming zone in the West. He wanted to consult with Wells on the matter but worried that they would not be able to secure "a sure title" to a large enough tract of land to proceed.[104] Known documents do not reveal Cody's plans as to the purchase of hunting grounds in Arizona, Colorado, or Utah, and the endeavor failed to materialize.[105]

⁓⁓⁓⁓

Even as Buffalo Bill privately pursued business ventures in Utah, he also made public remarks about Mormons following his 1892 expedition. After his proximity to Latter-day Saints and time spent in Mormon homes and with Mormon families, Cody praised them. He commented that everywhere the expedition went, "the Mormons treated us with great consideration." Remarking on their devotion to family and piety, the international celebrity said, "Those Mormons are the greatest people to pray I ever saw, and they have the regular old Methodist twang about it." Though subtle, Cody made a direct connection between Mormonism and a prominent mainline Protestant denomination, thereby giving a knowing nod to their growing respectability and acceptability. Further commenting on the Latter-day Saint habit for prayer, Buffalo Bill quipped, "They can pray for more things and for a longer space of time than any set of people in the world. They had me down on my knees eight or ten times a day."[106]

Cody's public remarks did not shy away from the pervasive problem of polygamy among the Mormons. "The Mormons," Cody told the *Washington Post* after his visit to Utah, "are law-abiding, energetic, and hard-working people" and, as far as he could judge, "good American citizens."[107] Such a statement reversed the barbarous and anti-American image of Mormons presented in his earlier stage performances. In another newspaper Cody commented further that, though they abided the law, the Saints he interacted with were bitter about it. "They think the law should have prohibited from the date of its passage any more polygamous marriage, but should allow those who were married in that way before the passage of the bill to have continued in that relation until death severed the bonds," Buffalo Bill observed. He did not give his opinion on this observation, but one can read sympathy in the words that followed. He remarked that "ex-plural wives of the men and their children are in all the towns living in virtual widowhood," only able to see their ex-husband on an occasional supervised visit.[108] Whatever his private feelings about the Mormon homes and families he saw on his trip, Buffalo Bill was encouraged by the positive direction the Saints were headed.

In his interview with the *Washington Post*, Cody further expressed satisfaction and even pleasure at a January 4, 1893, proclamation by President Benjamin Harrison. The president had granted amnesty and pardons to Mormons who had forsaken their unlawful cohabitations and plural marriages to "faithfully obey the laws of the United States." In fact, Cody and his colleague Prentiss Ingraham further lauded Latter-day Saints when they informed the *Post* that "Mormons in Utah were living up to the letter of the law against polygamy."[109] Such a statement would have pleased Latter-day Saint leaders, who remained on the defensive against the entrenched image of Mormon polygamy. But more important than pleasing Latter-day Saint leaders, the public-facing remarks that the most popular American showman gave about the faith and its peoples had shifted.

For nearly two decades, Buffalo Bill and his associates had presented Mormons to the public as deviants from and dangerous to the American family. Now, having spent time in the Mormon home and observing these people of faith in their environment, Buffalo Bill saw the individuals of this group differently. He witnessed their positive accomplishments and redeeming attributes. Cody viewed them as more complex than the singular negative character type of his previous performances. His statements provided signals that Mormons could now be accepted as respectable American citizens. Junius F. Wells had declared that "the homes of the 'Mormon' people are homes constructed upon the principles of purity and virtue," as he once extended an open invitation to visit these homes. Wells led Buffalo Bill Cody into the Mormon home and the great showman was impressed, even convinced, by the virtue he witnessed. As a man with great prestige and cultural and social influence, his remarks about Latter-day Saints held great potential to further dispel the ignorance and prejudice toward the faith. What Buffalo Bill observed in Utah would soon be on display on a global stage.

— *4* —

Buffalo Bill and the Mormons on the World's Stage

In the late nineteenth century, world's fairs were premier venues for displays of and contests over societal norms and values. Both the Mormons and Buffalo Bill planned to be at the Chicago World's Fair in 1893. Against the backdrop of a constructed white city, the Chicago World's Fair (also called the World's Columbian Exposition) feted the triumph of whiteness. It did so by linking the best of contemporary America with the heritage of western cultural, political, diplomatic, and economic dominance. Individuals from around the globe gathered for the American cultural celebration.

Buffalo Bill, the influential performer and storyteller, would not miss this opportunity to deliver an epic new performance on the world's stage. Nor would the Latter-day Saints. Their engagement with the public in this arena demonstrated in the most visible way to date their contributions to the expansion of white America. At the world's fair, the Saints began to cement their place alongside western individuals like William F. Cody as American pioneers.

※

After the southwestern expedition through the Grand Canyon and up to Salt Lake City, Buffalo Bill Cody took the train east to see his European friends off in New York, then he headed to Chicago. There, just months later, at Jackson Park on the Lake Michigan shore of the Second City's south side, Buffalo Bill introduced the world to a new spectacle. Cody established a fourteen-acre arena just outside the fair's entrance at the intersection of East Sixty-Second Street and Stony Island Avenue in Chicago.[1] All roads, one advertisement decreed, led to Buffalo Bill's presentation of the Wild West.[2]

From May to November, Cody treated spectators to not only the Wild West but also to a new exhibition: the Congress of Rough Riders of the World. Nate Salsbury, the vice president and manager of Buffalo Bill's Wild West show described the new attraction as an "assemblage of primitive horsemen" from far distant countries, "differing in race, language, habits, customs, dress, as well as in skill, style and methods of horsemanship."[3] At its inception the Congress of Rough Riders featured American Indian, white American, Black American, Mexican, European, and South American men. Other men, including Arab, Cuban, Hawaiian, Puerto Rican, Filipino, and South African, were introduced during the first decade of Rough Rider performances. The international equestrian cohort displayed a cosmopolitan variety of masculine specimens in competition against one another. The congress emphasized a common masculine character illustrated through fearlessness, athleticism, strength, and equestrian ability, while it simultaneously highlighted difference, through the equestrians' race or nationality.[4]

Buffalo Bill's Wild West show had featured the western American man, whether cowboy, cavalry, plainsman, scout, or pioneer, as battling Native peoples and colonizing their lands to pave the way for expansion surging westward. The Congress of Rough Riders of the World exhibit now specifically highlighted the white American cowboy, with Cody himself depicted as the "finest horseman of them all."[5] The racial aspect to the congress was crucial. It represented a hierarchy with white men sitting triumphantly on top.

At the same time as Cody's Rough Riders premiered, American conceptions of masculinity were shifting as a part of a cultural response to widespread concerns about rapid urbanization, industrialization, corporate consolidation, and immigration. Alongside the rise of modern technology and urbanization, eager consumerism and concentrated wealth generated an imbalance and a grinding poverty that befell large swaths of the population.[6] Especially with women more active in politics and public spaces and with negotiations around the place of Black Americans in society following the Reconstruction era, gender and racial antagonisms increased.

Feeling beleaguered, emasculated, disrespected, and weakened by the social and economic transformations in their society, white American men promoted even more strongly images of heroic whites as the superior masculine brand. The self-made and self-controlled manhood of the previous generation transitioned to a form more indulgent, ambitious, aggressive, tough, strong, sexual, and passionate. The body itself became a vital component of manhood: strength, appearance, and athletic skill mattered more than in previous centuries.[7] Body strength and the combination of intelligence and ability to harness natural power provided the core of what it meant to be the ideal man.

In its depiction of Buffalo Bill Cody, the official program of the Wild West and Congress of Rough Riders identified him as the ideal man: "Young, sturdy, a remarkable specimen of manly beauty, with the brain to conceive and the nerve to execute, Buffalo Bill *par excellence* is the exemplar of the strong and unique traits that characterize *a true American frontiersman*."[8] Cowboys in the show represented virile manhood that helped tame nature and move the outposts of civilization westward. The 1893 program likewise depicted the cowboy as "brave, generous, free-hearted, self-sacrificing rough riders of the plains, literally living in the saddle, enduring exposure, hunger, risk of health and life" to conquer the West.[9]

White American men had surged westward in the second half of the nineteenth century and battled Native Americans in the United States' frontier experience, the story of which Cody repackaged and used as his own claim to masculine supremacy. In Wild West promotional materials, the "American Indian frontier wars" provided the "finest school for the development of military horsemanship."[10] That Cody constructed white masculinity around the reenactment of the conquest of western land and Native peoples foregrounds how dependent his model was on subjugating or denigrating an "other" to elevate white male superiority. Following a decade's worth of performances showcasing living history in the form of the white man rebuffing Native American attacks on the settler's cabin and emigrant wagon trains, Buffalo Bill responded to societal changes with the addition of the Congress of Rough Riders of the World. The congress provided audiences potent symbols; none was more important than the cowboy, the symbolic conqueror of the vast spaces of the West and the man who could properly harness the horse and his animal instincts.

The cowboy came to represent the virtues of self-discipline, knowledge, ingenuity, excellent judgment, and "a capacity to continue in the face of total exhaustion and overwhelming odds."[11] The white cowboy also embodied the classic American republican virtues of self-sacrifice and liberty so important to white men in a nation they felt was beset and inundated by immigrants, racial minorities, and women in the workplace.[12] The western version of what it meant to be an American stuck and became prevalent in the understanding of American whiteness and its supremacy. The cowboy proved a popular symbol but one that depended on racial and gender hierarchies.[13]

The key to engaging the public in demonstrations of ideal manhood came through comparative descriptions and portrayals of members of the congress, primarily through the live show itself, and spread through promotional materials and press reports of the Wild West show.[14] Cody's Wild West entertainment had featured the gun-toting Annie Oakley and frontier women in feats of daring equestrianism, but the introduction of male Rough Riders from around the world allowed spectators of all classes the opportunity to witness elements of innate manliness. Audiences could compare the cowboys to exotic riders from Mexico, Europe, North America, South America, and Asia. Most of these riders were people of color and their riding styles described as "wild," "strange," or other adjectives demarcating their difference from or inferiority to the ideal American cowboy. In the Wild West and Congress of Rough Riders of the World, Cody sought to prove that in horsemanship white cowboys were second to none.

The congress reinforced the underlying premise of contested manhood in "the race of races," which presented "the juxtaposition between different peoples of the world," where "the viewers could always tell the cowboys from the Indians."[15] Until the 1897 season, riders in Buffalo Bill's congress participated in "a horse race between a Cow-boy, a Cossack, a Mexican, an Arab, a Gaucho, and an Indian," but by 1898 the program called the same event a "Race of Races," which was, perhaps, the most overt and efficient expression of racial manhood as a contest.[16] Billy McGinty, an Oklahoma cowboy who later joined Buffalo Bill's congress, wrote in his recollections that the winner of the race varied because the horses were well matched but that the "races were fixed, so the American horses got the majority of wins over the entire season."[17] So while Cody valued all the men of the congress for their equestrian abilities and athleticism, the audience clearly understood that the American cowboy had the superior grade of true manhood.[18]

The presentation of the congress highlighted a crystallizing definition of manhood. It also offered a takeaway lesson for audiences. Its many features, including races and displays of athleticism, indicated that manhood must be proved—and proved constantly. Cody sold this construction first to the fairgoers in Chicago, then to American audiences nationwide, and finally to the western world. All these audiences, in the throes of increasing industrialization, mechanization, urbanization, racial diversity, disparities of income, and deplorable working conditions, gravitated toward the majesty and freedom of the horse riders and the racial hierarchy the congress represented.[19]

In Cody's construction of popular masculinity, the white western American cowboy ultimately reigned supreme because he could properly harness the natural and innate elements of manliness and simultaneously display a greater, and often more practical, balance of intelligence, gentility, and civility than the other men.[20] Buffalo Bill himself was the paragon of this archetype. His presentation of the congress facilitated and encouraged identification with virility and primitive masculinity for white men.[21] It was a profitable sale, as white urban Americans felt increasingly weighed down by these factors of late nineteenth-century society. Seeing the pioneer protect his cabin and the cowboy tame the horse, a male observer could visualize and project himself into the scene or onto the animal's back and win the Race of Races, thereby mentally revitalizing his own vitality. It was a resounding success. Millions of observers witnessed the stunning spectacle and absorbed the message of Buffalo Bill's Wild West and Congress of Rough Riders of the World while in Chicago in 1893.

From outside the walls of the world's fair, Buffalo Bill's performances sent a loud, popular message about masculinity, whiteness, and history. His public history entertainment converged with the intellectual in Chicago. From inside the walls, others, including the distinguished historian Frederick Jackson Turner, provided a similar message. At a meeting of the American Historical Association held in conjunction with the world's fair, Turner delivered a paper defining American identity, institutions, democracy, and social progress from a western, white male perspective.[22] For Turner, in 1893, the last lines of settlement had been filled as white men led families that colonized the plains states and beyond. He concluded that the western American frontier was closed. Turner's theory posited that the frontier was the key to the vitality of American democracy, social stability, and prosperity. Turner argued that on the frontier, the white pioneer gave up aspects of comfortable, civilized life to struggle against indigeneity and extend the American empire. In this process the white man sought to supplant, exterminate, and remake the lands and people in a white image.

These were ordinary men carving out a living for their families and simultaneously establishing the roots of American democracy in the West. In these efforts, which resulted in the conquering of a region, western men had developed a formula for a superior strain of manhood (one that Buffalo Bill presented in his Wild West and Congress of Rough Riders). For Turner individual men leading their individual families, just as in earlier generations of American history, represented the true foundations of progress. In this well-received paper, Turner summarized contemporary thinking about the triumph of the western individual, who was the agent of and the face for American democracy. Turner's "Frontier Thesis" gained great influence and catapulted its author into historical eminence. At this opportune moment, when the world gathered in Chicago, Frederick Jackson Turner enlightened his fellow historians and the public of the triumph of white men. He also encouraged those same men to seek out new frontiers to extend American influence and remake the world in a white image.[23]

Like Turner, Buffalo Bill considered himself an educator. He presented a live-action version of the history that Turner described in academic prose. Both influential in different ways, Turner and Cody provided messaging in lockstep, though Cody's form took a greater hold of the public's imagination.[24] Their vision focused on the individual white male. Though family and home remained important in the background to their vision of society and progress, women's contributions were largely invisible in Turner's history or in Cody's Wild West and Congress of Rough Riders. It became more about the man and his masculinity than it was about family. This trend mirrored Cody's life. He himself was increasingly on his own; his family life, and especially his marriage, suffered as he poured more of his time and energy into his performing enterprise. With the Congress of Rough Riders taking the top billing in the show, individualism emerged paramount, and the cowboy in Cody's performances was the quintessential individual. The attack on the settler's cabin remained in the performance, but that attack on the individual family was now supplanted in prominence by the new feature of individual men in competition. And Buffalo Bill's tough, intelligent, and self-reliant cowboy character helped cement the image of the hardworking, individualist white male as vital to the successful growth and development of the American West.

Buffalo Bill Cody's living-history exhibit proved immensely popular with fairgoers. Every one of Buffalo Bill's performances attracted large crowds of all classes of people; Cody even invited members of the American Historical Association to witness his spectacle. Buffalo Bill's audiences were filled with what one newspaper called "ordinary visitors" and "distinguished parties." During one week in September, Cody not only entertained the governors of New York, Pennsylvania, Maryland, and Wisconsin but also welcomed hosts of friends, "a large party of distinguished prelates" of the Catholic Church, and a number of Latter-day Saints. Among the Saints were many members of the Mormon Tabernacle Choir and Wilford Woodruff, George Q. Cannon, and Joseph F. Smith; they were respectively president, first counselor, and second counselor in the church's governing First Presidency.[25] These three religious leaders were in Chicago in September in connection with their faith group's participation in the international exposition. These major figures of faith were part of a multitude of Latter-day Saint voices at the fair who in harmonious accord combated preconceived notions about their faith and its place in the American narrative. They presented to the world their version of their religion, history, and contributions to American society.

Wilford Woodruff and his two counselors had the good fortune to meet with Buffalo Bill Cody on September 7, 1893. Nearly a year had passed since Buffalo Bill had met with Woodruff and Cannon in Salt Lake City. Now in Chicago visiting the world's fair, the Latter-day Saint leaders seized an opportunity to renew their friendly acquaintance with the world-famous showman. Alexander Majors, whose freighting firm had supplied the federal troops bound for Utah in 1857 and who was a longtime friend of Buffalo Bill's, took Woodruff, Cannon, and Smith to visit Cody that late summer afternoon. Sitting with Cody in his luxurious tent, the men "had a pleasant interview." During this visit with Buffalo Bill, Joseph F. Smith received a souvenir that he kept the rest of his life: an autographed photo of the great showman.[26] Following their meeting, Buffalo Bill admitted his Latter-day Saint guests free of charge to his epic show. "At 3 oclock P.M.," Wilford Woodruff wrote in his journal, "we visited Buffalo Bill's Wild West Show and Enjoyed it very much."[27]

Woodruff, Cannon, and Smith were enthralled by the pageantry of Buffalo Bill's extravaganza, watching as white pioneers protected their homes against violent threats and as white cowboys showed their masculine superiority in equestrian competition with men from all over the world. Like the millions of others who witnessed the Wild West and Congress of Rough Riders spectacle in Chicago, they certainly would have taken note of the respectability given to and predominance demonstrated by white men in the arena.

Reveling in the Wild West and Congress of Rough Riders of the World performance was just one event on a busy schedule for the Latter-day Saint presidency during their Chicago sojourn. The next day, at the Utah Building on the far north end of the fairgrounds just east of the Fifty-Sixth

16. Autographed picture of "Col. W. F. Cody 'Buffalo Bill,'" given to the then second counselor in the First Presidency of The Church of Jesus Christ of Latter-day Saints, Joseph F. Smith, at the Chicago World's Fair, 1893. Courtesy of the Church History Library, The Church of Jesus Christ of Latter-day Saints, Salt Lake City.

Street entrance, Wilford Woodruff addressed an assembled, focused crowd. Each state and territory had the opportunity to construct a building or site from which representatives showcased the resources and advertised the people and potential of their respective geopolitical entity.

When Woodruff spoke from the Utah Building on September 8, 1893, he did so "not in his capacity of President of the Mormon Church, but

as a Pioneer," according to George Q. Cannon's recounting.[28] In his brief
remarks, Woodruff concentrated on his and his faith's role in conquering
the Intermountain West and making it a place for American families.
Nearly three years removed from his manifesto barring new plural marriages among the Latter-day Saints, Woodruff's message recalibrated the
narrative of a new identity for his church, one in which he and his fellow
Saints were pioneers that contributed to and revered American expansion.[29]

The narrative emerging from not only Woodruff's speech but also the
entirety of the Latter-day Saint display in Chicago was one highlighting
the foundational framework Latter-day Saints had laid for the progress of
American civilization.[30] Latter-day Saints were white men who directed
their families through industriousness, intelligence, hardiness, and self-
reliance. They had proven their manhood by colonizing arid lands and
establishing successful homes. They deserved to be counted among the
nation's pioneers, those western individuals celebrated by Buffalo Bill
and Frederick Jackson Turner. That night, following his remarks and
after shaking hands "with several hundred person[s] from the various
Nations of the Earth," the aging Latter-day Saint president retired to bed,
worn out but satisfied by what he said, what he meant, and the goodwill
he had received in Chicago.[31]

Wilford Woodruff's message only vocalized the powerful representations Latter-day Saints were making in Chicago during the world's fair.
Following decades of rhetoric and portrayals of them as anti-American
others, Mormons wanted to be seen as American as Uncle Sam. Taking
control of their public relations, representation, and image making, the
Saints rode a growing wave of positive publicity to the Windy City. Railroad
companies had largely omitted negative commentary about Latter-day
Saints in their advertising as the 1880s wore on and began to emphasize
instead their positive contributions in the West.[32] Buffalo Bill Cody had
publicly lauded the religious group after seeing the fruits of the Mormon
home during his 1892 trip. He had seen firsthand that the Saints and their
homes were not so outrageously different as previously reported, and he
did not shy away from making that known.

Buffalo Bill lent his name to other publications, doubling down on his affirmation of the Latter-day Saints. In a book published in 1893 for the world's fair, Col. Prentiss Ingraham, who had also recently visited the Mormon home with Cody, collaborated with Buffalo Bill and Alexander Majors on a memoir of Majors's life on the frontier. It was a hot commodity, and vendors could hardly keep it in stock, as more and more visitors descended on the Chicago fairgrounds. In the memoir Majors described Brigham Young as "one of the smartest men, if not the ablest man, it was ever my fortune to meet." In describing the religious edifice of the Salt Lake Temple, Majors applauded the Latter-day Saint work ethic: "No better illustration of the infinite patience, the ceaseless industry, and the religious zeal of the Mormon people could be given than they have manifested in this work." "It was a stupendous undertaking," the author stated.[33] Far from the images engendered just a decade earlier of Brigham Young as a tyrannical threat and the temple as a nefarious space for strange religious practices, Majors's popular account now presented Young, and by extension his faith group, as a productive contributor to western expansion. The memoir's messaging echoed the words Buffalo Bill spoke about Latter-day Saints just months earlier. Cody, Majors, and Ingraham were noteworthy voices in a swelling chorus of individuals singing the praises of the Latter-day Saints in the arid West. Acceptability and respectability only grew for the faith group as more voices offered them praise.

⁓⁓⁓

The acclaim offered by Cody, Ingraham, and Majors was only part of a growing trend in depictions of Latter-day Saints. For example, just ahead of the Chicago World's Fair, *Harper's Weekly* printed a lengthy report about the Mormon home and adopted homeland. Julian Ralph, the *Harper's* writer, published an exposé in April 1893 about his recent weeklong visit to Salt Lake City. Ralph wrote about the people, and he, like Alexander Majors, commented glowingly about the Latter-day Saint temple. The temple, which Wilford Woodruff had just dedicated after its forty years under construction, Ralph pronounced, both elevated "the soul and eye alike." The *Harper's* reporter remarked, "I was surprised and affected by the beauty of the city," located at the base of the Wasatch Mountains. He found the city, "so lavishly set with beautiful trees," to be incomparable to any other town or city in the arid West at that time. Mormon wonderworkers had brought about this splendid transformation from desert expanse to beautiful and productive oasis.[34]

Contrary to the industrial and urban decay threatening to overtake eastern cities, the *Harper's* writer stated, Salt Lake City boasted homes "which whole families feel the pride and joy of independence, of all that goes with true homes." "Why, I believe," Ralph posited, "that no one thing contributes more to America's greatness than her unparalleled number of citizens who are their own landlords."[35] The Latter-day Saint settlement had become, in this example, not only the exemplar of the American home but also an antidote to the cacophony of complaints facing eastern cities of the United States. Writers like Ralph and men like Buffalo Bill Cody increasingly portrayed the Saints as contributors to the nation's prestige and as an archetype portending the opportunities and possibilities for growth and development in the American West.

Julian Ralph then explained what made the beautification and productivity of the Salt Lake Valley possible: irrigation. The irrigation ditches constructed and maintained by Latter-day Saints provided the secret to the rich greenery of Salt Lake City and the success of Mormon families. This was not much of a secret, however. Visitors to the Salt Lake Valley had, since at least 1850, acknowledged the value of the Saints' waterworks. The eminent explorer John Wesley Powell had alerted government officials in his 1878 report on arid lands that the abundant agriculture in Utah Territory was dependent on irrigation.[36] Powell's report emphasized the importance of irrigation infrastructure to agricultural interests in the West and became the backbone for American thinking about expanding settlement in the arid region.[37]

For Powell and Ralph, Utah and its Latter-day Saint–produced canal networks provided the example of just how to make the arid lands of the West flourish. Controlling and appropriately distributing the sparse water to settlements and fields allowed the fruits of the Mormon home and family to become a beacon to others moving westward. Ralph wrote that vast waterworks, like those produced in Utah, would give hope to the people of the Dakotas, Wyoming, Idaho, Montana, Colorado, Arizona, New Mexico, and Nevada "to duplicate in the West the imperial wealth of the agriculture of the East."[38] With the right tools and infrastructure, the parched and barren lands could support a growing population with homes and livelihoods. Writers like Ralph underscored the rich opportunities for frontier development at a time when frontiers appeared to be closing and white men had become emasculated by urbanization, industrialization, and immigration.

Reclamation of western waters would benefit the nation by increasing its wealth and population and providing relief to congested eastern cities. As individuals, families, and communities looked for land and opportunity in the West, they only had to look at the Latter-day Saint example in Utah to understand how a desolate landscape could become beautified and productive. Buffalo Bill Cody observed this firsthand while touring through Utah and visiting Latter-day Saint homes in late 1892. Now the world had the opportunity to see the industriousness, irrigation, and fruits of the Mormon home on display in Chicago.

At the Utah Building inside the exposition fairgrounds, Latter-day Saints instructed visitors about life in Utah, especially in the art of canal development and water application. The Utah Building was a stately modern renaissance edifice situated on a beautiful plot of ground designed to highlight the accomplishments and possibilities of Utah and the West. In his writings about the Chicago World's Fair, E. A. McDaniel, secretary of the Utah World's Fair Commission, described at length the displays seen at the Utah Agricultural Pavilion.[39] The pavilion's innovative irrigation diagrams and maps, which detailed "how the Mormon pioneers had made the Territory's desert 'blossom as the rose,'" captivated hundreds of thousands of curious visitors at the world's fair.[40]

A relief map of the Bear River Canal was one of the most interesting features. Foreign experts and emissaries visiting the fair carefully studied the Utah method of canal construction, water application, and farming, later rendering "elaborate reports to their respective governments, all of which were published and circulated extensively."[41] In his February 1894 report to the Utah legislature summarizing the events at the Utah

Building during the world's fair, McDaniel extolled the irrigation and agricultural displays: "It was clearly demonstrated that Utah yields more wealth from the soil per capita, counting only the farming population, than any other State. The irrigation relief map was a wonderful attraction, and gave the Utah Agricultural exhibit a great deal of prominence. The statistics showing the yield per acre, taken in conjunction with the map, served to make the Utah agricultural exhibit one of the most practical and instructive in the Agricultural Building."[42] Utah's agricultural displays demonstrated that Latter-day Saint farming by means of irrigation "was not a crude and clumsy method, but was really scientific."[43]

The Chicago World's Fair displays attached a value to Mormonism.[44] That value came in several forms, but perhaps its most potent was in the narrative reformulation that this recognition brought. Mormon Utah set an example for how arid lands might be brought together under cultivation by irrigation. They were the pioneers of American irrigation. They controlled the water and therefore controlled growth that saw irrigated lands grow from 16,000 acres in 1850 to more than 263,000 by 1890. Those lands produced a wide variety of crops, from wheat and hay to potatoes to oats, corn, rye, and sugar beets, that not only supported a population over two hundred thousand people in the Salt Lake Valley but also allowed farmers to sell their crops for profits. Such growth was not possible without irrigation.[45]

In addition to the irrigation and agricultural exhibits, Utah mining and mineral wealth, manufactures, fine arts, and women's work (highlighting artistic designs and workwomanship in the silk industry) were prominently displayed. Latter-day Saint women also spoke at a variety of venues at the fair, seeking to debunk demeaning stereotypes and misrepresentations by reframing the narrative around their own pioneer patriotism. Refashioning their image from treasonous, hapless victims of, and even slaves to, polygamy to contributors to America's greatness, one Mormon woman explicitly stated, "We love our grand American Government, her colonizers, her sacred institutions, her Constitution, her flag, her Independence! We are taught to support and defend her every legal authority."[46] Mormon women positioned themselves as pioneers at a time when the country began to revere these colonizing figures. The church also sent its Tabernacle Choir to the fair as a significant component of its public-relations efforts.[47] The choir, women's ingenuity, and irrigation innovations helped weaken prejudice against the Latter-day Saints. By the end of the world's fair, Utah and its Latter-day Saint populace was better advertised than ever before.

More than ten thousand people visited the Utah Building each day during the duration of the fair, with an estimated two million witnesses having observed the fruits of the Latter-day Saint home. Certainly Buffalo Bill's Wild West and Congress of Rough Riders of the World performed in front of more people in total, but both the Wild West and the Utah agricultural displays instructed millions of people about the history of and potential for white men in the West. "The World's Columbian Exposition was a wonderful educator," E. A. McDaniel wrote.[48] Both Buffalo Bill and the Latter-day Saints benefited from the lessons they taught. It was not just the education but also the impression created in visitors from around the world that benefited especially the white inhabitants of the Intermountain West. Irrigation represented the controlling of waters, a new frontier for the American people to provide for the prosperity and stability of white families in the West. Water resources development promised to be the next big business venture.

The success of Latter-day Saint labor in the Intermountain West allowed legislators, businessmen, and speculators to dream of the possibilities for population growth in the western half of the United States. Those dreams depended on the ability to harness and manage the limited water in the region. The Latter-day Saints on display at the Chicago World's Fair were not the cowboys as exhibited in Buffalo Bill's Congress of Rough Riders, but at a time when mechanizing, industrializing, and urbanizing processes were considered to be weakening American men in the East, the Saints had shown a pioneering spirit of strength, intellect, and conquest like unto their western cowboy brethren. They were representatives of the pioneering spirit of the American West because they had built a vast irrigation network that produced an agrarian society in an inhospitable region. They were white, hardy individuals who led their families and reclaimed a desert landscape. They provided a blueprint for successful growth in the new West.

<div align="center">~~~~~~</div>

Hearkening back to the Jeffersonian ideal of the yeoman farmer promoting the small family farm as the hallmark and mainstay of American democracy, Latter-day Saints in Utah had provided the model for growing this ideal in arid lands. In this paradigm America's vitality was wedded to the land, and though Frederick Jackson Turner had declared an end to the American frontier, irrigation in arid America offered the opportunity for a renewed agrarian frontier experience.[49] The Utah example had therefore elucidated the possibilities for making the West a new crucible of democracy.

That their faith group was almost all physically white from Euro-American heritage opened the door to their acceptance. That is the ease of physical whiteness; it allows for a quick incorporation into the dominant group.[50] Pioneering in irrigation made this religious group palatable to their fellow non-Mormon Americans.[51] Americans could recognize this version of Mormons, the canal builders and successful agriculturalists, as pioneers, and that acceptance helped open the door to them into the white mainstream.

Perhaps no individual better narrated the role and position of Latter-day Saints as white pioneers than newspaper editor and writer William Ellsworth Smythe, born in Worcester, Massachusetts, in 1861. Smythe's New England heritage shaped the way that he viewed societal norms and developments. As the nation grew westward, he moved to Nebraska and began to apply his thinking about American homes and communities to an arid land. Smythe became a crusader for irrigation and reclamation. He began to publish a periodical titled *Irrigation Age*, which promoted land settlement for white families in western lands and the potential immense profits offered by those lands through water resources development and management. He wrote of irrigation as a social tool to promote democracy, cooperation, order, and unity of village life against the wave of urban decay befalling the nation's eastern cities. He sought to "bring the landless man to the manless land."[52] As part of his efforts, Smythe had helped organize the first annual National Irrigation Congress held in Salt Lake City in 1891, where he, like Buffalo Bill Cody, saw firsthand how bringing water to the dry lands would allow the yeoman farmer ideal to flourish and develop the western economy.

In his later book, *The Conquest of Arid America*, William Smythe wrote at length about the agricultural, industrial, and economic success of Utah. Such prosperity was built on the foundation of irrigation. Smythe lauded Salt Lake City's canal networks, which furnished a water supply for the sixty-thousand-inhabitant metropolis. Moreover, he praised the Mormons as pioneer irrigators who allowed American civilization to flourish in Utah. Utah, Smythe wrote, is America's "classic land of irrigation." The Latter-day Saints "had staked their whole future upon a region which could not produce a spear of tame grass, an ear of corn, nor a kernel of wheat without skillful irrigation." They possessed no capital—just brains, industry, and "hard hands" to construct canals and a water system that allowed their people and economy to prosper. "The forces that have made the civilization of Utah will make the civilization of western America," Smythe declared and had therefore "given the Mormons their just claim as the pioneer irrigators of the United States."[53] They had physically altered and transformed the land to unveil the economic and growth potential of a region. By adapting irrigation techniques, Latter-day Saints thrived amid difficult climatic conditions and generated material prosperity in the Great Basin. They were conquerors of arid America. They had redeemed a supposed wilderness and could therefore be perceived as contributors to the country's economic, political, and social development.

Writings by individuals like Smythe helped to advance the perception of Latter-day Saints as tolerable to the white mainstream. During the previous six decades, just about everyone with a voice had constructed an image of the Saints as un-American, undemocratic polygamists. They were not considered white.[54] Racism and racial thinking permeated so much of late nineteenth-century culture, especially in determining what was and what was not quintessentially American.[55] Much like the way racist ideas were generated and consumed about people of color

in nineteenth-century America, Mormons were looked down on as a
social problem.[56]

In the 1890s and into the early 1900s, commentators, politicians, and
the public now had a justification to graft Mormons into the story of white
male pioneers who were respectable and enhanced America's greatness.
Their water management networks had blown open a new frontier. Their
denunciation of polygamy had made them acceptable. Smythe's writings
only highlighted what Latter-day Saints at the world's fair had already
demonstrated: Utah illustrated the opportunities and possibilities for
individuals, families, and communities in the West at a time when that
region offered the nation so much potential. Individuals like Smythe,
Wilford Woodruff, and Buffalo Bill Cody used the contemporary need
for irrigation and western settlement to create a usable past that allowed
people to set aside the sensational aspects of Latter-day Saint history and
instead focus on their contributions to conquering arid lands. Thinking
about the religious group in the latter way helped cement a narrative that
they were industrious white men who led good families. They were now
viewed as a compelling example of how proper American people could
settle in proper American homes in an arid land. In the West, lands were
available to be reclaimed. In the West, men and families would not be
bogged down by widespread immigration, industrialization, and urbanization. In the West, opportunities abounded.

~~~~~~

Through the 1890s Latter-day Saints presented themselves as ideal settlers.
They promoted themselves through this now-accepted identity that fit
better with how they saw themselves: a persecuted faith group who fled
to the desert, making it blossom and prosper to become a beacon to the
world. This rhetoric and imagery were about whiteness, and it permeated the fifty-year jubilee of the Saints' entrance into the Salt Lake Valley,
held in July 1897. This jubilee took place just eighteen months after Utah
had been admitted to the American Union following a nearly fifty-year
battle to gain statehood. In a letter encouraging U.S. president William
McKinley to attend the festivities, Utah governor Heber M. Wells wrote,

This land then belonged to Mexico and was a forbidding desert, inhabited by no white man but roamed over by Indians and wild beasts. These pioneers had fought their way through the wilderness more than a thousand miles beyond the Western frontier, and one of their first acts upon arriving here was to erect upon a mountain overlooking this valley the ensign of liberty. The glorious Stars and Stripes. They were therefore more than the founders of Utah, they were the conquerors of arid America, the forerunners of western civilization, the envoys of the United States in the acquisition of a new and mighty empire.[57]

Though he did not attend the celebration, William McKinley acknowledged the Mormon pioneers as the purveyors of American civilization in the West and as loyal citizens of the United States.[58] Another observer wrote, "All of the States in the great arid belt will participate in the celebration, because the establishing of this colony on the shores of Great Salt Lake, is looked upon as the founding of the Western empire."[59]

In an address delivered at the conclusion of Jubilee Week, Joseph F. Smith "pointed out that the pioneers of 1847 looked to 'build up a great commonwealth,' one that not only enshrined religious but also civil liberty. The Pageant of Progress and the Jubilee promotional materials pointed to a Utah that had embraced American political values and first planted them in the yet fully developed regions of the West."[60] Though religious imperatives shaped the hard work to make the desert "blossom as the rose," Latter-day Saint narrators spoke only of the diligence and industry of white male pioneers who developed a barren land into a space for economic prosperity and political and social progress. This was language familiar to American notions of Manifest Destiny and westward expansion.[61]

It was important for the Saints to obtain the title of pioneer, especially as the nineteenth century ended and the nation was beset by ongoing changes and fears associated with immigration, industrialization, and urbanization. The promise of America was and is that everyone is potentially welcome. However, as the historian Elliott West has articulated, "widening the United States' political community has meant constricting

its cultural boundaries, and the greater the political inclusion the greater
the apparent need for cultural exclusion—and the greater the need to
tighten what it has meant to be American."[62] What it meant to be a true
American was indeed tightening in the 1890s.[63]

Pioneering became a national narrative, and the white pioneer, like other
white western individualists, was considered the quintessential American
in the drama of the nation's continual western expansion.[64] Buffalo Bill's
shows, Frederick Jackson Turner's "Frontier Thesis," and others made
the westering experience the epic story of the United States, as white
homemaking coincided with nation building at the expense of people
of color. In this western saga, America owed its greatness and a debt to
its white male pioneers who conquered peoples and lands and advanced
American civilization across the continent to the Pacific Ocean.[65] It was
a time in which white supremacy solidified, and Mormons took their
place among the ranks of the pioneers, as the nation and even the world
shifted its focus on the politics, culture, and opportunities of the American West. In the 1890s Latter-day Saints were embraced by the nation,
and they in turn embraced patriotism, nationalism, and whiteness.[66] This
new narrative simplified a complex past. It was a nationalist story that
endured. Latter-day Saints had long revered their heroic pioneers, and
they continue to do so in rhetoric and in worship.[67]

In the 1890s William F. Cody looked for new investment opportunities.
Not even a year after his triumph at the Chicago World's Fair, Cody was
introduced to Wyoming's majestic Big Horn Basin. On a topographical
map, the Big Horn Basin pops out of northwest Wyoming as a nearly perfect oval, cradled by the Big Horn Mountains on the east, the Owl Creek
and Bridger Mountains on the south, and the Absaroka Mountains on
the west. It is stunning country of approximately twenty thousand square
miles just east of Yellowstone National Park. Running through it is the
Shoshone River, a major tributary of the magnificent Bighorn River. Cody
believed in the superior potential of this basin.[68]

George Washington Thornton Beck, an eager entrepreneur and hopeful politician, had explored the basin with Cody in the fall of 1894. Beck was an athletic, imposing man, always well-groomed, with piercing eyes and a formidable mustache. He and Cody became friends and eventually business partners. In his memoir Beck told of their 1894 visit.[69] He recalled that one evening during their travels through the basin they attended a dance and spent the night in the small Mormon settlement of Burlington, located on the Greybull River. David Woodruff, a son of the Latter-day Saint president Wilford Woodruff, with whom Buffalo Bill had become acquainted, had recently established this small settlement in northwest Wyoming.

In recounting the events, Beck puts his "puckish sense of humor" on display. He had heard of an old Mormon man in that town who had two daughters, the youngest of whom was considered a great beauty and the other quite the opposite. Beck and a local sheriff named Virgil Rice told Buffalo Bill "at great length about the raving beauty." They never said a word about her age or perhaps even that she had a less fortunate-looking sister. After Cody, Beck, and Rice arrived at the dance, Cody was introduced to the father. The showman requested of "the old Mormon" a dance with his daughter. The father gladly obliged. He found his oldest daughter to introduce her to the world-famous entertainer. Buffalo Bill must have been taken aback by the eldest daughter's appearance but was a man of his word and had a dance with her. Beck, likely with a mischievous grin on his countenance, observed. Beck remembered that this Mormon daughter then stayed by Bill's side all evening "like a leech." Cody was stuck and "couldn't get away from her," but Beck figured that the showman "had probably danced with enough of the world's beauties in his travels to be able to stand up under one dull evening in a little western town." Besides this encounter with the Mormon's daughter, Beck also recalled that some Mormons, though against their religion, had imbibed alcohol and smoked cigars with Cody that night. When Cody and Beck awoke in the settlement the next day, the Mormons had fleeced them for everything except their clothes. It was a memorable, amusing night, at least for Beck.[70]

Though he did not find the Mormon beauty of Burlington as advertised, Buffalo Bill was smitten with the allure and grandeur of the Big

Horn Basin. Off the Shoshone River, near the western edge of the basin, William Cody saw the place he hoped to build the next great metropolis of the West: a town he would name Cody, Wyoming, thereby further bolstering his own legacy and that of his family. George Beck and others saw the potential of the area as well. Beck was a key partner in founding the town, having surveyed the land, drawn a map, and driven a stake in the center of what would become the town of Cody.[71]

Others also observed with interest the potential of the Big Horn Basin. Railroad companies, for example, explored the region in search of viable, and profitable, new routes. The Chicago, Burlington, and Quincy Railroad was rapidly expanding its rail network during the last decades of the nineteenth century, looking to become a transcontinental company rather than just a midwestern company. The company's executives looked for up-and-coming locations in the West to build line connections from Denver, Colorado, and Billings, Montana, the westernmost cities the company then served. Charles E. Perkins, the incisive, effective, and commanding president of the Chicago, Burlington, and Quincy Railroad, hired Charles H. Morrill, president of the Nebraska-based Lincoln Land Company, to investigate northwest Wyoming for viable new railroad routes. In his report to Perkins, Morrill extolled the opportunities he saw: "This is a wonderful country and will sometime be almost an empire of itself. Inside of the basin rim there is about 6,500,000 acres of land. I should say that it is possible to irrigate from 1,000,000 to 1,500,000 acres from the Shoshone, Greybull, Clark's Fork and numerous small streams."[72]

Buffalo Bill became infatuated with the area and set his mind to its development. The dry, arid climate and harsh terrain of the basin, however, mandated that water be efficiently and effectively diverted from the Shoshone River and its branches to sustain a growing population. Cody knew the importance of infrastructure for town development, and he started with the most essential piece: irrigation. He set to work to build a proper system of irrigation that would pour water "upon a rainless desert" to make "it blossom under the tropic sun as if some magician's wand had been waved over it." He envisioned a business venture that would take control of the water flow and bring a scarce and valuable resource to make the land agriculturally abundant and profitable. If he could provide adequate access to the water of the Shoshone River, he could sell the water and the land in his pioneer paradise, thereby bringing people to the basin and money to his coffers. Cody would emphasize the potential and downplay the realities of the harsh environment.[73]

Buffalo Bill began using the fortune he had amassed as an internationally known showman to promote and develop the land to bring settlers to the Big Horn Basin. Cody claimed that the impetus for his "extraordinarily successful and popular" Wild West and Congress of Rough Riders of the World exhibition was to generate profits and capital necessary for "agricultural and commercial development." With his funds and those of some friends, Buffalo Bill invested in the Big Horn Basin to "reclaim a vast territory, establish a city, and lead whole communities to prosperity." In thinly veiled and racially charged language, Buffalo Bill viewed himself as a "great public benefactor" for white Americans in his "efforts to provide cheap and fruitful homes for toiling millions" and reclaim the land "from savage hands."[74] He could provide opportunities for cheap homes because he took advantage of the recently passed Carey Act.

Wyoming was the first state to enact legislation to enable the transfer of lands under the federal law that allowed private companies to build irrigation systems and profit from the sale of water in western states. This law, known as the Carey Act, after Wyoming senator Joseph Carey, who believed the irrigation business would increase his wealth and that of his state, was passed in August 1894 to induce capitalists to build canals and sell water rights to settlers.[75] The Carey Act gave the state key rights in water and the ability to decide who got a private right to water as well as the volume, timing, and use of that water. Western states, like Wyoming, became highly involved and interested in water rights.[76]

Buffalo Bill founded the Shoshone Land and Irrigation Company, which became one of the first companies to make an application under the Carey Act. In 1895 his company first applied to divert water from the south fork of the Shoshone River to irrigate more than twenty-five thousand acres of basin land. Cody's friend and business partner George Beck managed the construction of the Cody Canal to water the eponymic

town. Wyoming state engineer Elwood Mead called the Cody Canal "one
of the most important and valuable projects ever inaugurated in this
State," and he believed that it was "destined to exercise great influence on
our growth in wealth and population." "It will open to settlers a region
having vast and varied resources," Mead continued, before offering this
endorsement: "I know of no place in this country which offers to prudent and industrious farmers greater assurances of material prosperity
and physical comfort than the Big Horn Basin."[77] The development of
irrigation systems to bring water to the dry land, however, would require
a substantial outlay of capital.

A nationwide economic depression that lasted from 1893 through 1897
hindered work on the canal. Nevertheless, Cody and Beck persuaded
investors from Buffalo, New York, and philanthropist Phoebe Hearst to
help fund the building of the Cody Canal, which initially cost in the neighborhood of $150,000.[78] The canal started providing water to the townsite
in 1897, on which Cody would ultimately build a two-story house, along
with a hotel, general store, and school. Buffalo Bill would also subsidize the
publication of a newspaper (the Cody Enterprise, which he co-published
with Col. John H. Peake); organize and lead hunting parties composed
of wealthy potential investors; and announce his intention to retire in the
Big Horn Basin.[79] Major storms the following year, however, destroyed
parts of the canal, requiring more money, more work, and more time to
repair and then extend the irrigation system.

Despite the setback to the Cody Canal, Buffalo Bill and his company
set their sights on more. They hoarded claims to land and water rights in
the basin, eventually amassing hundreds of thousands of acres of rights. In
essence, Cody monopolized the best land to control development thereon.
Like everything else in Cody's public life, he embarked on ambitious irrigation projects that he confidently believed would attract the multitudes.
To produce a system of canals sufficient to make the basin bloom was
estimated to be at least another $250,000.[80]

Construction on the irrigation canals, however, moved very slowly. To
make things worse, Cody and his business partners did not have enough
funds to continuously pay the one hundred workers already laboring on

17. The Cody Canal, circa 1897. University of Wyoming, American Heritage Center, George T. Beck Papers, accession number 59, box 31, folder 12.

the Cody Canal.[81] Buffalo Bill's traveling exhibition cost more and more each season, and Cody diverted funds needed for canal construction to his Wild West performances. The work to build canals quickly became a money pit. Cody had capital, but not enough to cover the costs for the construction and maintenance of such a significant irrigation system. And he certainly did not have enough manpower to carry out the work. Such was a problem across the arid West in the 1890s, as companies like the Shoshone Land and Irrigation Company waited years to bring water to their intended locations and for the settlers to follow.[82] The private capital and paid labor necessary for the development of irrigation was not the only model. Cooperative labor, such as what had been done with great success in Utah, was another option.[83] With a need for water and settlers in the Big Horn Basin, Cody knew where to turn.

As the 1890s drew to a close, William F. Cody needed some pioneers to reclaim the hinterlands of northwest Wyoming and turn that space into a pioneer's paradise. He needed a population of cheap laborers. The

Latter-day Saints fit the bill. They had become known as hardworking and had developed an archetype for irrigation. By 1898 the former star and producer of the anti-Mormon stage play *May Cody* had become so favorable toward Utah and the Latter-day Saints that he indeed viewed them as a model for Big Horn Basin settlement.

His inclination toward the religious minority seems to have been part of a growing mindset toward equality and inclusivity. Increasingly, he sought to do right by others "doing good" to help whenever and wherever he could.[84] For example, employment in Cody's Wild West show provided opportunities to people with a variety of racial and ethnic backgrounds, and though the performance was meant to publicly display white male superiority, he generally gave all employees equal pay for equal work. That went for a mixed-gender workforce as well. In April 1898 Cody told a reporter that if a woman could do the same job as a man, she should receive the same pay.[85]

That same month Buffalo Bill penned a dispatch to C. B. Jones, a land agent from Galesburg, Illinois, who had been helping to bring settlers to the northwest Wyoming basin. In his message to Jones, Cody outlined the characteristics and qualities of people needed not just to endure but to flourish in the region. Patience, persistence, and long suffering through hardship, Cody explained, were essential qualities. The showman asserted, "The possibilities of the new region I have no fears are as grand as any which have followed other pioneers in the older Western States. We have only to look at what the Mormons have done in the great Salt Lake Valley, which at the time of its settlement was the most desolate of deserts; they have made it blossom as the rose, and today there is no more prosperous and wealthy state on the continent, taking into consideration all the circumstances, than Utah." Cody, like many Americans, had accepted the Latter-day Saint characterization of the work they accomplished in the Great Basin. Now he promoted his own interests by using their story as a model. "We have in the Big Horn Basin, resources that are not only infinitely greater and more varied than in Utah," Buffalo Bill declared, "and I have no doubt that one season's effective work by our well to do settlers will show as great results as have been accomplished there."[86]

Cody's vision of attracting American families and homes to make the Big Horn Basin bloom mirrored his observations of Mormons and their own efforts in the Salt Lake Valley. Great commonwealths had arisen from suffering hardships and, in the West, by applying irrigated water to dry lands. That was the implication of Cody's reference to the Latter-day Saints having made the Salt Lake Valley "blossom as the rose." When it came to water, irrigation, and making the arid lands of the Big Horn Basin productive, Buffalo Bill, like most other observers, believed in the Mormons. They provided a useful, alternative model to private capitalization. They had planned and constructed irrigation systems for entire communities, large and small, throughout the Intermountain West. They could do so again.

Buffalo Bill's private letter to Jones was not the only writing attributed to the celebrity entertainer praising the Saints at this time. In a book authored by Col. Henry Inman and Buffalo Bill titled *The Great Salt Lake Trail*, published in 1898, the same year as Cody's letter to Jones, the Latter-day Saints and their pioneering industry take center stage. "Out of the most desolate of our vast arid interior areas," the authors proclaimed, and "in less than half a century has been evolved not only a magnificent garden spot, but a great city with all the adjuncts of our most modern civilization. Rich in its architecture, progressive in its art, with a literature that is marvelous when the conditions from which it has sprung are seriously considered, the Mormon community meets all the demands of our ever advancing civilization."[87]

Cody and his coauthor also addressed the Mountain Meadows Massacre. With the benefit of distance and the relationships Cody had built with church members in the intervening years, he and Inman ultimately came to a softer conclusion of the atrocity than most Americans. Of the second trial and the conviction of John D. Lee, they wrote, "It was proved that the Mormon Church had nothing to do with the massacre; that Lee, in fact, had acted in direct opposition to the officers of the Church. It was shown that he was a villain and a murderer of the deepest dye."[88]

Inman and Cody then spent an entire chapter in their book extolling the Latter-day Saint work ethic, organization, cooperation, and systematic program of expansion that produced a fruitful network of canals, roads, agricultural fields, and, most important, homes. The authors further heralded the Utahns, noting, "The same system of irrigation which flows through the streets to nourish the trees, the water runs into every garden spot, and produces a beauty of verdure in what was once the most barren of wastes."[89] The Mormons were the first commercially successful irrigators in North America. In their history and by their example, Buffalo Bill Cody found a new hope for his own endeavor.

иишии

Against the background of a nation being transformed by immigration, urbanization, environmental crisis, political stalemate, new technologies, the creation of powerful corporations, income inequality, failures of governance, mounting class conflict, and increasing social, cultural, and religious diversity, during the 1890s, and especially from the Chicago World's Fair forward, the Latter-day Saints had ingratiated themselves into public perception as proper Americans. Buffalo Bill Cody had long been seen as an embodiment and interpreter of the American standard of civilization and progress. He was a white western man who had paved the way for other white men and their families to populate the American West.

Latter-day Saints were now viewed in a similar vein. They too were agents of American expansion, pioneers with irrigation works that modeled the possibilities for productivity and growth in the arid region. No longer viewed as a threat to the American home and family as it grew in the West, they could now be, and by many were, seen as active participants in empire and the standard-bearers for establishing productive settlements. Theirs was a pioneer identity that proved foundational for civilization's success in the American West. They were white American pioneers who claimed ownership for their place in the American narratives of Manifest Destiny and empire.

Buffalo Bill Cody was a man of action, and he recognized what the Latter-day Saint experience and model could bring to the infrastructure he was building. These Latter-day Saints who conquered the arid lands and made them "blossom as the rose" were the type of men Cody could respect. He had embraced the heroic pioneer narrative that had increased Latter-day Saint respectability. And soon he would also embrace these western men in his determination to develop the Big Horn Basin. He had used caricatures of Mormons as feared outsiders to sell profitable dramas. Now, having spent time in proximity with individuals of the religious group, he viewed them primarily as productive pioneers. Did Cody have a true change of heart about Latter-day Saints? Or did he simply see them as a business opportunity?

ACT II

— 5 —

Negotiating Opportunities

In 1899 Buffalo Bill seized on a unique opportunity to promote his vision of white masculinity—and to grow his personal wealth at the same time. The United States had just emerged victorious from the short-lived Spanish-American War, which had been launched by the explosion of a vessel—the USS *Maine*—in Cuba's Havana Harbor in February 1898. From April through August 1898, U.S. troops engaged in armed conflict against Spanish forces, to both aid the Cuban fight for liberation and bolster American interests in the Caribbean.

The Spanish-American War was a popular conflict; more U.S. men tried to volunteer than the armed forces could accept. One volunteer regiment, the First U.S. Volunteer Cavalry, later nicknamed the Rough Riders (likely borrowing the moniker from Buffalo Bill's famous cowboy cadre) under Theodore Roosevelt's leadership, gained fame and notoriety during the war. The regiment was made up of riders and riflemen of the Rockies and Great Plains who became recognized by the public as brave, fearless, strong, athletic, and discerning equestrian men.[1] As Roosevelt himself later wrote of the group, "They were a splendid set of men . . . tall and sinewy, with resolute, weather-beaten faces, and eyes that looked a man straight in the face without flinching." In all the world, Roosevelt proclaimed, "there could be no better material for soldiers than that afforded by these grim hunters of the mountains, these wild rough riders of the plains."[2]

The Battle of San Juan Hill, fought in Cuba on July 1, 1898, became the bloodiest and most famous battle of the Spanish-American War. It also served as the location of the greatest victory for Roosevelt's Rough Riders. Roosevelt claimed that the Spanish-American War had finally driven the

Spanish from the Western Hemisphere. To Roosevelt and his contemporaries, the Spanish-American War proved the strength and exceptional-
ism of the American cowboy, a figure Buffalo Bill had been extolling in
his shows for the previous five years. Buffalo Bill Cody's Rough Riders
had exhibited masculinity that foreshadowed Roosevelt's exploits, but
real warfare and victory in Cuba led by a contingent of white American
Rough Riders made those exhibitions a reality.

Capitalizing on the popularity of Roosevelt's Rough Riders and their
victory in Cuba, Buffalo Bill Cody added members of the volunteer regiment to the 1899 season of the Wild West and Congress of Rough Riders of the World. Cody followed the pulse of the nation and knew that
highlighting these heroes would bring large, enthusiastic crowds to his
show. Those fellows were paid alongside other performers to reenact the
Battle of San Juan Hill for showgoers all over the United States. Their
addition to the show further celebrated the full potential of white American manhood on a global stage, as they had proven their masculinity
in the laboratory of actual combat. The Battle of San Juan Hill provided
the climax to Cody's show from 1899 to 1900 in the United States and
from 1902 to 1904 in Great Britain. In 1899 the San Juan Hill production
replaced the performance of the Battle of Little Bighorn, signaling a shift
in Cody's presentation from the conquering of the West to America's
place in a new global, imperial frontier.[3] The reproduction of the Battle
of San Juan Hill was "as historically accurate as possible" and portrayed
Roosevelt's Rough Riders as national heroes.[4] The valiant, daring charge
up San Juan Hill proved that white American masculinity had lost none
of its potency. Cody sought to popularize that idea in an international
drama and on an international stage.

The breakthrough popularity of the label "Rough Riders" presented a
new opportunity for Buffalo Bill and his company to advertise the Big
Horn Basin. Hoping to lure settlers, they ran prominent ads in each of the
thousands of programs distributed at performances of Buffalo Bill's Wild
West and Congress of Rough Riders of the World.[5] In addition, Buffalo Bill

started publishing a new periodical, the *Rough Rider* magazine, in 1899, to capitalize on the widespread admiration of his own and Roosevelt's Rough Riders. In the pages of this new periodical, Cody promoted his irrigation project and hopeful empire. He wrote letters and published promotional articles and pamphlets, lauding the basin as a "pioneer's paradise."[6] The magazine further christened Cody "a great public benefactor" because he had devoted his means and energy to the agricultural and commercial "development of that far Great West, in whose reclamation from savage hands he played so brave and conspicuous a part." In the pages of this periodical, Buffalo Bill effectively tied the heroic cowboy symbol with reclamation and water resource development.[7]

In the first issue of the *Rough Rider*, an article asserted that Buffalo Bill had his Wyoming development project in mind when he created his epic performance in 1893. "That was the ulterior object in view when 'Buffalo Bill's Wild West and Congress of Rough Riders of the World' was first organized," according to the magazine column, "and the profits resulting from the extraordinarily successful and popular exhibition have been largely dedicated to its accomplishment." Buffalo Bill had long looked for investment opportunities in places of settlement and even big-game preserves in the West but had come to devote himself to the Big Horn Basin. The narrative that Buffalo Bill's periodical established provided the hope of great prosperity for large communities of white American families who would fill the basin. Not shy about Cody's magnanimity, the promotional piece also acknowledged the costly enterprise of bringing water to the basin to make the showman's dream a reality.[8]

To encourage potential settlers, the *Rough Rider*'s Big Horn Basin promotional page included an endorsement from Elwood Mead, the Wyoming state engineer who would go on to become the commissioner of the U.S. Bureau of Reclamation. Mead was effusive in his praise of Buffalo Bill's efforts. He characterized the Cody irrigation canal as one of the most beneficial infrastructure projects initiated in the state. "I know of no place in this country which offers to prudent and industrious farmers greater assurances of material prosperity and physical comfort than the Big Horn Basin," Mead boasted.[9]

While the efficacy of the advertising is uncertain—though apparently largely fruitless, due to the small number of settlers who ultimately relocated to Cody and the Big Horn Basin—it did not go unnoticed. One letter demonstrates that the publicity at least piqued some interest. From Jackson, Michigan, approximately seventy-five miles west of Detroit, A. H. Whitaker wrote to George Beck, the operational manager of Cody's land and irrigation companies, requesting more information about settlement opportunities in the Big Horn Basin after reading the *Rough Rider* magazine. "Seeing in the 'Rough Rider,' a brief description of the 'Shoshone Irrigation Co's,' enterprise," Whitaker stated, "I have often thought of such a colony in the west, and have frequently been asked to organize one. I think the description, (as far as it goes) of the land and climate in the 'Rough Rider' suits my idea of a Western home."[10] Cody and his associates had promoted the interests of his Big Horn Basin endeavors for years; the popularity of the Rough Rider label, he hoped, would generate greater settlement.

The showman turned land and water salesman also highlighted Utah and its Mormon population in his advertisements and brochures for the Big Horn Basin. Cody's company employed the Saints as a clear example of success in irrigated agriculture. "Brigham Young realized its advantages and made it the foundation of his social system in planning the colonies of Utah," Cody's company declared, before marketing "the plateaus, valleys, mesas and parks adjoining the lands under the Shoshone Irrigation Company's Canal" that could be subdivided for villages of family farmers.[11] Buffalo Bill's company had water rights for hundreds of thousands of acres, tens of thousands of which were ready for immediate development. The success of the whole project rested on two interrelated factors: people and water. Cody needed laborers to bring the water, and he needed enough people to settle and farm the land once it became irrigable.[12] But he could not seem to get one without the other.

Though Buffalo Bill remained optimistic and determined, the town of Cody was struggling. A few years into the town-building project, the population remained stagnant. Some estimates were as high as "about 150 or 200 people," though land company president and Burlington Railroad confidante Charles Morrill lamented in November 1899, "There is prob-

18. View of the town of Cody, Wyoming, December 1899.
University of Wyoming, American Heritage Center, George T. Beck
Papers, accession number 59, box 31, folder 11.

ably not more than 10 settlers," on Cody's irrigated lands.[13] Settlers had certainly not swarmed to the region. Beyond the need to bring water to the land, Buffalo Bill knew access to the railroad was critical, a painful lesson he had learned thirty years earlier during his first town-building endeavor at Rome, Kansas. He recognized the importance of attracting the railroad and what it would mean for settlement and the regional economy. Anxieties lingered from his Kansas town-building failure. He knew he was up against a tough sale, but he had become savvier, he had connections, and he had cultural and political capital. He knew northwest Wyoming had untapped potential.

The Big Horn Basin had many attractive features, including coal deposits, mining, scenery, landscapes, and game-hunting opportunities. It had tremendous economic potential, and Cody was trying everything he could to sell people on it. Officials of the Chicago, Burlington, and Quincy Railroad carefully watched Cody's efforts. They understood the region's potential but were perceptive enough to see that the irrigation infrastructure and the population were still lacking. Cody had made repeated overtures to railroad officials and executives to convince them to build a line to his town. The town could command the business of the basin, but without a railroad line, residents would have no access to outside markets and could not grow economically.[14]

Buffalo Bill had solicited dozens of potential investors with minimal success. With few desirous to invest in expensive infrastructure projects in the basin, settlement stalled.[15] Cody wrote letter after letter about the financial liabilities he faced and the lack of investors to push the work forward.[16] Cody and his business partners took much of their frustration out on George Beck for what they considered mismanagement of the Cody Canal project. "This habit of doing the work on that ditch in a piecemeal way, has become something of a chestnut to me," Nate Salsbury scoffed in one letter to Beck.[17] He demanded that Beck complete the canal, but a lack of resources, human and financial, made that impractical.

By late 1899 a "properly constructed ditch" had still not been completed in Cody's town. Railroad companies and Wyoming state officials (anxious to see the region populated) were eager for Cody's endeavors to materialize. Buffalo Bill remained confident. "When we get a rail road," Bill wrote to George Beck, "which will be in side of three years—and our town numbers thousands and land worth $100 an acre—then I wont have such hard work getting my colleagues to put up."[18] Cody encouraged potential settlers to get in on the ground floor before the railroad arrived to guarantee their financial success. But settlers wanted to be assured of a railroad, while railroad officials demanded larger numbers of settlers. Cody faced the same conundrum with the railroad as he did with building vital irrigation infrastructure.

Buffalo Bill spent most of his efforts courting the Chicago, Burlington, and Quincy Railroad. Burlington officials were concerned about money, not just the price tag of constructing a railroad but the cost of irrigating the basin lands and whether anyone, including Cody, could or would pay the price. They recognized that the water supply from the Shoshone River was sufficient to water the lands, but to undertake a new canal project large enough to divert a sufficient capacity of water to other parts of the basin, Charles Morrill estimated to Burlington executive Charles Perkins, "would cost at least $250,000." Morrill struck a dire tone when he said, "At Cody there are less than a dozen houses, and only one store. There is no water in Cody, even for the irrigation of gardens. The Cody ditch scheme has been a failure." Regarding the future success of Cody's project, he said it was "improbable unless somebody else took hold of it."[19] Though Buffalo Bill remained outwardly confident in his efforts to coax the railroad, these letters strike a more apprehensive tone about the value of building a line to Cody's town. For the time being, Burlington officials kept a close eye on Buffalo Bill and developments in the basin.

мимим

While the Burlington Railroad officials observed Cody's progress in the Big Horn Basin, the Latter-day Saints also looked to its potential. Despite the displays of Utah's abundance at the Chicago World's Fair, the national economic depression of the 1890s hit the Great Basin Saints hard, especially those agriculturists who saw their products' prices plummet. Growing families and the continuing immigration of new Latter-day Saint converts created a difficult economic climate in Utah, wherein too many people were looking for too few jobs, and there was not enough land for those who wanted to farm.[20] By 1900, as one Utahn said, "it was apparent the country was too small for everyone to make a good living."[21] With few social services providing a safety net and The Church of Jesus Christ of Latter-day Saints millions of dollars in debt, largely to investment bankers, from the decades of struggling to build settlements in new places and from the more recent confiscation of church properties by the federal government, Latter-day Saint leaders increasingly looked for new economic opportunities, including those outside of Utah.[22]

Since the arrival of the Saints in the Intermountain West, church leaders had directed the movement and settlement of Saints to advantageous locations to spread their message of faith and to provide economic benefits for individuals and the church. These colonization policies helped create a Mormon corridor from southern California to eastern Idaho and southwestern Wyoming, with settlements ranging from northern Mexico to southern Canada. At the turn of the twentieth century, they did not have to look far for additional land, however, as their neighbor to the northeast, Wyoming, had an ample supply to offer. Like other places in the arid West, however, infrastructure and the needed human capital to develop the latent land resources was desperately needed.[23] There were plenty of Latter-day Saints who could provide the needed human capital and who were on the lookout for new economic opportunities. Plus, the faith group had a proven track record in developing the most important of western infrastructure: irrigation canals.

Northwest Wyoming appeared to be a natural extension for Latter-day Saint colonization, and in the summer of 1899 church leaders, including a young, energetic, and handsome apostle named Abraham Owen Woodruff, set their sights on the Big Horn Basin. In July 1899 Woodruff received authorization from church president Lorenzo Snow to travel to the Big Horn Basin to organize wards (Latter-day Saint ecclesiastical units arranged by geography) and "attend to whatever business may come up."[24] Woodruff—the son of former Latter-day Saint church president Wilford Woodruff, who had had the opportunity to befriend William F. Cody and who had recently passed away in September 1898—was only twenty-four years old when his father ordained him an apostle in 1896. Abraham was the youngest member of that quorum, the church's second-highest governing body. Abraham was born to Wilford, and his plural wife Emma Smith Woodruff. He grew up working on the family farm, fishing, and hunting. Prior to his calling as an apostle, Woodruff served a mission for his faith for three years in Germany before returning to Utah in 1896, where he married Helen May Winters on June 30. The young newlyweds faced long periods of separation, as Abraham the apostle traveled throughout Utah, Wyoming, Canada, and Mexico to oversee units of the church.

In the summer of 1899, as he prepared to visit the Big Horn Basin, Woodruff communicated with Charles Kingston, a land agent in Evanston, Wyoming, who served as the Wyoming representative for the church's interests in that state. Kingston's connections with Wyoming state officials and his communications became critical as the plans to settle Latter-day Saints in the Big Horn Basin unfolded.[25] Woodruff left Salt Lake City in July and arrived in Burlington, Wyoming, in the Big Horn Basin later that month. There he met one of his older brothers, David Woodruff, who had been born to Wilford (their mutual father) and another of his plural wives, Sarah Brown, in 1854 and whom Abraham had not seen for eight years.[26] David had settled in the Big Horn Basin in the early 1890s.

19. Portrait of Abraham Owen Woodruff, circa 1900. Courtesy of the Church
History Library, The Church of Jesus Christ of Latter-day Saints, Salt Lake City.

He established a ranch near Meeteetse and a settlement in the town of
Burlington (which Buffalo Bill and George Beck had visited in 1894),
both of which he helped to irrigate. David's small, yet successful efforts
demonstrated to his brother and others the potential for Latter-day Saint
communities in the basin. Abraham now looked to establish Latter-day
Saint settlements in the region on a much larger scale.

While in the basin, Abraham Woodruff noticed the plentiful game and observed, as he drove over thousands of acres, that the land was "of fine quality" and "can easily be irrigated" from the Shoshone River. There were suitable tracts of land to support thousands of people on either side of the river. He had reached the same conclusion about the land that Buffalo Bill Cody had: this land was a pioneer's paradise with immense potential. Woodruff organized the Burlington Ward of The Church of Jesus Christ of Latter-day Saints before he headed home to Salt Lake City.[27]

Abraham wasted no time in taking steps toward establishing a Latter-day Saint settlement in the Big Horn Basin. On his way home to Salt Lake City, Woodruff stopped in Evanston, Wyoming, and met with Charles Kingston as well as various attorneys and Wyoming legislators about "getting out a permit for the settlement of certain lands in Big Horn Basin." Upon his return home, Woodruff shared his excitement about the Big Horn Basin's potential with church president Lorenzo Snow, who, Woodruff noted in his journal, was "unqualifiedly in favor of pushing things in that part and told me to go ahead." Snow eventually appointed Woodruff the colonization agent for the church, making him a committee of one to carry out measures to help Latter-day Saint settlers colonize new areas, including Wyoming's Big Horn Basin. "A Committee of one," Lorenzo Snow told Woodruff, "is always best."[28]

Following his summer visit to northwest Wyoming, Woodruff communicated frequently with Kingston to push their settlement forward. Kingston, having many connections and understanding the proverbial lay of the land, reached out to several contacts, including Shoshone Irrigation Company manager George Beck. "I have been requested by the leaders of the Mormon Church, to visit our Colony at Burlington," Kingston informed Beck, with an eye toward looking "over the Big Horn country with a view of its settlement by our people." "I would like, while there," Kingston said further, "to see and talk with you relative to your canal scheme, so that I may get a general idea of the facilities of the country, for settlement."[29] Whether Kingston acted on his own knowledge or by directive of Woodruff is not known; nevertheless, his overture to Buffalo

Bill's irrigation company generated intense interest from some of Wyoming's most influential power brokers.

※※※※

Having heard of the Latter-day Saints' interest in the Big Horn Basin, Curtis Hinkle of the State Board of Land Commissioners wrote to Abraham O. Woodruff, hoping that the Latter-day Saints and the state "might come to some understanding" in settling and reclaiming land under the Cincinnati Canal, a large land proposition on the north side of Shoshone River between the present-day towns of Cowley and Byron, Wyoming, and approximately forty miles northeast from the townsite of Cody.[30] The land was excellent for farming and in proximity to timber on the Pryor Mountains just over a dozen miles away.

An understanding, however, required the consent of the current rights holders. Nate Salsbury and William F. Cody owned the land and water rights under the Cincinnati Canal proposition, obtaining them in 1898 after the Cincinnati Canal Company abandoned a project it started there in 1896. There were twenty-six thousand acres in the Cincinnati Canal tract, and the estimated cost to build the canal was $75,000 (more than $2.6 million in 2022 U.S. dollars). By the end of 1899, Cody's company had not yet started any work on it. Wyoming officials were hopeful they could negotiate an agreement between Salsbury and Cody, the Latter-day Saints, and the state, whereby Salsbury and Cody would relinquish their rights to the enterprising group of settlers from Utah, thereby leaving them financially unencumbered to construct the canals and develop the land under the Cincinnati plan. The cost for settlers would be relatively low. The margin for error was slim, Kingston noted, but the opportunity to allow settlers to build the canal and benefit from their labors without owing a cent to a private irrigation company was worth the investment.[31]

Another Wyoming power broker added his voice to the negotiations. In late December 1899 Buffalo Bill Cody wrote to Charles Kingston in Evanston about the possibility of working together. It is likely that Cody's business partner George Beck had filled Cody in about the initial correspondence he had been having with Kingston, the Latter-day Saint land agent for Wyoming. Wanting to press the matter, the influential showman addressed a letter directly to Kingston. Knowing what Mormons had accomplished in making the Salt Lake Valley "blossom as the rose," the celebrated plainsman asked if his Shoshone Irrigation Company could do business with the Mormons.[32]

Charles Kingston replied in a letter dated December 29, 1899, that Latter-day Saint leadership in Salt Lake City "was unanimous" on the idea of church members moving to the Big Horn Basin. "However," Kingston informed Cody, "it was considered best to allow those who might move into the Basin to make their own selection of location and conditions. The Church will not go farther than to recommend the Basin as a good place in which to obtain homes." Kingston ended his letter on an encouraging note, suggesting the good prospects that "quite a number" of Latter-day Saints would move into the basin in the coming season "but whether they would care to enter into contract with your Company is a matter for the individual to determine."[33] Kingston understood the desperate situation of Buffalo Bill and that Mormons held the upper hand.[34]

The Mormons wanted to have their own land and water rights. Kingston wrote, "It is a settled fact, that our people will not settle any of the lands under the various canal schemes now in operation there. Our idea is to let the people have all the benefits of their labor; this is the only way in which we will or can get settlers there."[35] The Latter-day Saint leaders were not interested in purchasing the water rights from Cody's company because it would not benefit the poor among them. Buffalo Bill needed money to fund his own canal work, but Kingston and Woodruff made clear at the outset that the Saints would not pay him for the privilege of settling in the region. They were "doubtful whether a poor settler could ever free himself from such obligations, and at the same time develop and obtain a living from his land."[36] Instead of working for Cody or purchasing land or water rights from his company, the church officials sought to obtain unencumbered opportunities for their people and free rights to usable land.

Abraham Woodruff wrote to Wyoming governor DeForest Richards, a fifty-three-year-old bespeckled politician and former banker who strongly supported the railroad, irrigation, and growth in his adopted home state. The apostle told the governor of the droves of Latter-day Saints anxious to move to the Big Horn Basin who would take the initiative to build canals and make the arid lands productive. These religious families needed autonomy, Woodruff informed the governor, and the apostle did not want to see them "have to deal with any middle men."[37] Charles Kingston also lobbied on the Saints' behalf. He told the governor directly, "Our idea is to let the people have all the benefits of their labor; this is the only way in which we will or can get settlers there." The Latter-day Saint leaders wanted their people to control their own destiny. That, coupled with religious devotion and strong morality, had provided the blueprint for transforming territory unfit for cultivation into successful communities. Controlling the water meant controlling the land, and that meant power to provide fruitful opportunities and livelihoods for their co-religionists and protect them from "undesirable parties" and elements.[38] It was a successful formula, and there was no reason to deviate from a winning strategy.

The promise of large-scale Mormon immigration made Buffalo Bill bullish on the basin's prospects. Though the Latter-day Saints were clear that they would not purchase land from him, Cody used the promise of a large Latter-day Saint colonization to further promote his development of the basin. Around the same time as he corresponded with Kingston, Cody wrote to his longtime friend Michael R. Russell. "Everything is booming at Cody," Buffalo Bill exclaimed. "The Mormon church want to buy us out—the Canal and all our land—everything but the townsite of Cody—that we wish to keep." He maintained a promotional tone in his friendly letter, declaring that at least one railroad would come into Cody within the next year.[39] But in reality the Saints were not interested in buying any property from Cody's company, and the timing of the railroad's arrival remained uncertain.[40] But the prospect of a large community of devoted workers building waterworks in the region enlivened hope in the great showman.

Buffalo Bill was not the only western speculator or town builder anxious for Mormon settlers to establish irrigation systems in the Intermountain West at the turn of the twentieth century. Investment brokers, real-estate agents, and irrigation companies in Montana, Idaho, Colorado, and Wyoming all worked to attract Mormon settlement.[41] These entities felt the same way as Buffalo Bill when he described Mormons as "the greatest irrigators on earth."[42] Latter-day Saint leadership quickly dismissed many of the propositions made, but the Big Horn Basin was different. It was perfectly suited for the Mormons' agricultural plans. The Mormons became Buffalo Bill's best hope to salvage development in his fledgling western town. The twin self-interested opportunities aligned. Buffalo Bill and his partners were anxious to bring settlers to the Big Horn Basin, and Mormons were anxious to find new economic opportunities.[43]

*

Buffalo Bill was not the only Wyoming-based individual with a vested interest in encouraging immigration of Mormons to the state. Wyoming government officials had long tried to recruit and retain settlers, especially outside of the primary towns—like Cheyenne and Laramie—along the Union Pacific line through the southern part of the state. Seeing an opportunity to promote immigration from their industrious neighbors to the southwest, Governor DeForest Richards began to strongly encourage the movement of Latter-day Saints to his state. Richards was a proponent of irrigation development, considering it of "paramount importance" and "great interest" to his state, the region, and the nation as a whole.[44]

Willing to do anything in his power to promote the interests of the Latter-day Saints, Charles Kingston had written to Governor Richards, asking for his help in clearing any obstacles to obtaining the lands under the Cincinnati Canal but also filing a permit on another tract of land previously filed on by Cody and his business partner Nate Salsbury in 1897. Like on the Cincinnati lands, Cody and Salsbury had not begun work on this land south of the Shoshone River below Eagle's Nest station. Since work had not begun on the land, Kingston and Abraham Woodruff were hopeful that meant it was unencumbered. They hoped that gaining rights to the south-side lands, approximately eight thousand acres, would be another simple process. The Cincinnati tract and the south-side lands combined, Kingston and Woodruff thought, would provide the perfect amount of land for the Saints' early colonization efforts. If given the opportunity to add this second tract, Kingston told the governor, the Saints would "go there and certainly succeed."[45] No filing on the land could take place until December 1902, when Cody's permit expired, and unless the state engineer could annul the contract or get Cody's company to relinquish, nothing could be done to assure the Latter-day Saint leaders they would gain rights to these lands.

The governor tried to refocus the conversation. Rather than see this as a zero-sum game, of the Saints getting both tracts of land or nothing, Richards encouraged Kingston, and by extension Woodruff, to concentrate first on settling the lands under the Cincinnati Canal. Governor Richards wrote in reply to Kingston, "I beg to assure you of my earnest desire that you take up this proposition, and that you will have my hearty co-operation toward a successful prosecution of this enterprise, should you embark in it."[46] Richards urged the Latter-day Saint leaders to take their immigration and colonization one step at a time. Doing so would bring them goodwill and prevent unnecessary conflict with other settlers and interests in the state. But the Saints remained eager.

Charles Kingston kept Abraham Woodruff apprised of every letter he received and every new development on the Big Horn Basin. He ended one letter on a particularly hopeful note: "It seems to me that our way is being opened up before us."[47] Building on Kingston's hopeful messages, Woodruff seized the opportunity and built on the momentum. He spent the bulk of his time in January 1900 attending to business matters relative to the Big Horn Basin.[48] Early that month he asked William H. Packard of Burlington, Wyoming, to make a survey of the Cincinnati Canal proposition. He also declared his intent of taking hold of the Cincinnati Canal lands in a letter to Governor DeForest Richards.[49] Woodruff wanted both the Cincinnati lands and the south-side lands, but he was not willing to go all in on them at this point. Woodruff viewed the Cincinnati Canal lands as a sure thing and wanted a strong foothold in the basin. But he still needed to work with Wyoming officials and Buffalo Bill to ensure the uninhibited access to those lands and water rights. That would require negotiating with Buffalo Bill himself.

Still trying to woo a railroad company to build into the Big Horn Basin town of Cody, Buffalo Bill's Shoshone Irrigation Company manager, George Beck, reported to the company's directors that the Northern Pacific Railroad manager, John W. Kendrick, was encouraged by the prospect of Latter-day Saint colonization in the area.[50] Shortly after Kendrick's visit to the basin, Beck wrote to Charles Kingston, hoping to expedite Latter-day Saint settlement in the area.[51] Beck, Kingston knew, was desperate. With time rapidly expiring to complete work on various canal projects, especially the Cincinnati venture, and the failure to entice the railroad or attract settlers, Kingston believed that Cody's company would be "pleased to have us take the enterprise off their hands, and on our own terms, that is, before very long."[52]

William F. Cody was not shy about encouraging Latter-day Saint settlement in the basin. Persisting in his goal "to open this new country and settle it with happy and prosperous people," Buffalo Bill told a midwestern newspaper reporter in mid-January 1900, "I am going up to my town in the Big Horn basin in Northwest Wyoming. . . . Ive got 200,000 acres of land up there and I am going to unload the whole 'rauakaboo' onto them Mormons." Though Kingston and Woodruff had made clear that they were not interested in purchasing land and water rights, Cody explained that he was negotiating for the sale of a portion of his land. To the reporter he stated, "The Mormons want to buy it—or at least a large part of it—and I'd just as soon sell to them as any one else." Though he misrepresented the sale of the lands (or perhaps he naively continued to hope for such a sale), in this interview the famous showman emphasized the Latter-day Saints as pioneer irrigators. To his interviewer Cody exclaimed, "Look what they did with the Salt Lake country! Well, I expect them to do the same thing in the way of irrigation in the Big Horn basin."[53] Buffalo Bill knew that access to water for agricultural purposes was vital to the success and continued growth of the basin. Work on Cody's irrigation canals was moving forward at a sluggish pace, but the Mormons were the most successful irrigators in the country, and Cody believed they could save his dreams for the Big Horn Basin.

By February Latter-day Saint officials, led by Abraham Woodruff, put their colonization plans into motion. They arranged to have Wyoming state officials visit Salt Lake City and the First Presidency of The Church of Jesus Christ of Latter-day Saints to discuss the proposal of the Saints colonizing lands in the northwest part of the state of Wyoming. DeForest Richards, Wyoming's governor, as well as Secretary of State Fenimore Chatterton and Judge Jesse Knight of the Wyoming Supreme Court arrived in Salt Lake City on February 5 for a meeting. In a room at the Knutsford Hotel, the Wyoming visitors expressed their gratification at the Saints' impending move to Wyoming. According to a *Deseret Evening News* account of the meeting, the Wyoming officials expressed their opinion that "Utah people [are] desirable citizens whom they are glad to see added to their population."[54] Following this goodwill meeting, at 8:45 p.m. that night, Woodruff left on the railroad for a business trip "connected with the matter of colonization." He headed north in company with Byron Sessions and Hyrum K. North, before being joined by Charles A. Welch, George H. Taggart, John Croft, and several other Latter-day Saint men in Ogden.[55] The party increased to more than a dozen as they traveled to the Big Horn Basin.[56] They arrived in Butte, Montana, on February 6 and had a church conference there. The apostle Abraham Woodruff taught the congregation in Butte on the resurrection of Jesus Christ. From there the party proceeded on to Red Lodge, Montana, where they stayed the night of February 7 at a hotel.[57]

On February 8 at 6:30 p.m., Woodruff and his delegation arrived at Eagle's Nest stage station, some fifteen miles northeast of Cody, Wyoming. It was a bitter cold evening, but the Latter-day Saints were warmed by the opportunity to meet an internationally known celebrity. Buffalo Bill had traveled from his home in Cody to greet the party, arriving with little fanfare just before dark. Cody had been amicably acquainted with Wilford Woodruff and now welcomed the chance to visit with his son Abraham. Woodruff and others were in awe at this chance to meet the international superstar. They described the showman as having "a striking personality" and being "a very genial man," while commenting on his physical appearance. Buffalo Bill stood "over six feet tall," and he was "very straight," though they also noted his aging features, particularly his graying hair.[58]

Following a supper meal together, Buffalo Bill regaled the Latter-day Saint men with stories of his life, while they listened with rapt attention.[59] According to Woodruff's journal, Cody "talked pleasantly of his experience with Johnson's Army when Lot Smith burnt them on the Sandy [River]." This referred to a story that Buffalo Bill first told in his 1879 autobiography. In that account, and thereafter, Cody claimed that he was part of the government wagon train traveling into the Intermountain West to support the army during the 1857 Utah War. His autobiography told in vivid detail of the harrowing experience, when Lot Smith and some "Mormon Danites" drove off cattle and burned the grass and government supply wagons that left the boy Cody and other freighters stranded that winter. His retelling of that event thrilled his Latter-day Saint guests. "We enjoyed this very much," commented Charles A. Welch. The Latter-day Saint men, some of whom had not been born or were very young when the Utah War occurred, then inquired about the conditions the army faced. Cody responded jovially with a tale of how the men subsided on mule meat.[60]

As discussed in a previous chapter, historians have long questioned whether Buffalo Bill did in fact participate in the 1857 Utah War. Uncertainty remains of his whereabouts, though the contemporary evidence does not support Cody being in Utah Territory at that time. What is certain is that Cody remained committed to the story that he had told in his autobiography, published at the height of anti-Mormon sentiment in the United States. Perhaps he had embraced the story so long that it had become part of his persona, and therefore it had become a constructed memory. The original purpose of the story as told in Cody's autobiography was to emphasize the danger and nefariousness of Mormons and Cody's heroic willingness to combat the danger, even as a young child. But now more than forty years removed from the actual event and more than twenty years removed from the writing of it in his autobiography, Cody struck a different chord. He was friendly, conciliatory, and lighthearted.

Cody's tone had already shifted markedly in talking about the Utah War. In an 1898 history of the West, titled *The Great Salt Lake Trail* and coauthored with Col. Henry Inman, Cody presented a brief history of the Utah War, as part of this epic of the West. Rather than presenting the Latter-day Saints as a violent threat, *The Great Salt Lake Trail* instead focused on the politics of a disgraced president. The Utah War was "merely a move on the President's political chess-board," Inman and Cody wrote. If it was a strategic move, it was a poor one. "There was, perhaps, no genuine basis of necessity upon which to organize the expensive and disastrous expedition against the Mormons," Inman and Cody asserted. Religious prejudice, the authors concluded, led to a "farcical demonstration on the part of the government."[61] Though Cody's earlier writings and stage performances had profited from that same religious prejudice, he now appeared to condemn it.

During the meeting at Eagle's Nest, Buffalo Bill expressed his admiration for the Latter-day Saints. "Colonel Cody spoke of his respect for the Mormon pioneers," observer Charles Welch wrote, "and particularly for Brigham Young because he was the master mind in the movement of so many thousands of people across the trackless plains into the Valley of the great Salt Lake."[62] According to this account from Welch and from other Latter-day Saint sources of the meeting at Eagle's Nest, William F. Cody spoke positively about the church's past and his early encounters with the religious group.[63] Buffalo Bill's meeting with the Latter-day Saints at Eagle's Nest symbolically reconciled the past to serve the present. This famous white man and this largely white religious group now existed on the same footing. No longer were the Saints portrayed as treacherous, polygamous Danites threatening the homes and families of the West. Now they were viewed as hearty pioneers who could provide homes for families in the arid West. The good-natured exchange between Cody and the Latter-day Saints demonstrated shared interest while prioritizing the present and future by allowing the differences of the past to remain there.

Cody and the Saints' mutual interest was in the development of the Big Horn Basin. It is not known what conversations or events had taken place, but by the time of the Saints' arrival, William F. Cody was prepared to give the religious group what they wanted. According to accounts by Charles A. Welch and his son Frederick Arza Welch, at this meeting "Mr. Cody agreed to relinquish both land and water rights to us if we could build a canal to irrigate the land."[64] Colonel Cody apparently said, "I have secured a permit to irrigate nearly all of the lands on the North side of the Shoshone River, from Eagles nest to the Big Horn River, but if the Mormons want to build a canal and irrigate the land down lower on the River I will relinquish both land and water to them, for if they will do this I know they are the kind of people who will do what they agree to do." Cody was referring to the lands under the Cincinnati Canal proposition, lands that Woodruff wanted. According to this account, Cody later told his business partner Nate Salsbury, "I have dreamed that I would live to see this country developed into a great agriculture region and now the Mormons will fulfill my dream."[65]

As the meeting between Cody and the Mormon group concluded, Buffalo Bill invited them to his home. This was a genuine gesture that held great symbolism. Buffalo Bill's character had protected the American home from the Mormons for decades, but the man had since visited the Mormon home and seen its goodness and virtues. Having experienced proximity to and familiarity with the once-maligned group, he was now ready to have them in his own home and settled in his adopted homeland. "Mr. Cody greatly desired us to visit his home and offered to entertain us if we would come," Charles A. Welch wrote. "However, our visit was to a different part of the basin and we could not accept of his kind invitation."[66] For the time Cody and the Mormon group parted ways as friends.

///////////

Abraham Woodruff's party spent the next ten days investigating the region and the potential for settlement in the area around the Cincinnati Canal proposition. Though Woodruff received a discouraging estimate of "$75,000 [for] the first ¾ miles" to build the canal, he ultimately concluded that not only could the Mormon people build a canal but that they would thrive on this "very fine tract of land."[67] Most important, for Woodruff, the church's colonization agent, "The canal will be built and owned by the people who will get the land and water at actual cost."[68]

The *Cody Enterprise* gleefully reported on the visit of the Mormon party in its February 8 issue. "The arrival of the twelve Utah gentlemen, headed by Mr. Woodruff, is an event of great importance to this section of the country," the *Enterprise* declared. The Cody newspaper applauded the Latter-day Saint endorsement "of the many favorable attributes of this region" before announcing that "thousands of industrious tillers of the soil" would soon settle in a basin that promised to provide them and all settlers "ample reward, and peace, contentment and prosperity."[69]

Other newspapers likewise reported on this development. Cody told representatives of the *Omaha World-Herald* later in February that he had "closed a deal with the representatives of seventy-five Mormon families whereby they will each be given a fifty-acre tract of land situated along the Cody canal for a certain price, water to be furnished for a number of years."[70] His comments appear to be deliberately misleading, with erroneous details about the Latter-day Saints purchasing lands. Nevertheless, he praised the recent visit of the religious group. The *Salt Lake Herald* reprinted a *Cheyenne Tribune* column quoting Cody, who reported,

Without doubt a large number of Mormons will migrate into Wyoming in the near future. Perhaps it is safe to say, as has been asserted by the Salt Lake papers, that before the end of the summer there will be not less than 30,000 Mormons who will have taken up permanent homes along the banks of the Shoshone river and the Cody canal. They are the greatest colonizers in the world, and the state authorities never made a wiser move then when they interested the Mormon church in the agricultural possibilities of western Wyoming.

In that interview he backed off of the rumor that a deal had been struck with the Mormons for sale of the land but said of the group, "They are excellent agriculturalists and it would be a paying move" to bring them to the basin.[71] Buffalo Bill's words reveal his open enthusiasm for the settlement of the Saints. Abraham Woodruff was even more excited. He returned to Salt Lake City on February 18, and the next day he made his report to Latter-day Saint church president Lorenzo Snow, glorifying the opportunities for Mormon settlers in the Big Horn Basin.[72]

In early March 1900, in a move calculated to encourage the growth and settlement he desired for the Big Horn Basin, William F. Cody relinquished, for no charge, his company's right to twenty-one thousand acres of land and water rights to the Cincinnati Canal on the Shoshone River.[73] During their early February visit, Colonel Cody had promised, according to Latter-day Saint Charles Welch's recollection, that he would relinquish land and water rights to the Latter-day Saints for free because he found them to be trustworthy and knew that they would build the canal and unleash the potential of the basin.[74] Free land and water rights to a substantial tract of land showed both Buffalo Bill's desperation and generosity.

But it was not as easy as Welch remembered. On March 2, 1900, Abraham Woodruff received a letter from Wyoming secretary of state Fenimore Chatterton, "in which he stated there seemed to be some complication with Wm. F. Cody regarding the application for water right to Cincinnati tract." "This news," Woodruff confided to his journal, "caused me considerable anxiety though I have faith that it will end all right." Though Cody had apparently given a verbal agreement to relinquish his right to the Cincinnati land, a question of whether he would follow through remained. The next day, March 3, Woodruff set off to meet with Wyoming state officials in Cheyenne. To the governor; secretary of state; Fred Bond, the state engineer; and Curtis Hinkle, the chief clerk of the State Land Board, Woodruff said, "We did not care to take hold of the Canal proposition in the Big Horn Basin if any cloud should attach to the title."[75] Woodruff remained firm that they wanted the unfettered right to the land and water.

While the men were meeting, a prominent Cheyenne lawyer, Charles W. Burdick, identified by Woodruff as "Mr. Cody's atty" arrived and guaranteed that Buffalo Bill would relinquish his rights as he had said. Woodruff was relieved and left Cheyenne that evening, elated with this development. His plans were coming together just as he hoped. But he waited impatiently for the final word and the paperwork. He wrote to Fenimore Chatterton just days later that he awaited "some word regarding the relinquishment of Mr. Cody, as some of our officials feel that, that is quite an important matter." Woodruff assured Chatterton that there was considerable interest manifest among the Saints to build a new colony in the Big Horn Basin.[76] The church colonization agent expressed confidence that they would make a success of the Cincinnati tract and that there would be a great many people who will want to find homes there. Woodruff closed his letter: "I hope it will not be long before we hear something from Mr. Cody."[77] Woodruff did not have to wait much longer. On March 9, 1900, William F. Cody and his business partner Nate Salsbury signed the official papers relinquishing to the state of Wyoming their rights "acquired by us to divert and appropriate the waters of the Shoshone River for use on or irrigation of any of the lands segregated" under the Cincinnati Canal permit.[78]

For his part Nate Salsbury was not thrilled with the arrangement Cody had made. Salsbury had insisted the Mormons pay $20,000 for the rights, but Buffalo Bill refused.[79] During an exchange about the land relinquishment, the celebrity showman apparently told Salsbury, "Now my dream will be realized, for I have thought that I should live to see this country developed into a great agricultural region and now the Mormons will fulfill my dream." After Salsbury persisted in his demand that the religious group pay for the land and water rights, Cody offered the following retort: "When you die it will be said of you, 'Here lies Nate Salisbury, who made a million dollars in the show business and kept it,' but when I die people will say, 'Here lies Bill Cody, who made a million dollars in the show business and distributed it among his friends.'"[80] The famous scout saw more value in his liberal offering; hundreds of settlers willing to fund and construct their own canals that would in turn create essential infrastructure to bring in more settlement and business opportunities to his pioneer paradise was incalculable to Cody.

Abraham Woodruff was also delighted by the development. In a letter to Wyoming secretary of state Fenimore Chatterton, he expressed his gratitude for Chatterton's help in the matter. The apostle exclaimed, "Am happy that you succeeded so well in the matter with Mr. Cody," before assuring the secretary of state that "we have a fine class of men who are preparing to leave here about April 15th or May 1st." But he was not entirely satisfied. Woodruff and the Latter-day Saints still had their eyes on a roughly twenty-thousand-acre tract of land on the south side of the Shoshone River below Eagle's Nest. Now that they had gained a foothold in the basin, Woodruff looked to leverage their settlement to gain even more land. William F. Cody owned about eight thousand of those acres on the south side as part of another canal scheme, and Woodruff asked Chatterton and Governor Richards for help to acquire the parcel from Cody.[81] Woodruff claimed he would practice patience, but he remained persistent in his mission to secure the south-side lands.

The young apostle then took an impudent, audacious step. He wrote directly to William F. Cody. Perhaps thinking that the goodwill enjoyed between them during Woodruff's early February visit to the basin and emboldened by the backing of Wyoming state officials for his venture, Woodruff addressed a letter to Cody, who was now at his ranch in North Platte, Nebraska, on March 15, 1900. "I desire to thank you for the kindly feeling you have shown towards us as witnessed by this action," Woodruff began by addressing the Cincinnati Canal lands.[82] But he shifted gears quickly. He launched into a new request for more land to which Cody's company held the title, in hopes of taking advantage of Cody's lingering desperation to populate and develop the basin.

Attempting to show Buffalo Bill the upside of his proposition and perhaps trying to mask a growing avarice for the land, the young and eager Woodruff ventured into uncertain terrain. "There is another matter which I wish to mention to you which may affect the settlement of our people in the Basin some," he alluded before directly addressing the matter regarding Cody's "tract of land on the south side of the Shoshone River." The Latter-day Saint apostle then broached the subject of another relinquishment of lands by Cody to the faith group. Woodruff boldly asked for another eight thousand acres of land. Trying to persuade the showman that it would be in Cody's best interest (and to the benefit of his religious group), Woodruff claimed that another gift of land "would be a great means of advertising your property." Using some shrewd gamesmanship, he concluded his brazen letter to Buffalo Bill: "I hope to hear from you soon in regard to this matter as it may have its influence upon whatever we decide to do in the Big Horn Basin," after which he thanked Cody "for the kindly feeling you have always shown towards our people," a feeling of friendship that he hoped would continue.[83]

The same day that Woodruff wrote to Buffalo Bill, he also penned a letter to Governor DeForest Richards on the same subject. The Latter-day Saint apostle and colonization agent expressed concern that, given the immediate and wide interest among his fellow religionists in settling the area, the Cincinnati lands would be too small to accommodate the growth that the Saints promised to bring. Demonstrating to the governor that more lands would entice greater population growth, Woodruff brazenly asked, "If it would be possible for you, by some arrangement, to get Mr. Cody to relinquish his claim on the south side of the Shoshone River below Eagles Nest, I believe that I could see a prospect of the location of another colony of our people." Woodruff continued, "It appears to me that it would be advantageous to the state, to Mr. Cody and all parties concerned in the event that our people desired to undertake the irrigation and settlement of this nineteen thousand acres, for Mr. Cody to relinquish."[84] The eager apostle wanted the governor to convince Buffalo Bill that by allowing the Saints to establish two colonies, one on the Cincinnati tract and one on the south side of the river, it would draw attention and thus additional settlers to Cody's property. Woodruff wasted no time in testing his newfound allies.

Woodruff's request for more land perturbed William Cody. On March 20, 1900, upon receipt of Woodruff's presumptuous letter, Buffalo Bill quickly grabbed pen and paper to fire off a response. "I have been working this property for some time I have had two surveys made of it—as you know this costs money," he wrote brusquely. "I have giv[en] *your* people my rights of the Cincinnatti Canal," Cody continued. "You surely cant ask me to give all my rights to *your* people for nothing." Annoyed by Woodruff's audacity, Buffalo Bill became obstinate and uncooperative with the Mormon efforts to acquire the land south of the river below Eagle's Nest. He told Woodruff that he was "putting an outfit together to commence building a canal this spring to water all the lands under my concession," which would prevent Woodruff and the Saints from gaining access to the lands.[85] Whether this was a bluff or simply a hope remained an open question. Nevertheless, it is understandable why Cody responded the way he did. He had just given up more than twenty thousand acres of land and water rights for the settlement of Latter-day Saints in the Big Horn Basin. Now he felt those same people were taking advantage of his generosity.

Woodruff received Cody's letter two days later. In his rejoinder Woodruff backed off. He stated coyly, "You evidently misunderstood the meaning of my letter to you, as I had no desire to ask you to give our people anything, and expected of course that should you care to relinquish your tract on the south side of the Shoshone River that our people would reimburse you for expense of surveys, &c."[86] Woodruff had made no mention of reimbursement or pay of any kind in his initial overture, but it seemed now that he was determined to acquire more land for Latter-day Saints, even if he had to pay for it. There is no known response from Buffalo Bill to this letter, so it appears the matter was dropped for the moment. However, this would not be the last that Cody heard about relinquishing more land and water rights to these religious settlers; it became a source of private frustration for Buffalo Bill in the early years of the 1900s.

unun

Even as he grew privately frustrated by the faith group, Buffalo Bill understood that their willingness to settle in the Big Horn Basin could further his plans to entice the railroad to build into the basin. In early March 1900, Buffalo Bill wrote to Charles Manderson at the Burlington Railroad offices in Omaha and notified him of his meeting with the Mormons. Cody told Manderson that the Latter-day Saint visitors were "immensely pleased with the country for agricultural and stock raising." Embellishing their visit, Cody claimed he had been all over the basin with the Mormon delegation and that Abraham Woodruff "said that if a railroad was built into the basin that many thousands of their people would move at once to the basin, and go to farming and stock raising, but without a railroad, only a small number would come as it would take a railroad to move the crops for any great number of farmers." With such possibilities available, the ambitious Cody wondered aloud in his letter why the Burlington railroad would hesitate in extending its line to the Big Horn Basin.[87]

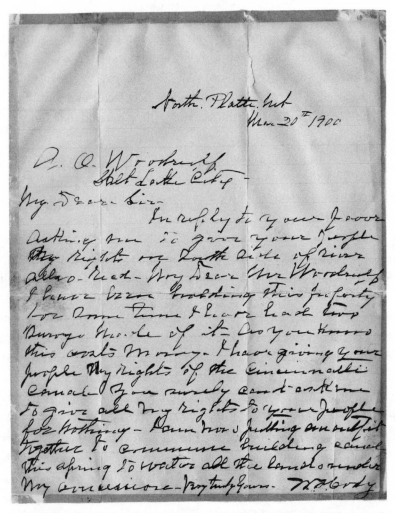

20. William F. Cody's handwritten letter to Abraham O. Woodruff about lands in the Big Horn Basin, March 20, 1900. Buffalo Bill Center of the West, Cody, Wyoming, Buffalo Bill Museum, MS006 William F. Cody Collection, MS6.1345.

Beyond a large and prosperous Mormon colony, Cody reminded the Burlington solicitor general of the plentiful copper, gold, lead, and coal mines; timber opportunities; and the vast tracts of rich farmland there. All that was needed to make the basin "the very richest portion of America" was a railroad. Ever the booster, Cody declared,

There is still room for many thousands of cattle, horses, and sheep. Stockmen will graze their stock on the grasses during the summer and fatten them for market from hay and grain raised by farmers, then the railroad moves it east. The very richest sugar beets has been raised in the Big Horn Basin; sugar beet factories are waiting to build there; brewery syndicates are waiting to build malt houses there; cities and towns will spring up; it will be by far the nearest route into the great National Park. There will be a good wagon road build from the town of Cody into the Park soon. The great hot and cold springs will attract thousands as soon as there is a railroad.[88]

Charles Manderson forwarded Cody's enthusiastic letter to Burlington president Charles E. Perkins. "Of course Buffalo Bill's interests in that locality compel enthusiasm," Manderson wrote, "but I have no doubt from what I hear from other sources that there is chance for tremendous development in the Big Horn Basin." In supporting Cody's assessment, he added "The Mormons of Utah and Idaho are increasing, by natural processes, very rapidly and there seems to be a shortage of water for irrigation purposes, which compels them to seek new localities."[89]

Manderson was not the only Burlington official to send the company president encouraging news about the Latter-day Saint move to Big Horn Basin. George W. Holdrege also wrote, though with exaggerated information. "Our General Agent at Salt Lake City has ascertained from the Officers of the Mormon Church that arrangements have been made to send five hundred (500) families to a location along the Stinking Water or Shoshone River," Holdrege asserted after observing that Latter-day Saint settlement had already begun to increase. These settlers had the experience and energy required to be successful, Holdrege assured the Burlington president. But perhaps most promising, Holdrege wrote, "They are not polygamists, and Governor Richards is very enthusiastic in the belief that this will be the commencement of a large settlement in the Basin country."[90]

Only a decade had passed since Latter-day Saint leaders publicly decreed an end to new plural marriages. Given the decades of upheaval over polygamy and the recent congressional controversy that ended with Latter-day Saint Brigham H. Roberts (who remained a practicing polygamist) being denied his seat in the House of Representatives, statements such as this were needed to remind the Burlington Railroad president that this development of a colony of Mormons moving to northwest Wyoming was not only palatable but essential to the railroad's interest in the region.[91] Ditching the rhetoric of Latter-day Saints as polygamist outlaws, they were now identified as good pioneers and law-abiding colonists who could appeal to government officials and business interests.

Perkins heard from William F. Cody on this matter as well. Buffalo Bill told the railroad president that he was willing to give a right of way to the railroad to ensure that the Burlington would build to his town site of Cody. Like his relinquishment of land and water rights to encourage Latter-day Saint settlement, he was willing to give up property to bring this needed infrastructure into the area. "You may be sure of the hearty co-operation of all concerned to further the interests of the Burlington in the Big Horn Basin," Cody pronounced before requesting a declaration from the railroad company president that the Burlington would extend its line to his town. Cody added a postscript about the Latter-day Saint settlement: "I let the Mormons have eleven thousand acres of farming land and now they want another tract of twenty-nine thousand acres," he declared (though he had confused his numbers) in his effort to highlight for the railroad executive that growth was happening and that the railroad would only bring more.[92]

Buffalo Bill had perhaps never felt closer to realizing his dream of seeing the Big Horn Basin prosper. Cody wanted to open the country and settle it with happy and prosperous people and leave a "landmark of something attempted, something done."[93] In that space families would find new opportunities to grow and flourish.

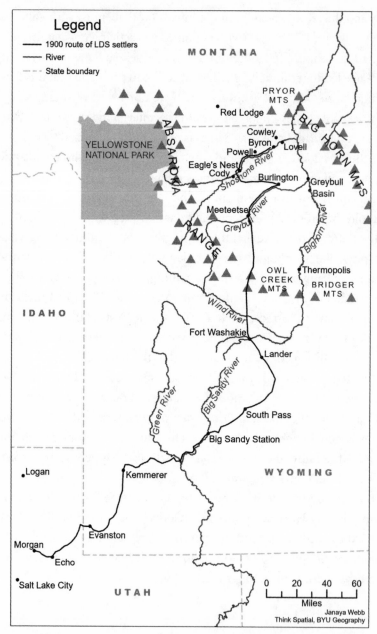

21. Big Horn Basin with geographic features and 1900 route of Latter-day Saint settlers from Utah to northwest Wyoming. Research by Brent M. Rogers. Map created by Janaya Webb, Think Spatial, BYU Geography.

— 6 —

The Saints Settle Cody Country

On April 6, 1900, the seventieth anniversary of the organization of The Church of Jesus Christ of Latter-day Saints, Abraham O. Woodruff met with the faith's leaders in Salt Lake City. That afternoon they drafted articles of agreement to establish the Big Horn Basin Colonization Company, a capital stock corporation that would direct the business and financial affairs of the Latter-day Saint settlers about to relocate to northwest Wyoming. Church president Lorenzo Snow had authorized Byron Sessions, Jesse W. Crosby, Charles Kingston, Charles A. Welch, and Abraham O. Woodruff, among a few others, to serve as company directors. These men and many others purchased stock in the newly formed company, contributing a total of $72,000 capital investment toward the construction of a canal in the northern Wyoming basin.[1] With the corporation set up and in place, Woodruff prepared to lead more than one hundred families from Utah's mountain valleys on an arduous journey to the place they would call home.

By late April the families who would establish a colony in Wyoming began their trek to the Big Horn Basin. Marching with teams and wagon loads of home goods and construction materials, these hopeful settlers encountered rocky trails, mountain passes, and river crossings. Abraham Woodruff met the emigrating families at a river crossing near Kemmerer, called Ham's Fork, in the southwestern part of the state. Woodruff organized the group into companies, creating an orderly caravan that traveled between fifteen and thirty-seven miles a day.[2]

On May 4, 1900, the party forded the Big Sandy River, a tributary of the Green River, just below the Big Sandy Station, a stage and Pony Express stop on the old emigrant trail. This location had some significance in

22. Latter-day Saint settlers traveling to the Big Horn Basin, pictured here having just crossed Kemmerer Bridge, Wyoming, April 1900. Courtesy of the Church History Library, The Church of Jesus Christ of Latter-day Saints, Salt Lake City.

Latter-day Saint history and, for this group of Saints, in its connection with Buffalo Bill Cody. Abraham Woodruff penned an entry in his journal that he "saw the place where Lott Smith burned Johnson's Armie's train of wagons."[3] Woodruff had heard Buffalo Bill's rehearsal of this dramatic 1857 Utah War event when he broke bread with the famous showman at Eagle's Nest nearly two months earlier. Cody's retelling apparently struck a chord with Woodruff, who reverently observed the shared moment of history between his religious group and their Big Horn Basin benefactor. The crossing at the Big Sandy on that spring day represented the crossing of differing sides of a common past and moving forward together toward a shared goal for the future.

After the Latter-day Saint caravan passed over the Big Sandy, it proceeded northeast through South Pass to Lander, then to Fort Washakie and through the Wind River Reservation traversing the Owl Creek Mountains.

From that point the colonists traveled north to Meeteetse then to Burlington before passing just east of Buffalo Bill's town of Cody, encamping near the confluence of Sage Creek and the Shoshone River.[4] The journey took weeks, but toward the end of May 1900, the caravan of Saints had made its way along the river to a point near the present-day town of Byron. Here they would camp and build the headgate to what would become a thirty-seven-mile irrigation canal that would eventually direct the water northeast from the Shoshone River to the towns of Byron and up to Cowley.[5]

The Saints wasted no time setting up camps, sawing wood, and placing survey stakes for the canal. "It was indeed a scene true to Mormonism to see about 35 men all working as hard as they could united in their labor," Abraham Woodruff rejoiced.[6] Like their forebears in Utah's Salt Lake Valley, these Latter-day settlers embraced order, unity, and community, seeing their labor as acts of religious devotion and a part of the sacred task of building up God's kingdom on the earth. Cultivating the sod was the same to a Latter-day Saint as cultivating the soul. To cultivate the land, however, required the construction of the irrigation canal. Upon her arrival in the Big Horn Basin, settler Patty Mann expressed bewilderment that "the land was more barren than we expected," but, she professed, with faith "we stuck it out."[7] Fellow colonist Rosa Vida Black similarly offered a maxim for the faithful: "to work hard at the job at hand is to know life's sublimest joy."[8] Hard work was indeed in front of the Big Horn Basin Saints. To create the soil-blooming, life-producing canal required the land to be cleared of waist-high sagebrush, followed by the breaking of the parched earth and the removal of hundreds of thousands of yards of dirt, rock, and gravel.

As the Saints industriously began their work, Abraham Woodruff felt the weight of this colonization venture. It was the first that he had the charge of, and he knew that church president Lorenzo Snow was carefully observing his leadership. Woodruff had led hundreds of individuals to a new settlement that they would have to build from the ground up. What if it failed? Living in the shadow of his respected father, the young apostle sat in his tent one night, mightily concerned about this "great undertaking." He prayed fervently to heaven. Despite having "a great deal of anxiety" about the canal-building project, the apostle pressed forward.[9] He organized an ecclesiastical unit for the colonists, and they held the first Latter-day Saint Sunday School on the Shoshone River on May 27, 1900. The next day Woodruff held groundbreaking ceremonies for the all-important canal project. At that event he took a firm grasp of the plow's handles. Byron Sessions, a middle-aged family man whom Woodruff had appointed as the settlement's ecclesiastical leader and canal-construction supervisor, sat just feet in front of him, driving the team. Sessions had uprooted his family after living in the same town for nearly thirty years. He sold his shares in a livestock company at a great loss, but with his wife, Idella, by his side he had accepted the responsibility to move to the Big Horn Basin and build the canal.[10] As Sessions drove, Woodruff held the plow to make the first furrow.[11]

Following the groundbreaking ceremonies, the settlers tied their efforts to religious devotion, as "all knelt before the Lord and petitioned his assistance and guidance" in their labors to build the canal. The digging of this canal was, for this group, a sacred task. Laborers then fitted out three teams with plows and scrapers and commenced work on the Sidon Canal, named after the city in ancient Phoenicia and the river of the same name found in the chapters of Alma in the Book of Mormon.[12] From dawn until dusk, day after day (except Sundays), workers drove horse teams that pulled plows and Fresno scrapers, digging up the earth to forge the canal. Others worked alongside them driving horses, hauling feed, or loading rocks to move the project forward. It was physically demanding and even dangerous labor. But the Latter-day Saints braved those dangers and the often-extreme weather and wind that blew dirt and sand into their faces and into the makeshift homes the families established along the canal's path.

Abraham Woodruff did not remain in the Big Horn Basin long. As work on the canal progressed into the summer, he felt the lure of home. He had a family, a wife, and young son in Salt Lake City, and his apostolic duties beckoned him. When he returned in July, Woodruff provided a favorable report to church leaders on the progress in northwest Wyoming.[13]

Even after he returned to Salt Lake City, Woodruff's attention was never far from the Big Horn Basin. Still interested in Buffalo Bill Cody's lands on the south side of the Shoshone River, Woodruff continually wrote to Wyoming governor DeForest Richards for assistance in obtaining the rights to that land. Richards kept in constant communication with the Latter-day Saint apostle. He informed Woodruff that he had conversations with Cody's attorney and had sent a personal letter to Cody, asking him to relinquish the south-side lands to Woodruff and the Saints. While Richards felt encouraged that the unnamed attorney would endorse the recommendation, he remained doubtful about Cody's desire to surrender those lands. He told Woodruff that if a deal could be made, it would cost the Saints this time. Buffalo Bill's magnanimity had run its course.[14]

As the situation developed, Woodruff and Charles Kingston worked together to press Governor Richards on the issue of the south-side lands. Like Woodruff, Kingston wrote to the governor several times, using whatever political capital he had accumulated to win the governor's assistance. In one letter to Richards, Kingston characterized Cody's actions as highway robbery or a "pure holdup." He encouraged the governor to work with the State Land Board to relieve Cody of his right to this land and award it to the Latter-day Saints, who would reclaim the "land without further delay." Richards, however, was not convinced that was the right course of action. He told Kingston he would not use his position to influence the board. "Unless Mr. Cody is willing to relinquish" the lands of his own accord, Richards wrote to Kingston, "we are powerless."[15] Nevertheless, Richards had declared his intent to "urge this matter with all the force" he could muster. "You can rely upon my doing all that I can for you," Richards had avowed in his correspondence with Woodruff.[16] Richards was certainly interested in seeing the land developed, and he knew the Saints would do it. But he also had a fine line to walk in keeping a good relationship with the world-famous William F. Cody.[17]

Cody did not engage with the Saints directly on this matter. He had already let Woodruff know, in quite certain terms, that he was not interested in giving up his rights to the lands south of the river. But Buffalo Bill was not silent on the matter either. Instead, he corresponded with the governor. Cody had claimed to have spent a great deal of money to survey that south-side land, and he was not yet willing to give up on his investment. Hoping to mediate an agreement, Governor Richards sent Cody a personal letter. The governor reminded Buffalo Bill that the Latter-day Saints were "most excellent citizens" and notified him that, because their work on the Sidon Canal had been proceeding so rapidly, they would need more land to accommodate more settlers.[18]

Trying to induce him to relinquish his rights to the land, Richards tried to demonstrate his and Cody's shared interest in building up northwest Wyoming. Richards argued that goal would be accomplished quicker and with less of the showman's money if he relinquished his south-side lands to the Latter-day Saints. "You have a very large and difficult enterprise on the north side of the river, involving an expenditure of not only a large amount of money but, also, of time," Richards stressed. Besides that, reclamation of the south-side lands, Richards reasoned, would require "a difficult and expensive engineering problem" for Cody to address. Richards implored Cody to relinquish the south-side lands so that the Saints would "go at once to work and build a large canal and reclaim not only what has been segregated for your benefit but quite a large tract of land besides." Richards tried to convince Buffalo Bill that this would be a win-win scenario, that giving up his interest in this land would "be a benefit rather than an injury" to his enterprise.[19] For his part William Cody was unmoved by Richards's plea and the continuing overtures from the Saints.

Cody did not consider further relinquishment of lands to Latter-day Saints as advantageous to his interests in building the basin. Nevertheless, he persisted in promoting and trying to lure more settlers to the Big Horn Basin. In June 1900 he published a lengthy article in *Success* magazine, identifying the basin as an "American Eden." Writing largely to American tourists considering a trip abroad, Cody encouraged them to see America first, a common promotional effort to market locations in the United States during the turn of the twentieth century. "America, and not Europe," Cody proclaimed, "will eventually become the paradise of tourists." Wanting readers to know something of the grandeur of their own country, Cody penned a verbose description of the many beautiful and unique physical features of the area: towering mountains, majestic rivers, and the natural wonderland of Yellowstone National Park. "In fact," Cody asserted, "the whole region seems to have been created in some wonderous fancy of the Great Spirit."[20]

From Buffalo Bill's vantage point, no physical feature of Europe could hold a candle to the Rocky Mountain region of western America, specifically the Big Horn Basin. Labeling it the "most poetic spot on earth," Cody informed his readers that the basin boasted a "perfection of climate, the healing power of its water, and the unsurpassed magnificence of its landscape." Irrigation from the great Shoshone River further enriched this garden spot, reclaiming it with artificial waterways that, if attempted in Europe, Cody proclaimed, would fill the European press with articles calling the canals "the greatest scientific accomplishments of modern times." He advised readers, perhaps encouraging their settlement in the basin, that the water supply in the region was inexhaustible, making farming by irrigation assured of success.[21]

The garden spot Cody had long advertised was under cultivation, thanks in no small part to his Latter-day Saint compatriots. In his *Success* article, Buffalo Bill even likened himself to Brigham Young. Like the Latter-day Saint leader who said, "Here we build the temple of Zion" when he arrived at the site of Salt Lake City, Cody pronounced, "I could not refrain from the expression regarding the Big Horn Country:—'This is my chosen land! Here I want my bones to rest!'" Buffalo Bill concluded his promotional piece by highlighting "the nucleus of a future great city, called Cody." Whether labeling the place an "American Eden" or a "Pioneer's Paradise," Buffalo Bill never wavered from his enthusiasm for the Big Horn Basin.[22]

Buffalo Bill spoke in grand terms of the sublime scenery and the paradisiacal potential of the Big Horn Basin. His words reflected his characteristic optimism and grandiloquent nature. He likely persuaded more than a few vacationers to make the basin the destination of their travels. For those settlers living on the ground, however, life did not match Cody's description of the "American Eden."

Those Latter-day Saint settlers who had moved to the basin just weeks prior to the publication of Buffalo Bill's *Success* article were met with a blazing sun, frequent dusty winds that blew dirt into every crevice of their tents or makeshift homes, and the buzzing of flies and rattlesnake tails. Men, women, and children toiled daily against these and other elements. Most of the men working on the canal faced physical exhaustion from laboring tirelessly under the hot sun. Confronting the same physical elements as men, women bore the brunt of nearly every other responsibility. They planted crops and flowers, tended the livestock, prepared and served meals, cared for children, sewed or weaved clothing and blankets, and built homes, among their many acts of labor. During the first few months, as they constructed permanent dwellings, the settlers lived in tents and wagons. Women tending these temporary dwellings became pest-control experts. Mary Welch, upon finding a large rattlesnake climbing into her wagon box, which was serving as the family home at the time, grabbed a shovel and detached the snake's head from its body. That was not an isolated incident. Women also faced stultifying isolation, which they remedied through creating church organizations, particularly the female Relief Society, and hosting social events such as dances. The Saints, male and female, young and old, faced severe challenges settling in and adapting to their new surroundings, which felt far from paradise.[23]

As summer turned to fall that first year in the basin, the Saints grew deeply concerned whether they could continue their work and settlement. Financial resources were scarce, as they had no source of income. The Big Horn Basin Colonization Company had the human resources, but the cost of labor and horsepower drained the coffers and by extension the ability to provide the necessities to continue work on the Sidon Canal. Seeing the troubles and the low morale among the people, the ecclesiastical leaders called the settlers together for daily morning and evening prayers. Big Horn Basin settler Charles A. Welch explained, "It is a part of the Mormon faith to pray as well as work."[24]

As fall settled in, the colonists struggled to feed themselves and their animals. The religious leaders called for the people to fast as they prayed. This must have been a difficult thing to ask of people already surviving on a meager diet. But the Saints proved faithful and began a two-day fast while praying that the Lord would provide an opportunity for them to earn much-needed money. Unbeknownst to the Big Horn settlers, Abraham Woodruff had been communicating with leaders of the Chicago, Burlington, and Quincy Railroad, seeking to secure work for the Saints.

During the second day of their fast, but hundreds of miles away, a meeting of the board of directors of the Chicago, Burlington, and Quincy Railroad was held in Chicago. This meeting would alter the lives of the Latter-day Saints in the Big Horn Basin and the trajectory of the city of Cody, Wyoming. The board discussed a contract for the construction of twenty miles of railroad grade along a branch line that would run from Toluca, Montana, to Cody, Wyoming. During the meeting the board heard of the colony of Latter-day Saints building the Sidon Canal. The chair of the board stopped the proceedings and said, "I think we should have the Mormons build this section of the road grade."[25] Mere days later, I. S. P. Weeks, chief engineer of Burlington railroad lines west of the Missouri River, traveled to the Big Horn Basin to meet with the Latter-day Saints.[26]

Towns in the West owed their growth to the arrival of rail lines. The Chicago, Burlington, and Quincy ignited a great burst of railroad construction into Wyoming in the 1880s and began to link northwest Wyoming to its national network due in part to the Mormon settlement in the area.[27] Railroad executives noted that, while there was an "apparent failure of Cody's people to accomplish anything in way of developing his county," the large amount of work done by the Latter-day Saints promised further development in the area. In short, the railroad powers observed that Mormons had commercially changed the situation in the Big Horn Basin, opening the way for their company's investment in the region.[28]

Burlington engineers eventually decided to build a route from Toluca to Cody. They believed, like Buffalo Bill Cody, that the basin's prospects were worth investing in. And they felt convinced of success, in large part because of the Latter-day Saint settlers. Since the building of the transcontinental railroad, the Saints had proven their ability to cut, dam, and grade railroad lines; their work had often been considered the standard of success.[29] Reporting on information received from the *Omaha World-Herald* and from Burlington executives, the *Cody Enterprise* declared, "The prosperity of the road is assured from the day of its completion" because of the settlers from Utah who would help grade and build the line.[30] Weeks, the Burlington representative, arrived in northwest Wyoming eager to contract the Latter-day Saint settlers as laborers. To make money to help support the building of the canal and their settlement, more than sixty-five Mormon men signed up and immediately went to work grading and constructing the new spur line.[31] Though the question of exactly where in the town of Cody the railroad would terminate remained an open conversation, that the town would be serviced by the Burlington was no longer in doubt. Buffalo Bill's town was finally getting a railroad.

The Saints were now engaged in building a canal and a railroad in the region. Jesse W. Crosby took charge of the railroad operations from the Pryor Gap on the Crow Indian reservation in Montana to Frannie, Wyoming.[32] Crosby wrote letters to Abraham Woodruff, detailing the railroad work and the pay. Crosby's crew of more than sixty men commenced work on October 15, 1900, with one plow behind a team of six horses. The rail workers were paid $1.75 to $2.25 per day to grade and lay track. Beyond that, board was afforded to the men at $4.00 per week. After a few months of work and at the end of 1900, Crosby provided Woodruff with a fuller picture of the economic benefits of working for the railroad. "Our expenses are quite heavy. Hay. Grain. Housing and clothing, etc. But we have been able to meet every account when it came due," Crosby informed the apostolic colonizing agent. Though the expenses to feed their animals was high, Crosby stated, "The first month we only worked five days and our check was over $500.00 the second month we led 30 to 40 teams and our check was over $3,500.00 and I beleave the third months check will reach $6,000." Crosby indicated that most of the workers would "save money enough to see them through another year." He further stated that the railroad contract provided the income needed for the Saints to continue to build the canal.[33]

By the end of 1900, greatly pleased with the work of the Latter-day Saint crews, I. S. P. Weeks offered Jesse Crosby another contract for the services of Latter-day Saint workers.[34] The Burlington Railroad contracts provided a pecuniary windfall that not only aided the ongoing canal building but also bolstered the overall economic interest for Latter-day Saint families in the Big Horn Basin. Byron Sessions, for example, articulated his joy for the circumstances the Saints found themselves in by the end of 1900. "We have this day," Sessions announced, "moved in to our log house [and] out of our tent." It was the first time in over seven months that he and his family had slept in a house.[35]

Characteristically, the Latter-day Saints took on the multiple tasks of canal building, railroad grading, and settling with zeal. Whether digging dirt or planting new life, they united in their labor. "The spirit of 'Mormonism' is seen on every hand," divulged the church's *Deseret Evening News* in its report of church members' efforts in the Big Horn Basin. "In their labors on the Sidon canal; in their devotional exercises, and in their pure home life; everything is conducted according to the spirit of the Gospel." Like Abraham Woodruff's remark that seeing the Saints united in the labor was a true symbol of their faith, the *Deseret Evening News* marveled at the Saints' efforts to subdue arid places and build infrastructure in northwest Wyoming. They were not interested in the aggrandizement and enrichment of investors. These Saints sought only "to bless their fellows, and to plant them firmly in a condition of independence."[36] The building of the canal and railroad was a means to that end.

Their work progressed well into 1901. That winter, however, proved exceedingly trying. Despite the lack of material goods, the settlers kept their determination. Many families still did not have permanent houses; they braved a harsh climate with frequent arctic wind blasts. One settler recalled, "It was not unusual on frost-chilled mornings, to see men sporting icicle coated beards and mustaches." He observed that the men worked doggedly on, even when their fingers and toes were numb with cold.[37] Christmas found the Saints short on gifts, but long on stories and scriptures. Through unique, even ingenious methods, mothers made candy in secret, dressed dolls, or cobbled together marbles to please their children and keep their spirits high during the holiday.[38] The women endured much for their hope that their efforts, and those of their families, would amply repay them for the sacrifices they made. Men and women alike layered their apparel to combat the bone-chilling cold. Many a canal or railroad worker donned heavy sheepskin coats and long boot-like socks that could be seen extending nearly to their knees. The many sacrifices were offset by dances, music, and games.[39]

The Saints earned over $20,000 from their work on the railroad through February 1901. The income, while initially viewed as a blessing, soon became a source of frustration and contention. Seeing the earning potential the railroad offered, many canal workers abandoned their jobs in favor of laboring on track grade. Jealousies arose as those workers carving out the canal were left to do more of that essential work with fewer men. They were also unable to make money for themselves and their families, further fueling their discontent with the wage earners on the railroad. Those who had abandoned the canal, the other canal workers believed, had forgotten why they took the job in the first place: to fund the construction of a canal that would turn their settlement into highly productive farmland.

The Saints were there to build canals and settle new towns; work on the railroad was meant to facilitate that, but funds only trickled from the railroad camp to those working on the canal. Latter-day Saint Charles Welch lamented that the canal workers "haven't a dollar to buy hay and grain while at work on the canal, nor to buy wire to fence with." "I did not think it possible for people to be so jealous and full of fault finding as some are," Welch complained in a letter to Abraham Woodruff.[40] The contention was short-lived, however, as church leaders worked together to right the proverbial ship. Through many meetings and teachings, the leaders reminded and assured each group of their value. Each group needed the other to accomplish the work that they migrated to the Big Horn Basin to do. The railroad contract provided a short-term windfall that would help finance the canal, which would provide the long-term stability the heads of household craved for their families. After putting the situation in perspective, the church leaders convinced canal workers to set aside their envy and to push their work forward.

By the summer of 1901, the Saints working on the railroad had earned approximately $90,000 for constructing more than twenty miles of rail-road grade; more than a third of that money went toward building the canal and saving the fledgling colony from financial ruin.[41] Those railroad workers pumped precious funds into the local economy. The railroad project was completed in August 1901, after more than ten months of sometimes excruciating labor. All crews then returned to canal construc-tion. By that time more than twenty miles of the canal had been dug with hand tools, wagons, and horse-drawn plows. One settler described the efforts of the Saints in the Big Horn Basin through the summer of 1901: "It has been work, work, work ever since we arrived in the country, and we have scarcely begun yet. The land and water has been blessed by our beloved Apostle Woodruff and we know this will be a great country and many of the Saints will find good homes in this once barren region. It needs the blessing of the Lord and the united effort of the Saints and the land yields her increase."[42] Though their unity was threatened by disputes over money, the religious settlers banded together over the importance of the life-providing canal.[43]

The railroad was only one of several building projects to which the Saints would contribute in the early 1900s. Other projects included road building. Because of their success grading the railroad, they earned a government contract to construct a road from the eastern end of Yel-lowstone Park to a county road leading into the town of Cody. Since at least 1895, Buffalo Bill had wanted to develop an eastern access road to Yellowstone Park through the mountain pass that separated the national park from his town in the Big Horn Basin.[44] "The building of the road into the park," the Cody Enterprise announced, "is of the greatest impor-tance to Cody and will assure a large amount of tourist travel going this way." The completion of the road "will be another great contributing ele-ment to Cody bringing thousands of people here each season and enable them to see and of course admire our beautiful region, spend a few days at the magnificent springs adjacent to town and in every respect add to the growing reputation of a spot that as we have once or twice remarked cannot help becoming one of the leading towns of the West."[45] It was an effort led by Byron Sessions and Charles A. Welch and constructed by men almost exclusively from the towns of Cowley and Byron, Latter-day Saint settlers building the infrastructure to help bring Buffalo Bill's dreams for northwest Wyoming closer to reality.

The accomplishments of the Big Horn Basin Saints won praise from a variety of sources. The *Deseret Evening News* reported frequently about progress in the basin. In September 1901 the newspaper published a laudatory assessment of the church settlements in general and of Abraham Woodruff in particular. "We consider that Elder Abraham O. Woodruff has shown the spirit of a true colonizer and exhibited great wisdom in thus selecting for the Latter-day Saint colonies so grand a country," the *News* article professed. The church's Salt Lake City newspaper reminded its readership that there were great opportunities for home seekers in northwest Wyoming. According to the article, "There is plenty of excellent land and an abundance of the very best water. The range for sheep and for cattle is practically inexhaustible. Timber of the choicest kind. . . . There is room for many new settlements and in the near future we hope to see not only the fifteen hundred now located there but fifteen thousand; and more than this number can be readily accommodated with homes for the taking."[46]

The *Cody Enterprise*, Buffalo Bill's newspaper, likewise expressed adulation in printed articles and editorials from the local perspective. Referring to the Saints as industrious people and good citizens, the Big Horn Basin newspaper asserted, "The progress these frugal and intelligent workers are making in this county borders upon the wonderful." The *Enterprise* lavished the religious settlers with superlatives such as "unfaltering courage," "heroic," "gritty determination," and "herculean," as its columns depicted the "success that has always followed their efforts."[47] As their religious forebears had in Utah, the Saints settled on uninviting land in the Big Horn Basin and through industry, patience, and perseverance succeeded in turning it into an attractive and productive place. The advancements they made in northwest Wyoming, Cody's newspaper averred, would be even greater than those they attained in Utah. Though some remained concerned about the influence the religious group would have on regional economics and politics, the standard narrative of the Latter-day Saints and their utility in fostering development to make the arid West "blossom as the rose" became entrenched because of their efforts in the Big Horn Basin.[48]

At the national level it was William Smythe, the renowned journalist and western reclamation promoter who had praised the Latter-day Saints at the Chicago World's Fair seven years earlier, that highlighted the progress and symbol of the religious group in northwest Wyoming. In *Harper's Weekly* in early 1901, the irrigation advocate published a glowing article about Mormon success and the brilliance of William F. Cody.[49] Smythe alluded to ongoing negotiations between church authorities in Salt Lake City and Colonel Cody to purchase large tracts of land and an irrigation enterprise in the Big Horn country. A potential of thirty thousand more Latter-day Saints could descend on the Wyoming basin, which, Smythe suggested, would only be the beginning of their colonization there. Though Cody had not begun his operations in the Big Horn Basin with the idea that it would be a Latter-day Saint colony, he did desire to see tens of thousands of homes and farms there as his enduring monument of his work in the West.

Smythe applauded Cody's genius for not only recognizing but also facilitating the Saints' success by providing them with land and water rights. The Church of Jesus Christ of Latter-day Saints was not just a religious institution, Smythe concluded, but a great business organization with brains, brawn, and far-reaching capital. He continued, "Upon that institution Colonel Cody deposited his burden and his dream. It was gladly accepted, and in the next few years homes and factories and temples will rise on the Virgin soil of another valley." While the small colony of church members labored diligently to prove the potential of the basin, their physical investment freed up Cody to proceed with town development, the reclamation of other lands, and other business ventures in the region.[50]

Intelligent businessmen like Cody, the reclamation expert declared, need only work with the Latter-day Saints to ensure their success in growth and development. Through their system of cooperation, which cheapened the costs for investors, they built a canal, a railroad, and towns. The Mormons had taught Cody and the nation how to unleash natural resources and provide homes. In other words, Smythe asserted once again, Latter-day Saint success had shown the way to develop the arid West. He closed by emphasizing that, despite lingering concerns about the religious group's Americanness, "if the opportunity be grasped in the right spirit the American people may yet acknowledge a debt of gratitude to their Mormon fellow citizens for having shown them the way."[51] The thrifty, industrious Saints were again praised for their role in converting a desert into a veritable garden spot. Their success was crucial to advertising the possibilities and opportunities of the West.

Alongside the religious, regional, and national voices praising the development of the Big Horn Basin, Buffalo Bill's sense of public optimism increased. He wrote more letters and published additional promotional articles and pamphlets lauding the basin as a "Pioneer's Paradise."[52] "My prospects never looked brighter," he wrote to a friend in 1901. "The Basin scheme is going to be a winner—and a big one."[53] In a pamphlet titled *Ideal Western Lands*, William F. Cody, as president of the Shoshone Irrigation Company, expounded on the choice region and the example of the Mormon settlers. Cody stated,

> It is indeed a "new empire," rich in natural resources, and the opportunities it offers to the intending settler, are not surpassed by any other section of country. Parties desiring to avail themselves of the opportunities offered must act at once, as a strong tide of immigration has already set in and the available land will soon all be occupied. Quite a number of farmers from the Great Salt Lake Valley have settled in this section and they consider it equal to, if not in many respects superior, to the Great Salt Lake Valley, where land sells at one hundred dollars an acre.[54]

Cody again used Mormons and the perceived success of agriculture in Utah in his efforts to demonstrate the potential of the basin and to encourage more non-Mormon immigration. The Saints had served their purpose for Buffalo Bill. They had constructed a canal that was watering some twenty thousand acres, and they helped facilitate the arrival of a railroad. They had built homes and communities. Now Cody wanted to see other settlers fill out the basin; settlers that would pay him for land and water rights.

Though newcomers to Cody's town were still few and far between, Buffalo Bill told a friend in spring 1901: "The town of Cody is booming— and so are all my interests."[55] Unflaggingly optimistic, Buffalo Bill never ceased from offering encouraging public rhetoric about the basin he so dearly loved.[56] His confidence soared as the Chicago, Burlington, and Quincy line was completed to his town in November 1901. He continued to pour money into irrigation projects and set his sights on yet another undertaking, even as some of his reclamation projects remained unfinished (and in some cases not even started). He began building "a beautiful little hotel" in his town.[57] He would name the hotel "Irma" after his youngest daughter. While construction on the noteworthy lodge commenced, the showman continued to promote the region and the success of his Sho-shone Irrigation Company. He also worked to induce the government to build a thoroughfare that would connect the town of Cody to Yellowstone National Park, approximately fifty miles west, a road ultimately overseen by Latter-day Saint contractors and built largely by Latter-day Saint labor-ers. And he communicated the region's developments and news through the medium of his town's weekly periodical, the *Enterprise*, over which he was co-publisher.

᠁᠁

To fund his many enterprises in northwest Wyoming and elsewhere, Buffalo Bill continued to rely on his Wild West show for income. As winter turned to spring in 1902, Cody and his cast of hundreds of employees embarked on another nationwide performing tour. The official program for the sea-son featured many of the same acts that had thrilled audiences for years.

The show began with a patriotic overture of a cowboy band playing the "Star-Spangled Banner" and a grand review of the performers, before the crowd was captivated by the Race of Races containing horse riders

of different nationalities.[58] Classic Wild West acts, including the reenactment of an emigrant train crossing the plains and an attack on a settlers' cabin, showcased Buffalo Bill, cowboys, and scouts rescuing white
families from "marauding Indians." Traditional performances displaying
feats of marksmanship by Buffalo Bill and others and scenes of the Battle
of San Juan Hill and the heroism of Roosevelt's Rough Riders continued
to exhilarate audiences.[59] In 1902 Buffalo Bill also added the "Siege of
Peking," another armed confrontation that had recently occurred during
the Boxer Rebellion in China.[60] In an age of global imperialism, when
the United States increased its worldwide political and cultural influence,
these acts provided a platform for the Wild West and Congress of Rough
Riders to visually represent that growing sphere of influence of white
American manhood.

Cody's company began its nationwide tour, as it often did, in New York
City. The first show of the season took place on April 21. To maximize
profits the Wild West show stayed in the populous cities of the eastern
United States for the spring, then headed west. The performers boarded
a train in Boston on June 21 and reached Minneapolis by the end of July.
From Minnesota the Wild West show played in Lincoln, Nebraska, on
August 1 and then crossed the plains to the Mile High City of Denver to
perform there for two nights on August 6 and 7. A week later Buffalo Bill
was back in Utah, performing there for the first time since 1886, when his
acting troupe presented *Prairie Waif*, a drama filled with anti-Mormon
content. So much water had passed under the proverbial bridge that there
was not a hint or whispering of bad feelings toward the international
superstar in Utah. Instead, Utahns—Latter-day Saint or otherwise—eagerly
anticipated the arrival of Buffalo Bill's Wild West and Congress of Rough
Riders of the World.

On August 3, 1902, the *Salt Lake Tribune* alerted valley residents to the
Wild West show's pending visit on August 13 and 14. The advertisement
noted that Buffalo Bill's spectacle was "now in the Zenith of its Overwhelming and Triumphant Success" and reminded readers of the show's
apparent authenticity, stating that it was "an exhibition that teaches but
does not imitate." The *Tribune* alerted potential attendees that the two

performances each day would take place "Rain or Shine" and directed them to purchase tickets at the Smith drugstore on Main Street and Second South.[61] The auspicious advertisement proved prescient, as tens of thousands of Utahns flocked to the grounds on Eighth South and Fourth West to witness the great exhibition of "devil-may-care cowboys, the dashing cavalrymen, the gaudily painted Indians and the various other attractions that go to depict the strenuous life of the world."[62]

Alongside Cody and the Wild West show, John M. Burke also returned to Utah for the first time since he had accompanied the exploration party there in 1892. Burke, the show's press agent, expressed his astonishment at the "wonderful improvements which have been made around the city since that time." Burke christened the Latter-day Saint capital "one of the liveliest burgs he had struck since leaving Chicago."[63] Salt Lake City was certainly abuzz for Cody's display. Bystanders assembled on sidewalks early on the morning of August 13 to watch and cheer as Colonel Cody led his cast on parade from the exhibition grounds through the streets of downtown.[64] Men, women, and children occupied every seat at the exhibition grounds, and while many monopolized the standing areas, hundreds were denied admittance.[65] Between two performances an estimated thirty thousand people attended Buffalo Bill's spectacle that day. The audience found the Wild West show remarkable and appreciated its authentic feel. The front page of the August 14, 1902, *Deseret Evening News* declared, "Buffalo Bill is distinctly and unmistakably the man of the hour in Salt Lake."[66]

Buffalo Bill had a packed itinerary while in Salt Lake City thanks in part to Junius F. Wells, Cody's old friend who guided the superstar through the Grand Canyon nearly ten years earlier. Several days before Cody's arrival in Salt Lake City, Wells contacted the showman to arrange a series of visits and entertainments. Cody was excited to see his old friend and accepted Wells's kind invitations.[67] Following the Wild West afternoon performance on August 13, Cody met Utah governor Heber M. Wells, Junius's younger brother, for dinner. He then visited several other friends prior to the evening show, which, like the matinee, dazzled some fifteen thousand spectators.[68]

The next morning Wells arranged for Cody and his daughter, Irma, to meet with the Latter-day Saint First Presidency—Joseph F. Smith, Anthon H. Lund, and John Henry Smith—at the Beehive House, the historical home of Brigham Young and the church president's current residence. Joseph F. Smith had taken over the reins of the church a week after Lorenzo Snow passed away on October 10, 1901. Smith was the second counselor in the church's presidency when he first met Buffalo Bill at the Chicago World's Fair nearly a decade earlier. He remembered the entertainer fondly and still had the autographed photo Cody had given him then. This was the first time that Cody's daughter Irma, who would have been about eighteen years old at the time, had the opportunity to visit with Latter-day Saints in Utah with her father. No record of her experiences or thoughts has been located, but Anthon Lund described Irma as a "nice girl," when he wrote about the meeting in his journal.[69]

This informal gathering was pleasant for the Codys and the First Presidency alike. The *Deseret Evening News* described the meeting as an effort to cement the friendship that had developed between Cody and the Latter-day Saints. The newspaper declared that Buffalo Bill emerged from the meeting with "words of praise and commendation for the 'Mormon' people."[70] The *Salt Lake Telegram* focused its report on irrigation and the relationship between Buffalo Bill and the Saints in northwest Wyoming. According to its column, the meeting was "supposedly in connection with the colonization of the Big Horn district." The *Telegram* averred that Cody used the opportunity to consult with the religious heads about a new reclamation project and the diversion of water from the Shoshone River in the Big Horn region east of Yellowstone Park.[71]

Whatever the extent of the conversation that took place on the morning of August 14, Latter-day Saint leaders—conscious of their still-tenuous national reputation and with ongoing business and colonization interests in northwest Wyoming—sought to keep friendly relations with the showman. For his part Buffalo Bill continued to offer positive public statements about Latter-day Saints, despite some tension still brewing between him and the settlers in the Big Horn Basin, who were trying to acquire more prime land along the south side of the Shoshone River.[72]

23. Irma Cody, pictured here
about one year prior to her
visit to Salt Lake City, circa
1901. Buffalo Bill Center of the
West, Cody, Wyoming, Buffalo
Bill Museum, MS006 William
F. Cody Collection, P.699.1386.

Cody left his rendezvous with Latter-day Saint leaders and hurried to
the Mormon tabernacle to attend a special organ recital with his company of some three hundred individuals, a concert held specifically in
honor of Buffalo Bill and the Wild West performers. "This meeting,"
according to the *Deseret Evening News*, "was probably the most unique
gathering that ever assembled in the great building." The Wild West performers sat in the tabernacle dressed in their arena garb, awaiting the

24. Photochrom print of Temple Square, including the
tabernacle (*center*) and temple (*right*), Salt Lake City, circa
1900. Library of Congress, LC-DIG-ppmsca-17879.

concert, while residents and spectators poured into the galleries. Within
twenty minutes the tabernacle had an estimated ten thousand people in
its bowels, overflowing the building's capacity. Cody relished the event
and gave high compliments to the singers and organist. In a statement
to a *Deseret Evening News* reporter, he exclaimed, "Wonderful. The most
marvelous building, all things considered, I was ever in. And certainly
the most marvelous organ I have ever seen or heard—both the creations
of a wonderful, yes, a very wonderful people."[73]

Following the organ recital, Buffalo Bill and his cohort walked the
grounds around the Latter-day Saint temple, marveling at the magnificent
edifice that boasted beautiful Gothic and Romanesque architectural elements. After forty years in construction, the temple had been completed
and dedicated as a sacred space for the Latter-day Saints just over nine years
earlier. Once an icon of a nefarious faith group, the Salt Lake Temple had
come to represent an industrious, friendly people. Having toured the temple
grounds, Buffalo Bill and his performers paused for a photo opportunity.

An unidentified photographer gathered the international superstar
and close to two hundred Wild West entertainers on the building's south

25. Buffalo Bill's Wild West performers in front of the Salt Lake Temple, August 1902. Object ID 70.0304, Buffalo Bill Museum and Grave, Golden, Colorado.

side, near the base of the southeast spire. Bystanders gathered to witness the picturesque scene, as the assembly of men and women lined up in several rows on a slight slope from the ground up to the building. As the photographer peered into the camera, men in military dress appeared on the far left, cowboys were sprinkled throughout the group, band members with their trumpets, trombones, and other instruments stood toward the front right, while American Indians adorned with feathered headdresses huddled in the middle of the group. Standing prominently front and center, proud and steadfast, was Buffalo Bill. To the left stood his daughter, Irma. The photographer snapped a picture worth a hundred thousand words.

Following the photo opportunity, Buffalo Bill and his contingent dispersed, returning to the arena several blocks away to prepare for their afternoon and evening performances. The two Wild West shows of that day again filled the arena to the brim. Spectators cheered as Buffalo Bill and the cowboys rescued the emigrant trains and settlers' cabin from attacking invaders. The crowd roared watching horse races, daring feats of horsemanship, and expert shooting displays. The audience observed in reverent awe the spectacular triumph of Roosevelt's Rough Riders in the Battle of San Juan Hill. In all, more than sixty thousand people witnessed Cody's exhibition in its two-day run in Salt Lake City. The celebrated scout commented on the turnout: "It simply proves what has so often been said of Salt Lake. It is the greatest amusement center of its size in the country."[74] At the height of his international popularity, Buffalo Bill did big business in Utah's capital city.

The Wild West and Congress of Rough Riders of the World left an impression on those who witnessed it. Ranchers and farmers from Utah and Idaho left the shows full of nostalgia for days past. Lamenting that "there is little that is wild" in the present-day West, the old western-ers felt inspired by the spectacle they had witnessed.[75] They could show their children and grandchildren the best equestrians in the world and scenes of conflict that led to the white man's settlement of the vast, arid West. Sentiments such as this had long followed the Wild West show. Its emotion-producing authenticity had drawn praise from individuals, including Mark Twain, since its inception. Cody's display continued to stir memories and take youngsters back to the days of the Wild West.

The Wild West performances left an indelible imprint on Salt Lake City residents. It was so influential on one eleven-year-old that he decided to replicate the Wild West in his backyard. Merely a week after Buffalo Bill's contingent left the city, young Moroni Gillespie mimicked parts of the performance with a crowd of other boys. Byron Reid, an eight-year-old next-door neighbor, sat on the fence separating his parents' property from the Gillespies' to watch the juvenile production of Cody's show. During his attempt at marksmanship, Gillespie fired what was described as a toy gun (it may have been a BB gun) toward the fence line. The shot, however, went awry, striking Byron in the leg. He endured a painful wound but survived the accident.[76] Gillespie admired Buffalo Bill and wanted to be just like him, but at that time he lacked the showman's elite marksmanship.

Buffalo Bill and his Wild West troupe headed north to Idaho and Washington after departing from Salt Lake City and before turning south down the Pacific Coast in September. They performed in every major California city, including a weeklong stint in San Francisco. The Wild West show then traveled east through Arizona, New Mexico, and Texas. The 1902 season of Buffalo Bill's Wild West and Congress of Rough Riders of the World concluded in Memphis, Tennessee, on November 8. From there the famous scout immediately boarded yet another train, with the destination his Big Horn Basin home.[77]

On his way home, Cody sent letters of invitation to friends, acquaintances, dignitaries, and press all over the country to a party commemorating the opening of his new hotel: the Irma. The grand-opening celebration took place on November 18 in the town of Cody, Wyoming, just ten days after Cody had left Memphis. Hundreds attended the gala event in the stately new hotel, situated against a glorious backdrop of majestic mountains. The Irma, coined "Buffalo Bill's Hotel in the Rockies," quickly became the social center of the Big Horn Basin. The hotel had cost some $80,000 (equivalent to just over $2.7 million in 2022) to construct and was perhaps Cody's most successful, and lasting, building venture in the basin. Though it took funds and resources away from other projects, Buffalo Bill now had a new attraction to entice visitors and more settlers to the region.[78]

Buffalo Bill could not stay in his town for long that fall. Another tour beckoned. By December 1902 he was once again in New York City, preparing to take his spectacle overseas to entertain the masses in England. His Wild West and Congress of Rough Riders of the World opened a new season of performances at the Olympia Exhibition Centre in London on December 26, 1902. The British public was treated to one of the "largest scenes ever presented on any stage," featuring a "great show of Indians" appearing "in their native wilds" and a "representation of the battle of San Juan Hill, the most remarkable event of the Spanish-American War," among the show's others acts.[79]

Though Cody was physically separated from his town and the region he loved, the business of the Big Horn Basin did not cease. Correspondence and telegrams relating to reclamation and other enterprises kept Buffalo Bill connected and captured at least a part of his attention while he stayed across the pond. Cody also encountered new Latter-day Saint acquaintances on the isle, even as he pondered what to do with the lands south of the Shoshone River, where the faith group hoped to extend their own northwest Wyoming colonization.

—7—

Friends in the End

Buffalo Bill Cody and his massive cadre of performers had settled in at the Olympia, an iconic exhibition center in West Kensington, London, upon their arrival in December. Winter soon thawed into spring, as the Wild West and Congress of Rough Riders of the World mesmerized exuberant audiences in the capital city from December 6, 1902, through April 4, 1903. Following the four-month residence, Cody and his crew left London to tour the United Kingdom. They traveled more than two hundred miles northwest to Liverpool for an extended stay during the month of May. There Buffalo Bill had the opportunity to meet Francis M. Lyman, a Latter-day Saint apostle and president of The Church of Jesus Christ of Latter-day Saints' European mission, which was then headquartered in the seaport city. Liverpool was the landing place for the first Latter-day Saint missionaries in Great Britain in 1837 and a center of proselytizing activities for the faith ever since.[1] British citizens had flocked to Mormonism in the 1840s, first by the hundreds then by the thousands. From Liverpool tens of thousands of converted church members emigrated to the United States during the second half of the nineteenth century.

The rapid rise of the faith on the isle inevitably led to backlash. Anti-Mormonism had ebbed and flowed in England. Opponents in Britain, as in the United States, printed copious tracts and other materials portraying Mormon men as violent and as immoral sex traffickers. Some of the most vocal critics were former Latter-day Saints who had gone to America, only to become disillusioned with the faith's religious teachings, the pervasive presence of plural marriage, or life in Utah. They returned home to warn others of the nefarious faith and its preachers.

Sentiment against the church, its practices, and its people was strong and rising in Britain at the turn of the century. The proliferation of anti-Mormon tracts and messages found in popular works like Sir Arthur Conan Doyle's first Sherlock Holmes book, *A Study in Scarlet*, had staying power and swayed public opinion. These writings depicted lurid tales of Mormonism and murder, the horrors of forced marriage and sexual slavery, and strange religious rituals (not unlike the themes found in Buffalo Bill Cody's early stage performances and later dime novels). The damaging, even pornographic, imagery and stereotypes only stoked the fire burning brightly against Latter-day Saints in the English-reading world. Latter-day Saint preachers could not escape the negativity. They struggled to find people to listen to, let alone accept, their message of faith and conversion. By 1900 the once expanding and flourishing sect had dwindled to just over four thousand individuals in England.[2]

In such a cultural climate, separated by thousands of miles and far removed from his interests in the American West, it would have been easy for William F. Cody to dismiss a Latter-day Saint seeking an audience with him in the bustling port city of Liverpool. After all, he had a thriving business to attend to, and it was the first week of the Wild West show's monthlong residence in Liverpool. But the ever-sociable performer cordially welcomed the caller.

Francis Lyman knocked at the door. The international superstar opened it and greeted him with delight. For an hour and a half, Cody and Lyman waxed nostalgic about life on the American frontier. Lyman was ten years Cody's senior in frontier life, or so he claimed (Lyman was only six years older than Buffalo Bill), but it rather pleased the famous scout to meet an older pioneer.[3] The two then spoke of mutual acquaintances and friends. The great hero of the plains perked up upon hearing that the Latter-day Saint apostle was well acquainted with other Saints whom Cody had befriended. They spoke fondly of individuals such as Junius F. Wells and Daniel Seegmiller, who had piloted Buffalo Bill through the Grand Canyon in 1892, and Lyman's fellow apostle Abraham O. Woodruff, who had led the Saints' negotiations and efforts in northwest Wyoming. Lyman then pulled out a recent photograph of the church's First Presidency and

26. Buffalo Bill in England, 1903. Library of Congress, LC-USZ62-22029.

Quorum of the Twelve Apostles, the highest leaders of the faith, and showed it to Cody. Apparently Cody was taken with the image and asked for a copy. The apostle was ecstatic at the request and "promised to get him one at the earliest moment."[4]

After approximately ninety minutes of conversation, Buffalo Bill had to return to his work. Before he said goodbye, he gifted the Latter-day Saint apostle a dozen tickets to the "best seats at the show."[5] Lyman thanked

Buffalo Bill profusely for his generosity. Later that day Lyman took eleven other Latter-day Saints to witness Buffalo Bill's Wild West and Congress of Rough Riders of the World. They sat on the edge of their seats, cheering loudly and enjoying the marvelous performance. "Col. Cody is good to us," Lyman affirmed in one of the many letters he wrote to his children and fellow Saints about his encounter with the world's most well-known entertainer.[6]

One of the letters that Francis Lyman penned was to Junius Wells, who was then in London. "I want you to see Col Cody," Lyman urged, following his visit with the great showman. "He talks of you and remembers you very well," Lyman assured his fellow Saint.[7] Wells had been instrumental in showing Cody the Great Basin and its people. In many ways it was Wells who introduced Buffalo Bill to the real Mormon people. He had left an indelible mark on the great plainsman, who, despite ongoing frustrations with the Latter-day Saint quest for certain lands in the Big Horn Basin, continued to outwardly befriend and publicly support members of the long-embattled faith. It is unknown if Wells traveled to Liverpool at that time to visit Lyman and see Cody. At some point during Cody's British sojourn, the two did connect. It was Wells who put Lyman back in contact with Cody in October 1903.

By then Lyman had procured a copy of the photograph of the Latter-day Saint church leaders that he had shown the celebrity during their previous encounter. He had promised Cody he would get him the photo, and he intended to fulfill that promise. "I shall always feel a brotherly and sympathetic interest in you henceforth," Lyman declared in a letter that he sent the showman accompanying the photograph. The Latter-day Saint apostle further expressed hope that he could meet Cody again, whether in England, Wyoming, or Utah. He encouraged the entertainer to seek out Latter-day Saints in other British cities, whom he believed would be delighted to behold the Wild West and Congress of Rough Riders of the World spectacle. Lyman closed his correspondence bestowing blessings from heaven on Buffalo Bill.[8]

The responsive performer wasted no time. He immediately scrawled a short though amiable letter. "My Dear Brother Lyman," Cody addressed

27. This image is likely a copy of the Fox and Symons montage of the
First Presidency and Quorum of the Twelve Apostles that Francis Lyman
gave to Buffalo Bill in England in 1903. Courtesy of the Church History
Library, The Church of Jesus Christ of Latter-day Saints, Salt Lake City.

the letter, expressing gratitude for the photograph of the First Presidency
and Quorum of the Twelve Apostles of The Church of Jesus Christ of
Latter-day Saints. "I will have it framed and carry [it] with me," Buffalo
Bill professed, "for I like to gaze on good and true men—and Pioners."
Encounters and experiences with members of the religious group over
the previous decade had solidified in Cody's mind that Latter-day Saints
were indeed deserving of the pioneer label. They were, in Cody's words,
"men who help to make God's country blossom as the rose."⁹ Since at
least his 1892 trip with Junius Wells, Cody did not waver from his admiration of the work Latter-day Saints had done to make the arid lands of

the West productive. Among these were men he helped to lure to build infrastructure and grow the population in the Big Horn Basin, a region near and dear to his heart and business interests. He knew these religious believers toiled against the elements in making great settlements out of what others considered waste spaces. He knew it because he had seen it. And he did not forget it in his letter of sincere thanks to Francis M. Lyman.

Buffalo Bill had at least one other encounter with Latter-day Saints while touring England. In Hull, Buffalo Bill received a visit from two unidentified Latter-day Saint preachers. Despite Cody's busy schedule with the Wild West show and his many other appearances and engagements, he spent thirty minutes with the two church elders. According to their report to the *Deseret Evening News*, Buffalo Bill "was enthusiastic in his praise of the 'Mormon' people, and said that a finer body of people could not be found anywhere. He also stated that at one time when he had property in the Big Horn basin, his great desire was to get a colony of 'Mormons' on the place, as he knew they were the ones who could and would build it up, and make it a success." He also spoke "very highly of Apostle Woodruff." The following day Cody gave these two men passes to his performances, a courtesy he had extended to other Latter-day Saints during his time touring in England. Latter-day Saints never tired of hearing such praise from the world-famous entertainer. "It is not unpleasing to hear what those who really know us have to say about us," the *Deseret Evening News* remarked at a time rife with "hard and bitter things" being said and published about the Latter-day Saints.[10] The Saints had found a friend in Buffalo Bill Cody, and they glommed on to his admiration.

The Big Horn Basin was never far from Cody's mind. Even while thousands of miles east, performing day in and day out, Buffalo Bill kept tabs on business and developments in northwest Wyoming. In May 1903 Buffalo Bill received tragic news. Just four months into his second term as governor, DeForest Richards passed away from kidney disease on April 28, 1903. Richards and Cody had corresponded regularly about their mutual interests. Cody had recently told Richards, "No matter how many

English pounds I get, it will find its way to Wyoming."[11] Richards had also been a key supporter for the Latter-day Saints' growth in the basin. He was a helpful mediator between Abraham Woodruff and William F. Cody in long-standing conversations about the Latter-day Saints' desire to acquire more of Cody's land. Upon hearing of Richards' death, Cody assured Fenimore Chatterton, who succeeded Richards in office, that "I am perfectly willing to do whatever is best for the interests of the State."[12] Like his predecessor, Chatterton wanted to work with the celebrity because of the money and power he wielded, not only in the state of Wyoming but also internationally.

Among the many matters of business on his desk, the new governor was now thrust into the role of mediator in the standoff between Cody and the Mormons. As much as Buffalo Bill respected and even appreciated the work Latter-day Saints had done to build infrastructure in the region, he had refused to allow them to obtain more of the land and water rights that he had segregated to him. Doing so, he thought, was not in his best financial interests. Cody feared that, if Mormon settlers obtained more land to irrigate on the south side of the Shoshone River below Eagle's Nest, his company's remaining land and water rights would not generate the revenue needed to finance essential canal work or enrich himself, his company, and his investors.[13]

Abraham Woodruff had pushed Governor Richards hard to obtain this land, and the governor had resolved to make it happen. In February 1903, just prior to his death, Richards had told Cody in no uncertain terms: "The land on the south side, we are going to give to a Mormon colony." On account of the success of Latter-day Saint settlements in northwest Wyoming, Richards asserted, "They have proven to be a splendid lot of citizens and we desire very much to accommodate them with this strip of country."[14] Richards's death, however, changed the dynamics of these negotiations.

Just weeks after Cody's friendly visit with Latter-day Saint apostle Francis Lyman, he fired off a letter to the new Wyoming governor. He remained concerned that his vision for the pioneer's paradise would fail if the Mormons took hold of the south-side lands. He had previously told the Burlington Railroad general manager, George W. Holdrege, that he opposed the Mormons having these prime acres, especially when "60,000 acres on the upper end lay idle." He had cautioned that if the Mormons obtained the south-side lands, "the upper end will never be irrigated."[15] He worried that they would take control of the water in a choice location and supplant his influence in his own pioneer's paradise. Now, he similarly warned Chatterton, "as I have said before if the Mormons or anyone else is permitted to take out canals to irrigate cheaply the lower end of this tract of land it will not pay the government or any private individuals to take a canal out of the canyon."[16] The new governor faced a difficult decision. Would he follow through on his predecessor's plans to support the transition of lands and water rights to the Mormons? Or would he satiate the world-famous showman? Chatterton opted to remain neutral. By not taking action for the Mormons, the governor ultimately privileged Cody's interests.

Though tension characterized the private relationship of Buffalo Bill and the Mormons as they vied for prime lands at this time, Cody continued to use their efforts to his advantage in his public advertising. He commended the Saints who had succeeded in the Big Horn Basin and proved their mettle in settling, farming, railroad building, and constructing a thirty-seven-mile canal there at a cost of "upward of $125,000."[17] The canal allowed the settlers to irrigate fields of alfalfa for hay and oats, as well as wheat, a variety of vegetables, and sugar beets.[18]

The Latter-day Saints had successfully colonized the land. They were prolific, prosperous people contented in their efforts to build a growing settlement.[19] In her life story, Idella Twombly Sessions remarked, "We have never been well off, but a happier woman and family never lived."[20] That was plain to see, as the towns of Byron, Cowley, and Lovell grew despite the arid country. Stores, butcher shops, schoolhouses, churches, and homes sprang up alongside farms and ranches adjacent to the canal.[21] In Lovell alone were some 140 families engaged in cultivating seven thousand acres of land that produced crops of grain and vegetables of all kinds.[22] By applying the irrigation from the canal they had labored on so diligently, the settlers realized abundant crops and a very comfortable livelihood.[23]

Through toil, sacrifice, and dedication, these Saints had changed barren benchlands into waves of grain and helped to build a rail line for the iron horse to carry off their produce to the country and the world.[24]

In a pamphlet titled *Ideal Western Lands*, William F. Cody, as president of the Shoshone Irrigation Company, used Mormons in his efforts to advertise the basin and its economic promise. Buffalo Bill knew they would come into the Big Horn Basin and successfully build infrastructure that would help take it from a land of dust and sagebrush to one producing grains, fruits, and vegetables of all kinds. But his economic interests were different than theirs. Cody wanted to see more diversity in the basin and families who would pay him for land and water rights.

Water has always been a vital resource in the American West, and Mormon foresight and industry brought water to begin to make the basin bloom. For Buffalo Bill the simultaneous pricelessness and costliness of the Mormon experiment in the Big Horn Basin was incalculable. He gave the Mormon colonization company land and water rights for free, hoping to jump-start irrigation infrastructure and large-scale settlement to the basin. To a small degree, it worked. Mormon settlers showed the viability of Cody's "schemes" and the fruitfulness of the region. Their settlement provided the celebrity salesman with promotional fodder to encourage other industries and settlers to realize the business or personal economic opportunities that awaited them in northwest Wyoming. When he spoke of the "new empire" and rich resources available, Cody spoke of the emerging "New West" and its economy, which required technology and infrastructure to realize the fullness of its potential.[25]

During Cody's lengthy stay in Britain, a new party emerged to complicate the dynamics of canal building and regional development in the Big Horn Basin. By mid-June 1902 the U.S. Congress had passed, and President Theodore Roosevelt, the immortalized Rough Rider, had signed into law, the Newlands Reclamation Act. This revolutionary piece of legislation authorized the federal government to commission water diversion, retention, and transmission projects in the states of the Trans-Mississippi West.

Through the act Congress appropriated $50 million for water projects. It also established a new agency, the Reclamation Service (which became the Bureau of Reclamation in 1923) within the Department of the Interior, to administer what became a massive federal effort to bring water to arid lands, thereby opening those lands to greater settlement and population growth. By funding irrigation projects, the federal government moved aggressively to expand and strengthen agriculture, settlement, and access to water to meet the demands of a region primed for growth. Politicians and others believed that first harnessing or controlling the water, then bureaucratic management of the water would help the people in the western states master the elements. It was what Buffalo Bill wanted to do in the Big Horn and what the Latter-day Saints did in the Intermountain West. But this new effort would be done on an unprecedented scale.

Buffalo Bill anxiously sought information about the government's intentions and developments. He had heard that federal surveyors were in the canyon above Cody, planning to build the dam and canal network that he had always dreamed of to water his large Cody-Salsbury segregation.[26] Where Buffalo Bill could not raise the funds needed to construct this major system, Congress appropriated $2.25 million for the Shoshone Reclamation Project to provide irrigation water through dams, canals, and diversions to provide a dependable water supply to much of the Big Horn Basin, including the towns of Cody, Powell, and Lovell.[27] Under the Reclamation Act, however, the federal government needed to have state water permits for its irrigation projects, so it would need to acquire Buffalo Bill's permit to build the dam.[28] Within five years of beginning construction, the federal effort produced a 325-foot-high concrete arch dam in the canyon above the town of Cody. Completed in January 1910, the Shoshone Dam was the tallest dam in the world at the time of its completion. The dam, later renamed the Buffalo Bill Dam, created a water-storage reservoir that held over 450,000 acre-feet of water that could supply irrigable water to over 150,000 acres of land, which could in turn yield a wide variety of crops, including alfalfa, sugar beets, potatoes, fruits, and grains.

For this plan to proceed and succeed, William Cody had to act. In February 1904 he wanted the same thing he had always sought: to make the desert into valuable land and bring settlers to his pioneer's paradise. Four years earlier he had hosted Latter-day Saint visitors, hoping they would be the fulcrum that would unleash the waters of the Shoshone River onto the land in northwest Wyoming. He and his company had exhausted every effort to find people, investors, and funds to build the irrigation network that would realize his dream. As it became clear that the federal Reclamation Service was taking up the proposition to build a dam and canal system, Buffalo Bill determined he would not stand in its way.[29] In looking out for the best interests of the state of Wyoming and his own self-interest, in February 1904 Cody used the same tactic he had with the Latter-day Saints years earlier: he relinquished his water rights to and interests in a significant amount of land to spur development. In the latter case Buffalo Bill gave up his rights to more than sixty-five thousand acres of land within the Cody-Salsbury segregation on the north side of the Shoshone River to Ethan Allen Hitchcock, the U.S. secretary of the interior.[30] Where Cody had relinquished his land in the Cincinnati tract to Abraham Woodruff and the Latter-day Saints gratis, he did receive a ceremonial consideration of one dollar for his relinquishment to the federal government.[31]

Buffalo Bill's move was popular and much lauded. The Cody Town Council passed a resolution applauding Buffalo Bill, and "a rousing celebration was held" in town to express the joy and gratitude of the citizens that the government was going to build the dam and canal.[32] In the politics of irrigation development, the individual company could not compete with the federal government. Cody had "vastly underestimated the cost of irrigation," as had most other private capitalists hoping to turn a profit on irrigation investment in the West.[33] He wanted to create the equivalent to one of his popular shows, with people flooding in to northwest Wyoming, but neither Cody's celebrity nor Latter-day Saint efforts nor even the later federal infrastructure could bring about the population or development in the area for which Cody had once hoped. One newspaper summarized, "Some years ago, Buffalo Bill (Col. W. F. Cody) sensed what might be done in this season in the way of irrigation, and started out to organize a big irrigating company with a view to doing just what the government is now proposing to do. But it was not long before the immensity of the undertaking impelled him to halt, and enter negotiations with the government to take the job off his hands. Finally, about two years ago, Cody was induced to sign off all his claims to the lands immediately under the scope of the project, and then the government took hold."[34] William Cody's relinquishment of land and water rights to the federal government symbolized the death knell for the private investment in and funding of irrigation in the Big Horn Basin.

News of the Shoshone River project and of Buffalo Bill's relinquishment spread quickly. All over the West individuals and organizations watched the federal enterprise with interest. Those in Salt Lake City were especially intrigued. The *Deseret News* called it "one of the hugest undertakings of the kind that Uncle Sam has yet engaged in." Work on the project was directed and supervised out of Salt Lake City. But for those watching and waiting to realize the success of the project, it symbolized future prosperity for settlers, for farmers, for ranchers, and for all in the "waste places" of the West. The *Deseret News* maintained a special watch on the Shoshone project "because of the existence of two 'Mormon' settlements some 15 miles below the site of the proposed dam, and where nearly 1,000 of the Saints have established prosperous communities. The good people of these settlements will come within the immediate sphere of the project's operations, as their lands extend out under the lines being laid for the latterals to be connected with the main canal which is to be 50 miles long."[35] The Latter-day Saints in the Big Horn Basin likewise stood to benefit from the government works. But the Saints too had to give up something.

Since Abraham Woodruff had expressed interest in colonizing the area, church members in the basin coveted prime lands on the south side of the river. Buffalo Bill had firmly held his rights to these lands, not wanting to lose out on their potential high value. However, in early February 1904 Cody saw the writing on the wall. He gave up the fight. The same month that he relinquished the centerpiece to his Big Horn Basin empire to the federal government, Cody relented on the south-side lands as well. Charles A. Welch, one of the leaders of the Latter-day Saint Big Horn Basin Colonization Company, praised Chatterton and expressed his gratitude to Buffalo Bill. Welch and the Saints were intent to push their enterprise forward "with all possible speed." Welch assured the Wyoming governor that with these land and water rights his people would build another canal to irrigate the south-side lands and "redeem [it] from its barrenness."[36] The Mormons had finally got the desired rights to the sought-after tract.

Charles Welch's enthusiasm, however, was short-lived. Federal surveyors and engineers soon stepped in to negotiate with the Saints for the transfer of those lands to the government for the Shoshone project. The U.S. Reclamation Service wanted those highly favored south-side lands to complete its plan for the Big Horn Basin.[37] Welch turned the negotiations over to Byron Sessions and Jesse W. Crosby, the president and vice president of the church's Big Horn Basin Colonization Company. For months talks ensued between the religious leaders and the federal representative. Both the Saints and Cody had wanted to dictate growth and development in the region. Federal power had upended their strategies, but both Cody and the Latter-day Saints believed that they could still gain from the change.

In April 1905, just over a year after gaining the rights to the land, Sessions and Crosby decided "to turn over and formally assign to the Reclamation Service, without remuneration," the south-side tract, which consisted of approximately seven thousand acres of land, with all the water filings, applications, and permits pertaining to that land. The Saints went further in relinquishing the rights to over forty thousand more acres they had acquired in the Whistle Creek and Wilwood tracts.[38] On April 17, 1905, a telegram to the U.S. Geological Survey in Washington DC read simply, "Mormon people agree [to] formally transfer south side Shoshone land fifty thousand acres with Water rights . . . to reclamation service."[39] Though no formal payment was made to the Saints, the government reimbursed the Latter-day Saints for "moneys actually expended" by them for surveys and filing applications.[40] The formal assignment of water and land rights from the Latter-day Saint company to the U.S. Reclamation Service took place on May 20, 1905.[41] The federal government now dictated the waterworks in the Big Horn Basin, as it would throughout the arid West in the twentieth century and beyond.

Buffalo Bill Cody's interests in the basin continued. He hoped to build another new town in the heart of the lands the federal government was in the process of reclaiming. Cody planned to name the town, which would be located thirty miles east of the town of Cody, Ralston. Despite what he viewed as his magnanimity for relinquishing the Cody-Salsbury segregation to the federal government, Buffalo Bill felt that the Reclamation Service was not treating him fairly.

Upset about the turn of events, the legendary entertainer penned a letter directly to the president of the United States, his friend Theodore Roosevelt. "Mr. President: I have been the pioneer in the irrigation and reclamation of that arid country known as the Big Horn Basin, in northwestern Wyoming, and no one knows better than yourself what the pioneer has to contend with," Cody articulated as he launched into his complaint about his treatment by the U.S. Reclamation Service. He understood that the government would build a town near his proposed new townsite and that it would again interfere with his pecuniary interests. He explained, "I have spent nearly all that I possessed in opening up that country, making it possible for white men to live there." If the Reclamation Service was able to build a government town to compete with Cody's proposed town, Buffalo Bill pled with the president, "the old pioneer again meets with a hardship." He then asked the president to have the Reclamation Service build its "Government town in some other place so that it may not interfere with the interests that I have there."[42] Cody hoped that his letter was persuasive and that his friendship with the old Rough Rider would sway government development in the region in his favor.

Buffalo Bill also appealed directly to Frederick Haynes Newell, the first director of the U.S. Reclamation Service. Cody believed he was entitled to the water rights and land on which he would build Ralston in lieu of his relinquishing the lands for the Shoshone Project.[43] His appeal fell on deaf ears. So Cody returned to President Roosevelt, imploring him to at least help him obtain water rights to the land that would otherwise be worthless. He again reminded Roosevelt of his previous generosity and the tens of thousands of dollars he had expended on the Cody-Salsbury segregation lands. "It seems to me it would be bad faith on the part of the Government to refuse to let me have the water" for the land Buffalo Bill purchased to build Ralston, Cody argued, "after I turned my rights over to them without money and without price." "As you know Mr. President," the world-famous entertainer declared, "I have a great love for that country and I am very anxious to see it develop. For twenty years I have been pouring in every cent I can make and up to the present time there has never been a cent in it for Cody." In concluding his plea, William F. Cody brilliantly played on the president's well-used progressive political phrase "a square deal for every man." "It seems to me it would not be a square deal for the Government to make my land worthless for all time by refusing to let me have water. What do you say?" the great showman queried.[44]

Neither the director of the Reclamation Service nor the president gave Buffalo Bill the assurances he sought on this land. Instead, Cody found frustration with the government, like he had been frustrated by the designs of the Latter-day Saints in the basin. For their part government employees and agencies chalked up Cody's discontent to his own misunderstandings. In responding to a query from the president, the Reclamation Service praised Colonel Cody "as an entertaining companion" but stated unequivocally, "He has, however, an apparently erroneous idea that something was promised him, or that there existed some understanding which has not been carried out. Our records show that our dealings were primarily with the State Land Board of Wyoming. Our people are very certain that no promises were made to Colonel Cody. As a matter of fact, none could be made nor carried out, under existing law, unless embodied in a written contract."[45] The federal agency effectively ignored Buffalo Bill Cody.

The relationship between Buffalo Bill and the Latter-day Saints had grown perfunctory as federal reclamation expanded in the Big Horn Basin. Though the two no longer vied for lands in northwest Wyoming, links between the two kept them connected during the last decade of Cody's life. For one, popular dime novels featuring the great western hero's exploits reminded readers of ever-lingering concerns about Latter-day Saints in American politics and culture. And second, Buffalo Bill continued to tour the United States. Still needing the income that being a showman provided, Cody traversed the nation with new shows and circuses, returning to Utah's capital city on a few occasions.

⁓⁓⁓⁓

Echoes of past perceptions haunted the Utah-based faith, especially when it came to the dynamics of home and family, during the early twentieth century. Nowhere was this more visible than during the Reed Smoot Senate hearings from 1904 through 1907. The election of Reed Smoot to the U.S. Senate resurrected a national controversy surrounding Latter-day Saints, their practice of polygamy, and their political power. Smoot, a monogamist and an apostle for The Church of Jesus Christ of Latter-day Saints, won the vote to represent the state of Utah, but his eligibility to serve was quickly investigated by the Senate. Reports had surfaced that church leaders, including those in the Quorum of the Twelve Apostles, of which Smoot was a member, still approved, authorized, or participated in plural marriages, even though in 1890 then church president Wilford Woodruff issued a manifesto renouncing future plural marriages among good-standing members of the faith. Because plural marriages were illegal not only in Utah but also in the nation, pundits, politicians, and partisans strongly questioned whether Smoot could honorably support the Con-stitution while serving in a leading role in a church that had defied the laws of the nation, or at the very least placed God's laws above those of the nation, for so long. These questions and others prompted the inves-tigation into Smoot as an individual and into the church, its teachings, doctrine, and history.[46]

Those reports of church leaders approving, authorizing, and partici-pating in plural marriage were not unfounded. Though Smoot could not be counted among them, some members of the Quorum of the Twelve Apostles participated in postmanifesto polygamy. It has been estimated that approximately 250 plural marriages were solemnized between 1890 and 1904 and that half of the highest church leaders took an active part.[47] These marriages were kept secret and were denied in public to uphold the positive image that the church had worked to establish during those years. Some of these polygamists lived directly in William F. Cody's neck of the

28. Political cartoon from *Puck* magazine in 1904, titled *The Real Objection to Smoot*. In the illustration an old, bearded man representing the "Mormon Hierarchy" drops his puppet, labeled "R. Smoot," into the U.S. Senate to do his bidding. The Mormon character wears a coat stitched together from pieces of cloth emblazoned with "Polygamy," "Mormon Rebellion," "Mountain Meadow Massacre," "Resistance to Federal Authority," "Murder of Apostates," and "Blood Atonement," all elements that Buffalo Bill's character fought against in performances and dime novels. Library of Congress, LC-DIG-ppmsca-25844.

woods.[48] In fact, despite the outward claims to governors and railroad executives that those Latter-day Saints moving to the Big Horn Basin were not polygamists, some church members, including the apostle in charge of colonization to northwest Wyoming, Abraham O. Woodruff, had engaged in plural marriages after Abraham's father had renounced the practice.

Abraham Woodruff was the most prominent person associated with the Big Horn Basin to become a polygamist. By at least August 1900, just months after he had led families there to colonize an area along the Shoshone River, Woodruff was determined to enter into a plural marriage. He confided to his journal, "A subject has been troubling me of late so I have made it a matter of prayer and asked the Lord to reveal his will to me through Prest. Joseph F. Smith to whom I will present the matter at the Temple tomorrow." Woodruff approached Smith, then the second counselor in the church's presidency, about his desire to have a plural wife. On August 30, 1900, he talked of his bold desire with Smith, and the president "counseled me to follow the impression I have had. The matter is clear to me now and I mean to do it."[49] And he did. During his travel from Salt Lake City to the Big Horn Basin that summer, Woodruff passed through Wyoming's Star Valley, a place founded as a polygamous haven from federal prosecution in Utah, and spoke to a congregation of Saints.[50] There he met eighteen-year-old Eliza Avery Clark, who later wrote that during his address she was impressed with his "charming, majestic personality." Later that day, in conversation with her sister, Eliza (who went by Avery) "raved about his good looks, intelligence and personality," as she lamented that "there weren't more of his kind to be passed around so more deserving girls could get a worthy husband."[51] Avery was apparently quite taken with the young apostle, and though he did not leave a record of his impressions at that time, Woodruff also departed Star Valley intent on pursuing Avery as a plural wife.

Talk among church leaders surrounding plural marriages heated up as the cool weather of the fall of 1900 set in. On November 1 Abraham Woodruff went to a meeting at the Salt Lake Temple. There he heard Lorenzo Snow, then the faith's prophet and church president, declare that "he did not know how it would be done but Plural Marriage will again be restored." "I am just sure of it," Snow proclaimed.[52] Later that month, emboldened by what he heard from his prophet, Abraham Woodruff openly asserted, "No year will ever pass . . . from now until the coming of the Saviour, when children will not be born in plural marriage." Wood-ruff declared this divine prediction "in the name of Jesus Christ," as was customary among the faithful.[53] Just two months later, action supplanted words. Woodruff met Eliza Avery Clark in Preston, Idaho, where his fellow apostle Mathias F. Cowley sealed the two in plural marriage on January 18, 1901.[54] Avery had agreed to the marriage after learning that several of the brethren in high positions had been advised to take plural wives and after her sincere prayers to do what she believed was "the will of God at all times to live worthily in preparation for the celestial kingdom." The union was kept a secret from all but those closest to Abraham and Avery, though she had an ardent desire to "announce to the world that I was happily married to a grand person whom everyone admired."[55] After more than two years of marriage, Avery became pregnant and went to live in a Latter-day Saint colony in Mexico to hide the evidence of this plural marriage.[56]

Secrecy regarding these plural unions remained essential for the Saints' public standing and in the eyes of the nation, especially during the Reed Smoot hearings in the Senate. Investigators looked for clues and pieces of dirt on Smoot and the church as an institution, hoping to block Smoot's congressional seating. Early in the federal investigation, Reed Smoot typed a letter to Abraham Woodruff. He was already weary. "I am rather tired and a little worn out, for I have hardly had time to sleep lately," he confided to his fellow apostle. "I am not worry[ing] about the investiga-tion of myself," Smoot insisted. "The only thing that is troubling to me is the inclination of many, and the determination of some, to go into a never-ending investigation of the Mormon Church, and charge me with being responsible for the sayings of every man, and the actions of every member of the Church." Apparently unaware of Woodruff's foray into plural marriage and his being one of those individuals who would bring condemnation on the faith, the senator sent his best wishes for Woodruff's mother and first wife, Helen, as he closed his communication of January

21, 1904. About a month later Smoot sent another communication to
Woodruff, when he learned that Woodruff was not being subpoenaed as
a witness in the investigation.[57] This was apparently by design. Joseph F.
Smith, now the president of the church, had sent Woodruff, along with
his first wife and their children, to Mexico to avoid the possibility of
arrest and testifying in Smoot's trial. Upon his arrival in Colonia Juarez,
Abraham visited Avery and met for the first time the daughter they con-
ceived together.

For his part Smoot remained optimistic that, once the senators had "a
chance to meet our brethren," it would have a good effect. The monogamist
senator from Utah claimed that he had "no fear as to the final outcome of
my case," confident that neither he nor his church had anything to hide.[58]
Proximity to and the opportunities to interact with upstanding Latter-
day Saints, Smoot believed, as did Buffalo Bill Cody following his 1892
visit to Utah, would demonstrate their goodness and value as American
citizens. And though some in the highest ranks of church leadership did
have something to hide, those things remained hidden and were pushed
further underground when Joseph F. Smith presented a special declaration to the church at its semiannual conference in early April 1904, just
months after the Smoot investigation began. Smith publicly doubled
down on the 1890 manifesto, issuing what has become known as a "Second Manifesto," stating unequivocally that the laws of the land would
be upheld and that those members who entered new plural marriages
would be excommunicated from the church.[59] It was a bold move from a
church president who had tacitly approved of such marriages in the preceding years. Though Senate investigators and the press had dragged the
Latter-day Saints through the mud, Reed Smoot ultimately retained his
seat in the Senate, with the backing of U.S. president Theodore Roosevelt.
During this time Roosevelt, the old Rough Rider, praised the Mormon
people. In language like that used by Buffalo Bill, William Smythe, and a
chorus of important voices, the U.S. president lauded the faith group for
"literally—not figuratively" taking a "territory which at the outset was
called after the desert" and making "the wilderness blossom as the rose."[60]
And while Smoot would go on to serve an impressive thirty-year career

in the Senate, it was clear that, in spite of plaudits from some powerful people, the American people still feared the cohesion, power, and familial relations of Mormons.

⁓⁓⁓⁓

After more than a year's worth of the worst depictions and rehashed clichés of Latter-day Saints coming out of the Smoot trial, the New York City–based Street and Smith Publishing Company released the Buffalo Bill Stories. The series was a weekly publication devoted to the adventures of Buffalo Bill and to so-called border history. The Street and Smith publishers claimed their stories to be authentic tales of the king of scouts, cautioning their readers of imitations and fictitious stories and characters. In their words the Buffalo Bill Stories was the only weekly series containing the actual escapades and history of Col. William F. Cody. On June 24, 1905, Street and Smith released edition number 215, titled *Buffalo Bill's Mormon Quarrel, or At War with the Danites*. This dime novel resurrected stereotypes common to anti-Mormon perception that far predated even Buffalo Bill's stage career: the hoodwinking of religious converts, the control and power of religious leaders, the trafficking of women for nefarious purposes, and the omnipresence of religious violence within Mormonism.[61]

Buffalo Bill's adventure began as he and his associate Nick Wharton heard the hair-raising screams of a young woman. Cody and Wharton came on a harrowing scene: a father and his daughter had been captured by a Danite band threatening to cut their throats. The father had refused to add his daughter to the number of Brigham Young's wives and then attempted to flee with his beloved child from Salt Lake City to California. The Danites tracked and captured the runaways and now promised to spill their blood for disobedience to their prophet. Buffalo Bill and his partner came to the rescue, dispatching the captors and killing all but one who escaped to inform the religious authorities in Salt Lake City what had occurred. Knowing that this Danite would get reinforcements if he reached the Mormon capital, Buffalo Bill needed to intercept him.

The beautiful young woman then approached Cody and Wharton to commend them for their bravery. She held "out her hands in impulsive gratitude to the two scouts, who, with their natural chivalry, had stepped into the background to allow the father and daughter to have their reunion without being embarrassed by the observation of strangers." Upon learning the identity of her deliverer, the famous Buffalo Bill, the rescued daughter, Freda, fixed her gaze on the "handsome, athletic scout with new interest, and the admiration plainly written on her face made him turn his head away and hasten to change the subject."[62] A flirtation sparked between the two, with Cody caught stealing glances, as Freda's father, Peter Hanson, told the story of how he became ensnared in Mormonism. Peter came to see the sect as wicked and had enough of it when Brigham Young came to take his daughter as a plural wife.

After a series of encounters and adventures, the short novel reached its climax. A days-long battle between the scouts and their allies and the Mormons and the Indians had reached a standstill. Then, suddenly "a loud whoop was given by the chief of the Indians and a yell by the leader of the Mormons. At these concerted signals, the allied parties charged together down upon the wagons, racing over the intervening distance at tremendous speed." During the charge Freda and another young girl were seized by a couple of Danites, who forced the women to their knees and drew knives to their throats. The border king, Buffalo Bill, made an unexpected counterattack. He had noticed that one man had complete authority over the Mormons and their Indian allies as well. This man was now within a few paces of Buffalo Bill. Quick as a flash, Buffalo Bill leaped on the chief of the Danites, subdued him, and pressed a six-shooter to his head. With their leader held at gunpoint, the Danites and Indians immediately ceased fighting and let Freda and the others go. Then came the story's big reveal. The Danite leader was none other than Young, the first president of The Church of Jesus Christ of Latter-day Saints. The Mormon leader was revealed to be a coward, lips blue with terror and shivering like a leaf in his fright. Buffalo Bill, positively contrasted, was described as having nerves as strong as steel and being unafraid of ghosts, Native Americans, or Mormons. With leverage over Brigham Young, Cody ensured the safety of Freda and her father. "I will do as you say," Young said. "As soon as I get back to Salt Lake City, I will see that the names of yourself and your friends are stricken off the book of the blood atonement, and will give particular orders that not a hair of the heads of any one of you is to be harmed at any time."[63] Buffalo Bill had once again saved the day.

Buffalo Bill dime novels were short, action-packed stories featuring the heroic adventures and deeds of the eponymous figure. The readership for these fast-paced, lively, and dramatic stories was broad and diverse, encompassing a variety of classes, genders, generations, and nationalities. Dime novels published in the late nineteenth through the early twentieth century pandered to widely held prejudices and perceptions of definitive villains in American society. The content was entertaining; anti-Mormon stories continued to intrigue readers. Anti-Mormon content had been a part of Buffalo Bill dime novels since at least 1881, when Prentiss Ingraham had written *The Doomed Dozen, or Dolores, the Danite's Daughter*. Mormons were the villains in these tales. At the heart of their villainy was polygamy. They were cast as lustful, violent kidnappers of beautiful young women, providing the backdrop to and shaping of the melodramatic scenes of captivity, chase, and rescue. Buffalo Bill always came out of the scrums victorious. He was still a white knight against these threats to the American home and family.

Buffalo Bill's Mormon Quarrel was just one of a plethora of publications reminding the reading public of the perceived dangers of Mormonism. Though William F. Cody had come to know and even praise Latter-day Saints in general for their industry and Brigham Young in particular for his organizational leadership, the Buffalo Bill persona renewed a long-standing battle against the religious zealots and once again cast their faith in a negative light. This and other dime novels presented the same narrative formula popularized by Cody's stage plays and the culture of 1870s and 1880s America. The recycled tropes of religious control, power, violence, and polygamy found in Street and Smith's June 1905 publication surfaced regularly whenever problems with Mormons in American society emerged, and they continue to haunt the Latter-day Saints.

The continued inclusion of Latter-day Saints as villains in Buffalo Bill dime novels of the early twentieth century served as one reminder that, despite their status as pioneer irrigators, the minority religious group was

still considered suspect. For all the progress made in the actual relationship between Cody and the Latter-day Saints, the popular character of, or
persona represented by, Buffalo Bill was still "at odds with the Danites."[64]

annnn

Buffalo Bill Cody was never content to settle down. He had been traveling and performing for decades. He had expended substantial sums of
money in the Big Horn Basin. He had also financed numerous ventures,
ranging from cattle ranching in Nebraska to mining in Arizona. As an
international celebrity, he had become accustomed to living in luxury.
And he was always generous with friends and family. But his family life
had deteriorated. His daughter Arta died in January 1904, shortly after
he had petitioned for divorce from Louisa. William told the court of a
miserable marriage full of constant fighting between him and Louisa and
his choice to live life on the road spending time with others to escape
his unhappy home. He accused Louisa of trying to poison him and of
blocking his ability to provide cash for his show and business ventures.
Louisa told the court of her husband's absenteeism, his constant drunkenness when at home, and his infidelities. William was accused of being
"immoral with any woman that he met." It was a bitter, acrimonious trial
that tainted the public veneer of a man who had spent so many decades
carefully crafting a particular image.[65] The divorce was not granted, leaving Louisa and William married but still at odds.

Following his unsuccessful divorce trial, Cody became more introspec-
tive. In June 1905 he wrote to his sister Julia, a devout Christian who had
long encouraged him to turn to Christ. "In my old age," the performer
confided to his sister, "I have found God—And realize how easy it is to
abandon sin and serve him." Cody had long been ambivalent about religion, despite his mother's best efforts. He previously considered himself
too wicked to earnestly pray to God but had undergone a spiritual awakening that would bring him closer to a Christian faith that would have
pleased his sister and made his mother proud.[66]

Despite the challenges and turmoil that he was seeking to overcome in
his life, Buffalo Bill continued to tour, first in Europe and then the United

States, year after year. His shows still commanded large crowds, and in early September 1908 he returned to Salt Lake City with much fanfare. One Salt Lake newspaper claimed that this offering was "the best entertainment 'Buffalo Bill' has ever presented during the 25 years the Wild West has been before the public." The intrepid scout and Indian fighter's troop had ballooned to over 800 persons (127 of whom were American Indians) and more than 550 horses, carried in approximately fifty rail cars from city to city. This mass of humans and animals descended on Salt Lake City.[67]

Cody's crew set up tents on the same downtown fairgrounds where the Wild West show had been performed six years earlier. As it had for so many years, Buffalo Bill's production would present historical scenes of the settlement of the West along with the competition of horsemen from every clime. New features also attracted attention. A game of football played on horseback was among the most intriguing that season. The best riders from among the Native Americans and the cowboys squared off in the contest, as the riders attempted to push, kick, or shove an immense pigskin (six feet, three inches in diameter) through the goal posts at each end of the arena. This most novel competition fascinated the spectators in Salt Lake City, who watched in awe as the cowboys emerged victorious.[68]

The Salt Lake papers gave mixed reviews. "Buffalo Bill's Wild West Show," the *Deseret News* reported, "is not in the same class with the original show which came west some years ago." Even Buffalo Bill's shooting display "failed to arouse great enthusiasm" from the estimated fourteen thousand attendees (the *Salt Lake Herald* placed the number in attendance much higher, at twenty thousand). The *News* complained about the facilities and seating, which was "so poor that many hundreds left the tent before the show was half over. . . . The rows of iron chairs were placed so near together that either one must be satisfied with planting one's knees in the small of his neighbor's back, or in moving his own chair an inch and falling into the mysterious unlighted part of the tent."[69] In short, the *Deseret News* declared that the audience was ultimately disappointed in Buffalo Bill's offering. The *Salt Lake Herald* concurred, "The performance, however, showed a decided falling off in excellence when compared with the last show given by Buffalo Bill in Salt Lake."[70]

The *Inter-Mountain Republican*, on the other hand, claimed his "Wild West is well worth going to see." The vivid, realistic picture of frontier life, the *Republican* asserted, "will linger long in the memory. . . . It is ever new to those who love to hear of the early days of the West when men like Cody were wresting a great empire from the savages, and were paving the way for those who were to make the desert blossom as the rose."[71] Another area newspaper similarly commented on the show's importance for providing visual imagery of a bygone era: the show is "interesting to the young people because it depicts something which has entirely disappeared and will never be seen again, and to the old it is interesting because many of them remember the days when the name of Buffalo Bill was a name to conjure with in the West."[72] A "good portion" of the audiences in Salt Lake City were composed of children, who left the arena to emulate the cowboy through play. The Wild West show again left an indelible imprint on a new generation of witnesses.[73]

The newspapers also commented on Cody's age and appearance. Though his hair had turned white, and he had entrenched wrinkles on his face, the great showman appeared strong and imposing.[74] Despite his sixty-three years of age, Buffalo Bill, aging gracefully, was still the picture of power and vitality on horseback.[75] Spectators and reporters alike still recognized Cody as an imposing specimen of masculinity. This was still true when he made his foray into the burgeoning film industry a couple of years later. Of his early work in film, the *Los Angeles Herald* wrote, "Buffalo Bill intends to live for all generations—two hundred years from now our grandchildren's sons and daughters will look at the famous old scout and plainsman just as he is today—as active and as vigorous in sturdy manhood."[76] Just as he had depicted himself in his early autobiography and in Wild West promotional materials, Cody was, observers believed, not only the "master horseman of his generation" but also "the exemplar of the strong and unique traits" that characterized a white American cowboy, which Cody had helped to become one of the most enduring symbols of American masculinity.[77]

As another decade began, the old cowboy was ready for a change. Buffalo Bill had lived a hard life on the frontier and participated in scouting and combat for the military. With a vigor and vitality perhaps unmatched in entertainment in that era, he had been performing and touring for nearly forty years. Ready to say goodbye to the stage, he intended to launch a farewell tour in 1910. "After many years of almost constant devotion to my calling," Buffalo Bill proclaimed, "I have determined to retire from active service at the expiration of a final and complete tour of the American Continent."[78] Buffalo Bill declared his desire to walk away from entertainment in the public arena and ride off into a northwest Wyoming sunset. He wanted to live out the rest of his days in a quiet existence in his town in the Big Horn Basin. Like so many of the plans he had made in his life, however, the intent to retire did not work out as he had hoped. He poured money into several unprofitable business ventures. Stretched thin financially, Buffalo Bill ultimately could never fully step away from show life.

Declining receipts in 1913 and the burdensome expenses of the show and his far-flung enterprise forced Buffalo Bill to raise money. To do so he made a fateful blunder, taking a six-month $20,000 loan from a merciless businessman named Henry Tammen. Among his empire Tammen owned the Sells-Floto Circus and the *Denver Post*. The slick entrepreneur conspired to break Cody from his Wild West show. When Buffalo Bill could not make payments on the loan, Tammen worked through the courts to seize Cody's assets and sell his properties. Tammen effectively bankrupted the Wild West production, thereby ending the thirty-year reign of Buffalo Bill's signature show.[79]

After his own show went bankrupt, Cody reluctantly joined the Sells-Floto Circus and returned to the grind of touring, this time with his wife, Louisa, with whom he had finally reconciled, by his side. And though he remained a prominent feature of the performance of western life and history, the Sells-Floto show was more of a circus act than the performance that had shaped his celebrity. When Sells-Floto came to Salt Lake City in June 1914, the newspapers mentioned the return of Buffalo Bill, the "most famous American," but it was "the forty clowns . . . the pretty lady, the bearded woman, the skinny man and the menageries of wonderful animals" that seemed to attract the most attention.[80] Whether it was

Buffalo Bill or the circus curiosities, crowds swelling over ten thousand in the cities of Salt Lake City, Ogden, and Logan came out to experience the Sells-Floto show.[81]

While he was in Salt Lake City, Buffalo Bill renewed acquaintances and visited old friends. Cody attended a showing at the art gallery in the Social Hall. While there, his old-time friend Junius F. Wells, who had piloted him through the Grand Canyon in 1892 and with whom he had a reunion ten years later, presented the colonel with a beautiful cast of Avard Fairbanks's reproduction of a buffalo sculpture.[82] Cody was grateful for this kindness and for the opportunity to visit with Wells. He was, as he had been during his previous visits to the city, a guest of the First Presidency of The Church of Jesus Christ of Latter-day Saints. President Joseph F. Smith welcomed the distinguished frontiersman, and the two western contemporaries conversed about "the olden days in Utah, when the Indian was still a menace and the prairie was unscathed by the iron tooth of the railroad."[83] They reminisced about pioneer life and overcoming the land and peoples of the West, two common topics of conversation between Buffalo Bill and his Mormon friends.

President Smith and the church's First Presidency then treated Buffalo Bill and the entire company of circus performers to a special organ recital held in Cody's honor at the noted Latter-day Saint tabernacle on Temple Square. The presidency arranged for the renowned organist of the tabernacle, John J. McClellan, to play. McClellan, who had studied with international masters and was considered one of the best organists in the world, favored the large company and a public audience of thousands with an impressive array of pieces and arrangements that showcased his wide-ranging abilities.[84] The organist began with a showy selection from the famous overture to the 1845 German opera *Tannhäuser*, written by Richard Wagner, to impress the distinguished guest. McClellan then moved into a simpler, calm but haunting melodic arrangement with a piece by French composer and organist Théodore Dubois. He played other popular, lively pieces, including *Andantino in D-flat* by English organist and composer Edwin Lemare and *Ronde d'Amour* by Italian composer Niccolò van Westerhout, before finishing with a grand selection from

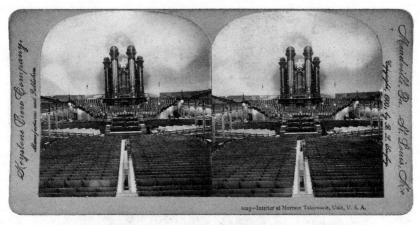

29. Interior of Salt Lake Tabernacle, as Buffalo Bill would have seen it, circa 1900. Library of Congress, LC-DIG-stereo-1s15741.

Cavalierra Rusticana, an opera in one act by Pietro Mascagni. McClellan's finale had big, beautiful dynamics filled with emotion and drama. Buffalo Bill was honored by the impressive concert and by his hosts, with whom he had so much history.

By the time of his 1914 stop in Salt Lake, Buffalo Bill's penultimate visit to Utah, a reconfiguration of memory had taken place. "In days of old," an *Ogden Standard* article proclaimed, "when they were not so well and favorably known and the practice of polygamy created almost universal prejudice against them, the great scout was one of the best friends of the Mormons, and was always ready to praise them for their industry, thrift, sobriety, honesty and other desirable characteristics, as he had observed them during their operations in the course of making the desert blossom as the rose, and establishing the nucleus of our now great and prosperous intermountain empire."[85] Cody's supposed role in the Utah War and anti-Mormon performances of the 1870s and 1880s had been long forgotten. Instead of a fascinating trajectory that began with pernicious perceptions of Mormons displayed onstage and concluded with mutual embrace and influence, this Utah newspaper column collapsed the narrative to highlight a constant positive connection between the place, its people, and the celebrity.

30. Buffalo Bill, as he appeared toward the end of his life, between 1913 and 1917. Library of Congress, LC-DIG-hec-03802.

Buffalo Bill himself likewise applauded the industrious religious group. Addressing the audience during his last performance in Utah in June 1915, the aging showman declared with a clear and resonant voice that it was his "pleasure to appear before an audience, many of whom were descendants of the hardy pioneers who trekked across the plains and 'made the valley of the Great Salt Lake blossom as the rose.'"[86] In that moment, like most of his public declarations about Latter-day Saints during the preceding twenty-three years, Cody collapsed his experience into a soundbite. The message he articulated had remained constant. His sentiments about Latter-day Saint industriousness and irrigation works had drawn praise since the early 1890s. With a conviction from which he had not wavered since that time, Buffalo Bill's last known words to a public audience in Utah revealed a deep admiration for the hardy pioneers of the Intermountain West.

Though friendship and mutual respect had won the day for both Buffalo Bill and the Mormons, when it came time to choose a faith, William F. Cody did not choose the Latter-day Saints. As Cody approached the end of his life, he made a decision about religion. Despite growing up in a Protestant Christian household and encountering a multitude of faiths during his life, he never claimed to belong to a particular religion. On January 9, 1917, the day before he died, Cody was in Denver, Colorado, at the home of his sister, Mary "May" Cody Decker, the namesake of his late 1870s anti-Mormon stage drama. They were visited by Father Christopher Walsh, a Catholic priest from the city. Cody told Walsh that he had always believed in God and that he wanted to die in the Catholic faith. Father Walsh administered to Cody and baptized him that day. After his baptism Cody received the sacrament, which according to the faith meant "that his soul was wiped absolutely clean of every fault." The *Denver Catholic Register* reported, "This is the most notable conversion ever made in Colorado." The next day Buffalo Bill passed away from kidney failure and "entered his promised land."[87]

Conclusion

Curtain Call

William F. "Buffalo Bill" Cody was a storyteller. Onstage and in the arena, he re-created the West and its history for audiences all over the world. He performed within their preconceived notions of what the West and its peoples were like. And he helped shape those very perceptions. A diverse multitude of peoples found reasons to embrace his shows and their message. A stunning array of individuals and groups found reasons to embrace the star performer, and he found reasons to embrace them. Buffalo Bill's character, both literal and figurative, and his person were at times in harmony and at times in conflict. Individuals are never one-dimensional—neither are groups or people within those groups, though perception and stereotypes of them might suggest otherwise. Through proximity and getting to know them and their stories, we can move beyond perception and see people and groups for who they truly are.

As his celebrity grew, Buffalo Bill Cody demonstrated that he valued people and relationships. At times he lent his voice and profound celebrity for the benefit of others. At other times he let the messages of his shows speak for themselves. He was a complex and complicated individual. His perception of and relationship with the members of The Church of Jesus Christ of Latter-day Saints help illuminate complexities: those of Cody, those of Latter-day Saints, and those of the culture, politics, and development of the American West. The factors that brought Buffalo Bill and the Latter-day Saints together coincided with trends that left an indelible imprint on the thought, perception, and history of the West.

One could say that Buffalo Bill was simply self-interested. Did he appropriate anti-Mormon images to profit from them? Yes. He grew up in a culture suffused with anti-Mormon prejudice, and he and those who authored his stories brilliantly played on the public aversion to the faith group. Cody used anti-Mormon imagery in his stage performances and dime novels to project himself as the antithesis of the Mormon people in a cultural, racial, and gendered way at a time of transition in American society. He was certainly not the first or the last to tread in anti-Mormon storytelling for personal gain. Cody generally reflected the thoughts about Mormons that Americans held, but this history reveals that he developed a more nuanced, if slightly softer, view of Mormons than did many of his era. It may have been for no other reason than it made sense for his bottom line. He used a representation of Mormons onstage, and then he used them to build up northwest Wyoming for his own personal gain. For Cody it could simply be said that Mormons were good for business.

But this simple explanation belies a more intricate, more complex, story. Cody became acquainted with real Latter-day Saints. He spent time with and among them. He learned that they were not necessarily the caricature that he and some other Americans had perceived them to be. Cody grew impressed by the Saints' industry that had turned arid lands into a thriving society. Buffalo Bill had emulated anti-Mormon stereotypes onstage but sought to emulate Mormon performance in irrigation and urban development in his own town-building endeavor. Whether because of financial interest, a genuine admiration, or something in-between, Cody championed the Latter-day Saints as white American pioneers at a time when most Americans did not seek to include diverse groups in their national story. He boasted of Mormons' success in settling harsh environments of the West and demonstrated his acceptance of the Mormon people. His observations and commentary about the religious group came at the height of his international celebrity. His words helped change the narrative about a reviled, downtrodden people. The Saints were efficient colonizers who had earned the outward acceptance of the most famous American. This helped them assume a veneer of respectability. Their acceptance as American pioneers even supplanted persecution as the primary narrative of the faithful. Even after their acceptance, however, the relationship between Cody and the

Mormons, like so many facets of individual and group life, was at times in harmony and at times in conflict.

The shared story of Buffalo Bill Cody and the Latter-day Saints has been mostly forgotten. There are only a few tangible reminders, most visible in Wyoming's Big Horn Basin. A researcher visiting the Harold McCracken Research Library at the Buffalo Bill Center of the West in Cody, Wyoming, for example, is greeted by a series of quotes from notable western figures plastered on the library's walls, visible on each surface near the ceiling. One of those quotes is from Brigham Young and reads, "This is the right place. Drive on." At first glance it seems odd to include Young's quote, which was so singular to the Mormon experience and settlement in Utah, among more poignant quotes from William F. Cody, Mark Twain, and Native American leaders. Upon deeper reflection, however, Young's quote speaks to the larger place of the West, the place that both Buffalo Bill Cody and the Mormons helped to build and came to represent. For both Buffalo Bill Cody and Mormon settlers, the Big Horn Basin was also the right place.

Just over 120 years after Buffalo Bill Cody met Abraham Woodruff at Eagle's Nest, Wyoming, a meeting that helped facilitate the Saints' settlement in the Big Horn Basin, the enduring presence and population of members of The Church of Jesus Christ of Latter-day Saints had grown to a size sufficient to support the construction of a temple in the region. The temple, a sacred space for religious rituals for believers, had once been a symbol of a suspect, sinister people. It was portrayed as such in Buffalo Bill's stage plays and dime novels. But William Cody came to understand the temple as a monument to Latter-day Saint faith, industry, and perseverance. For believers each temple is a holy place, symbolic for the potential eternal glory of individuals and families.

On October 3, 2021, Russell M. Nelson, president of The Church of Jesus Christ of Latter-day Saints, announced that the church would build a temple in Cody, Wyoming. The next day the *Cody Enterprise*, the newspaper founded by Buffalo Bill in 1899, reported the announcement and added that one in every nine residents of Wyoming, roughly sixty-eight thousand people, claimed membership in The Church of Jesus Christ of

Latter-day Saints. The news brought joy to local Latter-day Saint leader Andrew Jacobson, who declared, "To have a temple here will be a blessing for the entire Big Horn Basin." While the *Enterprise* noted that Wyoming has a significant place in the history of the Latter-day Saint faith, as pioneers had traversed it during their westward migration to Utah, primarily from the 1840s to the 1860s, it made no reference to the vibrant history of the origins of the Saints' settlement in the basin.[1] The announcement and eventual construction of the Latter-day Saint temple in Cody's town brings the story of Buffalo Bill and the Mormons full circle and forever unites the two.

Buffalo Bill was a storyteller, and the Mormons were a part of his story. He told the story of stereotypes, of prejudice, and of hate toward the religious group. He listened to their stories and shared experiences with the faith group. The showman and the faith group then told a shared story, though with different perspectives and desired outcomes. Together they ultimately told a story of friendship and admiration.

The stories we tell are important. Listening to the stories of others is even more important.

Notes

INTRODUCTION

1. The historian Robert E. Bonner has written that "Buffalo Bill was first introduced to the Big Horn Basin of Wyoming in 1894 by his son-in-law, Horton
Boal, and George T. Beck of Sheridan." Cody had interests in the town of
Sheridan but, as Bonner notes, "was looking for something more in the way
of investment when he heard that Beck was looking into irrigation possibilities on the upper reaches of the Stinking Water River, east of Yellowstone
National Park." Buffalo Bill founded the town of Cody in the Big Horn Basin
in 1896; it was incorporated in 1901. Bonner, "Buffalo Bill Cody," 434.

2. Audiences and reviewers of Buffalo Bill's stage performances recognized the
budding star as a "magnificent specimen of a man" and a "handsome fellow"
who moved across the stage in a captivating, graceful manner. Review of
Scouts of the Prairie, clipping, Buffalo Bill Stage Notices and Reviews, Business, Combination, Scrapbooks, 1873–80, Cody Collection, oversize box 40,
HMRL; "'Lost and Won' at the Opera House," *National Republican*, September
27, 1877; see also "Buffalo Bill's Wild West and Congress of Rough Riders of
the World," official programs, 1893–1903, Cody Collection, HMRL and DPL.

3. Cody, *Hon. William F. Cody*, 69–89; W. MacKinnon, *At Sword's Point*, 355–58;
for more on the supposed Mormon rebellion and the concomitant Utah War,
see Rogers, *Unpopular Sovereignty*.

4. "Sixth Annual Tour of the Buffalo Bill Combination in the New and Refined
Sensational Drama, May Cody, or Lost and Won!" Cody Collection, box 12,
folder 2, HMRL, 3; see also Walker, Turley, and Leonard, *Massacre at Mountain Meadows*.

5. M. Jones, *Performing American Identity*, 3.

6. "Buffalo Bill's Wild West and Congress of Rough Riders of the World," program, 1893, Wojtowicz Collection, HMRL, 4.

7. William F. Cody to C. B. Jones, April 9, 1898, Buffalo Bill Letters to George T.
Beck, AHC.

8. Rowley, *Bureau of Reclamation*, 56; Abruzzi, *Dam That River*, 16. The historian Colleen McDannell has stated, "Mormons saw plowing fields, digging ditches, and constructing homes as fundamentally religious acts." McDannell, *Sister Saints*, 4.

9. Twain, *Roughing It*, 92.

10. "The Wild West of Today," *Washington Post*, January 7, 1893.

11. "Buffalo Bill on Utah," *Utah Journal*, February 8, 1893.

12. McDaniel, *World's Columbian Exposition*, 37–38, 53.

13. A. E. Wood, Manager of Payette Valley Real Estate Agency, to Lorenzo Snow, December 27, 1898, Lorenzo Snow General Correspondence, box 2, folder 10, CHL; D. A. Richardson, Investment Broker, to Lorenzo Snow, March 9, 1900, Lorenzo Snow General Correspondence, box 1, folder 39, CHL; W. S. Wallace to Lorenzo Snow, May 8, 1900, Lorenzo Snow General Correspondence, box 2, folder 8, CHL.

14. "'Buffalo Bill' to Raise Horses," *Kansas City Star* (from the *Omaha Bee*), January 21, 1900.

15. Warren, *Buffalo Bill's America*, xi; Martin, "Grandest and Most Cosmopolitan"; Cody, *Hon. William F. Cody*, xv–xvi.

16. For more on the economic climate in Utah and the impetus for a colony in the Big Horn Basin, see, for example, Arrington, "Utah and the Depression," 6; Arrington, *Great Basin Kingdom*, 383; Alexander, *Mormonism in Transition*, 197; and Graham, "Mormon Migration," xi.

17. Graham, "Mormon Migration," 7.

18. C. Welch, *Big Horn Basin*, 52–54, 58.

19. "Lovell Man Recalls Early-Day Work on Yellowstone Park Roads," *Billings Gazette*, April 8, 1956, Irrigation Projects, Sidon Canal, Vertical Files, PCA.

20. C. Welch, *Big Horn Basin*, 58.

21. Wilford Woodruff, journal, March 3, 1900, Woodruff Papers, BYU; C. Welch, *Big Horn Basin*, 58; Bonner, *Cody's Wyoming Empire*, 189.

22. Whiteness is included as a tool of analysis in this history. For studies on and encouragement for the use of whiteness as an analytical tool in Latter-day Saint history, see Reeve, *Different Color*; and Nelson, "Saint History and Culture."

1. SETTING THE STAGE

1. Prior to his marriage to Mary Ann, Isaac had been a widower with one daughter named Martha. William was the third child of Mary Ann and Isaac, having been preceded in birth by Sam in 1841 and Julia in 1843. Warren, *Buffalo Bill's America*, 8; Fryxell, "The Codys in Le Claire"; Wetmore and Grey, *Buffalo Bill*, 1.

2. Articles about Mormons and the difficulties they had in Nauvoo were common features of regional newspapers. The *Davenport Gazette* newspaper, for example, contained numerous articles, editorials, and reports on Mormons each year dating to at least 1842.

3. Untitled, *Daily Missouri Republican*, February 13, 1846.

4. Untitled, *Daily Missouri Republican*, February 19, 1846.

5. Brigham Young, journal, January 18, 1846, CHL; Hosea Stout, journal, January 18, 1846, CHL.

6. Young, journal, January 1–February 3, 1846, CHL.

7. Orson Pratt, journal, July 21, 1847, CHL.

8. The historian Jared Farmer has explained that there is no record of Brigham Young uttering that exact, though now memorialized, phrase. See Farmer, "This Was the Place," 192. Wilford Woodruff wrote, "The camp was called togeather to say whear the City should be built. After a number had spoken on the subject a voat was calld for [and] unanimosiley aggread that this was the spot After that Pres Young said tha[t] he knew that this is the place. he knew it as soon as he came in sight of it and he had seen this vearey spot before." Journal, July 28, 1847, CHL.

9. Godfrey, Godfrey, and Derr, *Women's Voices*, 243; S. Rogers, Reminiscences and Diary, October 12, 1846, CHL.

10. Campbell, *Establishing Zion*, 135–36.

11. Turner, *Brigham Young*, 181–206.

12. Cody, *Hon. William F. Cody*, 19–20.

13. Friesen, "No Swearing or Drinking."

14. Cody, *Hon. William F. Cody*, 32–42; Louisa Frederici Cody, "Memories of Buffalo Bill," typescript, box 22, folder 1, HMRL.

15. Warren, *Buffalo Bill's America*, 9–12.

16. For more on the history of "Bleeding Kansas," see, for example, Etcheson, *Bleeding Kansas*.

17. Cody, *Hon. William F. Cody*, 45–69; Warren, *Buffalo Bill's America*, 10–13.

18. Warren, *Buffalo Bill's America*, 14–17.

19. See Rogers, *Unpopular Sovereignty*.

20. Catholics in New Mexico believed similarly about their religious leaders. See Lamar, *Far Southwest*, 77–87.

21. Sylvester Mowry suggested that several hundred Indians he encountered had received the same education. Lt. Col. Edward J. Steptoe of the U.S. Army, and the leader of Mowry's military contingent, earnestly asked the full support of the government to establish consistency in Indian administration in the territory because the Great Basin Indians did not understand their relation-

ship with the federal government, instead believing the Mormons to be the source of authority. See "List of Camps and Distances from Great Salt Lake City, Utah Territory, to Fort Tejon, California, via Lakes Utah and Sevier— the Santa Clara, Virgin and Mohave Rivers—San Bernardino and Pueblo De los Angeles, Observed by Lieut. J. G. Chandler, 3d Arty on a March under Lieut. S. Mowry 3d Arty in Spring of 1855," Records of the War Department, USHS, 12; and Rogers, *Unpopular Sovereignty*, 120–34.

22. See Rogers, *Unpopular Sovereignty*, 135–54.

23. Turner, *Brigham Young*, 4.

24. Buchanan, "First Annual Message."

25. Cody, *Hon. William F. Cody*, 73, 74; "Cody Chronology," Gray Research Papers, box 4, folder 32, Newberry Library.

26. Cody, *Hon. William F. Cody*, 69.

27. Helen spelled the last name of the general incorrectly; his name was Albert Sidney Johnston. Wetmore and Grey, *Buffalo Bill*, 39–40.

28. Cody, *Hon. William F. Cody*, 79–80, 83.

29. W. MacKinnon, *At Sword's Point*, 331–56.

30. Lewis Simpson, affidavit, November 13, 1857, Research Notebooks, Gray Research Papers, box 19, folder 155, Newberry Library.

31. Russell, *Lives and Legends*, 35; Wells, "Echo Canyon War."

32. William Eads, affidavit, Research Notebooks, Gray Research Papers, box 19, folder 155, Newberry Library.

33. Inman and Cody, *Great Salt Lake Trail*, 130.

34. W. MacKinnon, *At Sword's Point*, 355.

35. For a brief analysis of authorship of Cody's original autobiography, see Cody, *Hon. William F. Cody*, xxxv.

36. Cornwall and Arrington, "Perpetuation of a Myth," 147–49; "Danites."

37. Cornwall and Arrington, "Perpetuation of a Myth," 164–65.

38. Cody, *Hon. William F. Cody*, 85–89.

39. "Life of Buffalo Bill," Cody Collection, box 21, folder 4, HMRL.

40. Russell, "Julia Cody Goodman's Memoirs," 483.

41. Helen provided the wrong month for the Mountain Meadows Massacre, which happened in September, not June, 1857.

42. Wetmore and Grey, *Buffalo Bill*, 39–40.

43. Robert Morris Peck, "Reminiscences," typescript, Research Notebooks, Gray Research Papers, box 5, folder 33, Newberry Library.

44. L. Cody, "Memories of Buffalo Bill," HMRL, 17.

45. "Exploring the Big Horn Basin: Apostle Woodruff and Party Make an Extended Trip; A Land of Vast Resources: Plenty of Room for Homeseekers-

Irrigating Water Will Be Owned by Colonists," *Deseret Evening News*, February 19, 1900.

46. See Gray, "Fact versus Fiction," 12–14; and Warren, *Buffalo Bill's America*, 17–21.

47. Warren, *Buffalo Bill's America*, 22.

48. Ross and Wilson, "Constructing and Appraising"; Taves and Harper, "Joseph Smith's First Vision," 60.

49. Warren, *Buffalo Bill's America*, 21.

50. English, *Mormons*; "Burton's Theatre," *New York Times*, March 18, 1858; Meserve, "Social Awareness on Stage," 96–97.

51. English, *Mormons*.

52. George Clinton Odell, *Annals of the New York Stage*, vol. 8, quoted in Meserve, "Social Awareness on Stage," 96.

53. "Burton's Theatre."

54. Meserve, "Social Awareness on Stage," 96.

55. *Deseret Deserted*, 19.

56. Untitled, *Brooklyn Daily Eagle*, September 12, 1855.

57. See Sylvester Mowry to Edward J. Bicknall, September 17, 1854, Mowry Letters, CHL; and Rogers, *Unpopular Sovereignty*, chap. 2.

58. *Deseret Deserted*, 21.

59. See Rogers, *Unpopular Sovereignty*, 285.

60. An Act to Aid in the Construction of a Railroad and Telegraph Line from the Missouri River to the Pacific Ocean, and to Secure to the Government the Use of the Same for Postal, Military, and Other Purposes, 37th Cong., 2nd Sess. (1862), chap. 120, secs. 2, 9, in Sanger, *Statutes at Large*, 489–98, esp. 492.

61. An Act to Secure Homesteads to Actual Settlers on the Public Domain, 37th Cong. (1862), chap. 75, in Sanger, *Statutes at Large*, 392–93.

62. "Kansas Pacific Railroad," *Freedom's Champion*, August 9, 1862.

63. Richardson, *West from Appomattox*, 79–80.

64. D. R. Gorden, Pioneer Stories, SRL. Gorden arrived in Kansas in 1866 and worked alongside the railroad construction in various positions, including as a telegraph operator.

65. Warren, *Buffalo Bill's America*, 49.

66. J. K. Lull Jr. to Governor Samuel J. Crawford, August 26, 1867; and George W. Spencer to Governor Samuel J. Crawford, August 26, 1867, Records of the Governor's Office, box 32 27-03-06-05, folder 2, KHS.

67. *Denver News*, cited in "Fort Hays," *San Francisco Daily Evening Bulletin*, September 26, 1867.

68. W. E. Webb to Governor Samuel J. Crawford, October 8, 1867, Records of the Governor's Office, box 32 27-03-06-05, folder 18, KHS.

69. "Crumbling Ruins Mark Sites Where Fifty Kansas Towns Once Thrived," *Kansas City Journal-Post*, August 7, 1932, Kansas History Scrapbooks, SRL.

70. Cody, *Hon. William F. Cody*, 149–52.

71. Cody, *Hon. William F. Cody*, 175–88; Gorden, Pioneer Stories, SRL; John O. Stotts, History and War Record of J. O. Stotts, SRL. For more examples of seeing many herds of buffalo in and around urban areas, see *Leavenworth Conservative*, February 22, 1868, March 5, 7, 1868; "Chronology of the Construction of the Union Pacific Railroad the Old Kansas Pacific Railroad," Railroads History Collection, KHS.

72. "Buffalo Hunting," *Kansas Herald of Freedom*, October 10, 1867; "The Enterprise Says," *Freedom's Champion*, June 7, 1866.

73. "Buffalo Hunting," *Harper's Weekly*, December 14, 1867, 797–98.

74. Webb, *Buffalo Land*, 462.

75. Branch, *Hunting of the Buffalo*, 129.

76. "Sketches in the Far West," *Harper's Weekly*, March 21, 1874.

77. See Isenberg, *Destruction of the Bison*, 3, 136–63; and "Sketches in the Far West."

78. Branch, *Hunting of the Buffalo*, 139–40.

79. Cody, *Hon. William F. Cody*, 161–65.

80. "My Greatest Little Horse," Cody Collection, box 21, folder 11, HMRL.

81. J. White, "Hunting Buffalo."

82. Branch, *Hunting of the Buffalo*, 142–43.

83. R. White, *Republic*, 109–15.

84. Warren, *Buffalo Bill's America*, 160.

85. "Chronology of the Construction," KHS.

86. Cahill, "Indian Campaign," 125.

87. Cody, *Hon. William F. Cody*, 304; North, *Man of the Plains*, 114.

88. Cody, *Hon. William F. Cody*, 305–7, 362; Warren, *Buffalo Bill's America*, 113, 116.

89. Cody, *Hon. William F. Cody*, 362–63.

90. Cody, *Hon. William F. Cody*, 373.

91. "Nixon's Amphitheatre," *Chicago Tribune*, December 19, 1872.

2. ON THE STAGE

1. Untitled, *Chicago Tribune*, December 18, 1872.

2. *Scouts of the Prairie*, playbill, Buffalo Bill Stage Notices and Reviews, Business, Combination, Scrapbooks, 1873–80, Cody Collection, oversize box 40, HMRL; Sagala, *Buffalo Bill on Stage*, 22.

3. *Scouts of the Prairie*, playbill, HMRL.

4. *Scouts of the Prairie*, playbill, HMRL.

5. Newspaper clipping, n.d., Buffalo Bill Stage Notices and Reviews, Business, Combination, Scrapbooks, 1873–80, Cody Collection, oversize box 40, HMRL.

6. Sagala, *Buffalo Bill on Stage*, 33, 58; Hall, *Performing the American Frontier*, 58.

7. Newspaper clipping, n.d., HMRL.

8. Buffalo Bill's stage combination performed *The Scouts of the Prairie* in front of audiences in St. Louis, Cincinnati, Albany, Boston, and New York during the 1873 season.

9. H. Smith, *Virgin Land*.

10. Bold, *Selling the Wild West*, 10–12.

11. M. Jones, *Performing American Identity*, 52; Hall, *Performing the American Frontier*, 3.

12. Alexander, *Brigham Young*, 241; Daynes, *More Wives Than One*.

13. M. Jones, *Performing American Identity*, 72.

14. Walker, *Railroading Religion*, 14.

15. Alexander's first name has been alternately spelled as "Sara" and "Sarah"; I have opted for the former.

16. Brimhall, "Sara Alexander."

17. "Mormonism: Lecture Last Evening by Miss Sarah Alexander; Pictures of Salt Lake Society by an Escaped Actress," *Chicago Interocean*, December 2, 1872, Sara Alexander, scrapbooks, CHL; "From the Heart of Brigham Young's Family to the Lecture Field," *Chicago Times*, December 2, 1872, Alexander, scrapbook, CHL; "All the Way from Salt Lake: One of Brigham Young's Actresses in Chicago; A Few Words from Her Concerning the Prophet's Family," *Chicago Times*, December 19, 1872, Alexander, scrapbook, CHL.

18. "From the Heart."

19. Stenhouse, *Expose of Polygamy*; Walker, *Railroading Religion*, 138–43.

20. Beadle, *Brigham's Destroying Angel*; Twain, *Roughing It*, 90–91, 97.

21. "A Mormon Ukase," *Harper's Weekly*, n.d., clipping, Mercaldo Collection, HMRL.

22. Charles Rapp, Miners Delight, Wyoming Territory, to Eva Shepard, Columbia Center, New York, October 15, 1875, Rapp Collection, box 1, folder 6, HMRL.

23. [Francis Lieber], "The Mormons: Shall Utah Be Admitted into the Union?" *Putnam's Monthly*, March 1855, 234; Talbot, *Foreign Kingdom*, 133.

24. See Reeve, *Different Color*.

25. R. White, *Republic*, 5, 136–37.

26. Pearsall, *Polygamy*, 284.

27. Pearsall, *Polygamy*, 286.

28. R. White, *Republic*; Warren, *Buffalo Bill's America*; Richardson, *West from Appomattox*, 30–37.

29. Alexander, *Brigham Young*, 313–14.

30. Turner, *Brigham Young*, 386.

31. Young, *Wife No. 19*, 574–75; R. White, *Republic*, 384.

32. Young, *Wife No. 19*; Bunker and Bitton, *Mormon Graphic Image*, 41.

33. Young, *Wife No. 19*, 568, 108.

34. Young, *Wife No. 19*, 590, 591.

35. Young, *Wife No. 19*, 569.

36. Turner, *Brigham Young*, 387.

37. "The Mountain Meadows Massacre," *Harper's Weekly*, August 14, 1875.

38. Reeve, *Different Color*, 251.

39. "That Bloody Deed: The Press of the Country Put It Where It Belongs," *Salt Lake Daily Tribune*, July 28, 1875, reprinted from the *Virginia Enterprise*.

40. Walker, Turley, and Leonard, *Massacre at Mountain Meadows*, 229–31.

41. "Mountain Meadow Massacre," *Salt Lake Daily Herald*, August 5, 1875; "The Lee Trial," *Salt Lake Daily Tribune*, July 14, 16, 20, 23, August 5, 1875; "The Verdict," *Salt Lake Daily Tribune*, August 8, 1875.

42. "Territorial Dispatches," *Deseret News*, September 20, 1876.

43. "The Lee Trial," *Salt Lake Daily Tribune*, September 20, 21, 1876; "At Last," *Salt Lake Daily Herald*, September 21, 1876; "The Verdict," *Salt Lake Daily Tribune*, September 26, 1876; "John D. Lee," *Salt Lake Daily Herald*, October 11, 1876.

44. "The Great Mormon Crime," *New York Times*, March 24, 1877; "Going Crazy concerning Mormonism," *Deseret News*, April 4, 1877; "All Are Talking of Utah," *Deseret News*, April 11, 1877.

45. Lee, *Mormonism Unveiled*. This book title, interestingly, is almost identical to the first major anti-Mormon exposé: Eber D. Howe's 1834 book *Mormonism Unvailed*.

46. "Among the Mormons," *Harper's Weekly*, January 27, 1872.

47. Twain, *Roughing It*, 90–100.

48. M. Jones, *Performing American Identity*, 92, 103.

49. Hall, *Performing the American Frontier*, 9.

50. "Sixth Annual Tour," 3.

51. "Sixth Annual Tour," 3.

52. "Lost and Won."

53. Mattes, *Indians, Infants, and Infantry*, 242.

54. "Sixth Annual Tour," 3.

55. Austin and Parshall, *Dime Novel Mormons*, ix.

56. "Sixth Annual Tour," 3.

57. Historians and writers continue to grapple with such a representation, while others continue to debate Brigham Young's role in and responsibility for the Mountain Meadows Massacre. See, for example, Bagley, *Blood of the Prophets*; and Walker, Turley, and Leonard, *Massacre at Mountain Meadows*.

58. "Sixth Annual Tour," 3.

59. M. Jones, *Performing American Identity*, 49, 53.

60. "Lost and Won."

61. Since classical times the trope of the endangered female has been employed to stoke outrage among men whose gender identity demands that they protect "helpless" white women from those deemed other. See Greenberg, "Way of the Transgressor," 86.

62. "Amusements," *Washington Post*, September 19, 1878, 4.

63. Foner, *Reconstruction*, 606; Foner, *Short History*, 36; Blight, *Race and Reunion*, 280–85; Ayers, *Promise*.

64. Young, *Wife No. 19*, 32.

65. "May Cody," Business, Combination, Scrapbooks, 1879–80, Cody Collection, oversize box 40, HMRL, 19.

66. Mattes, *Indians, Infants, and Infantry*, 242.

67. Buffalo Bill used a similar formula of instructive object lessons and historical monuments in selling his Wild West show during the next decade. See Martin, "Grandest and Most Cosmopolitan," 93.

68. M. Jones, *Performing American Identity*, 66.

69. "Lost and Won"; Mattes, *Indians, Infants, and Infantry*, 242–44.

70. "The Stage," *Daily Alta California*, March 19, 1879.

71. Sagala, *Buffalo Bill on Stage*, 113.

72. Cody, *Hon. William F. Cody*, 425; Untitled, *Cheyenne Daily Sun*, May 7, 1878; Russell, *Lives and Legends*, 259.

73. Sagala, *Buffalo Bill on Stage*, 123; "Stage"; "Lost and Won"; "Amusements: National Theatre; Buffalo Bill," *National Republican*, September 16, 1878; "Amusements," *Washington Post*.

74. Russell, *Lives and Legends*, 259; "Amusements," *Quincy Daily Herald*, January 25, 1878.

75. "Metropolitan Theater," *Sacramento Daily Union*, April 19, 1879.

76. "Buffalo Bill," *Salt Lake Tribune*, May 1, 1879.

77. "Among the Mormons."

78. Walker, *Railroading Religion*, 159.

79. Sara Alexander, "Recollections of the Mormon Theatre," prepared expressly for the *Dramatic Magazine* from personal observations never before published, Alexander, scrapbook, CHL.

80. Walker, *Railroading Religion*, 163; Lindsay, *Mormons and the Theatre*.

81. Young, *Wife No. 19*, 381.

82. Brigham Young, discourse, March 6, 1862, *Journal of Discourses*, 9:243.

83. Newspaper article, n.d., Alexander, scrapbook, CHL; Alexander, "Recollections," CHL.

84. Advertisement, *Salt Lake Tribune*, May 1, 3, 1879; Sagala, *Buffalo Bill on Stage*, 118–19.

85. Sagala, *Buffalo Bill on Stage*, 118–19.

86. "Buffalo Bill," *Deseret Evening News*, May 3, 1879.

87. Wetmore and Grey, *Buffalo Bill*, xiii; Joy Kasson, *Buffalo Bill's Wild West*, 28.

88. The historian David Blight has written about memoirs among Civil War veterans catching the attention of the American public in the 1870s. See Blight, *Race and Reunion*, 161.

89. Joy Kasson, *Buffalo Bill's Wild West*, 28.

90. Cody, *Hon. William F. Cody*, xvi.

91. For more on the details of the Reynolds case and its place in the Reconstruction era, see Gordon, *Mormon Question*, 119–44.

92. Reynolds v. United States, 98 U.S. 145 (1879), 166.

93. Gordon, *Mormon Question*, 130.

94. Reynolds v. United States, 98 U.S. 145 (1879), 166; see also Gordon, *Mormon Question*, 119–44.

95. Hayes, "Third Annual Message."

96. Hayes, "Fourth Annual Message."

3. A SCENE CHANGE

1. "John A. Stevens Dead," *New York Times*, June 18, 1916.

2. "Buffalo Bill as a Man of His Word," *St. Paul Globe*, October 28, 1901.

3. "Amusements," *Milwaukee Chronicle*, n.d., "May Cody," HMRL, 19.

4. Warren, *Buffalo Bill's America*, 194.

5. Garfield, "Inaugural Address."

6. Arthur, "First Annual Message."

7. Talbot, *Foreign Kingdom*, 147.

8. "The Law and the Mormons," *Harper's Weekly*, December 31, 1881.

9. Utah Commission, *Edmunds Act*, 3–5; Amendment to 5350 U.S.C., in *Compiled Laws of Utah*, 110–13.

10. William Cody to Julia Cody Goodman, September 24, 1883; Ed Goodman to Al and Julia Goodman, March 17, 1887, both in Foote, *Letters from "Buffalo Bill,"* 33, 47.

11. Mason, *Mormon Menace*, 66.

12. For more on the early effort of Latter-day Saints to combat rhetoric about sexuality, see Rogers, *Unpopular Sovereignty*, 222–24.

13. Ulrich, *House Full of Females*, 241.

14. Jenson, *Latter-day Saint Biographical Encyclopedia*, 1:714.

15. Junius F. Wells, remarks delivered in the tabernacle, July 12, 1885, *Journal of Discourses*, 26:269–76.

16. Charles C. Goodwin, "The Mormon Situation," *Harper's Magazine*, October 1881, 763.

17. Thomas Nast, "More Cheap Help-Mates for Mr. Polygamist," *Harper's Weekly*, March 25, 1882.

18. James Buchanan to Lord Clarendon, confidential letter, April 8, 1859, in Moore, *Works of James Buchanan*, 318.

19. William M. Evarts to Diplomatic Officers of the United States, August 9, 1879, in *Papers Relating*, 11–12.

20. Lord Salisbury to W. J. Hoppin, September 5, 1879, in *Papers Relating*, 465.

21. Cleveland, "First Annual Message."

22. "Curiosities of Immigration," *San Francisco Daily Evening Bulletin*, August 9, 1879.

23. "The Question of Mormon Rights," *New York Times*, August 13, 1879.

24. Hirota, *Expelling the Poor*.

25. For more on the 1882 Chinese Exclusion Act in context and the virulent Sinophobia of the 1880s, see, for example, Painter, *History of White People*, 234; Hahn, *Nation without Borders*, 412; and R. White, *Republic*, 380–81.

26. "The Wild West: Buffalo Bill's Great Show Booked for Next Week," *Wheeling Register*, October 1, 1884.

27. Warren, *Buffalo Bill's America*, 212–28.

28. Basso, McCall, and Garceau, *Across the Great Divide*, 117.

29. Warren, *Buffalo Bill's America*, 215.

30. H. Smith, *Virgin Land*, 109.

31. Hopkins, *Life among the Piutes*.

32. "Buffalo Bill and His Play: From the Omaha Herald," *Salt Lake Herald*, February 25, 1886.

33. "Route Schedules, Season '86," Cody Collection, box 10, folder 2, HMRL; advertisement, *Ogden Herald*, February 23, 1886; "Buffalo Bill," *Ogden Herald*, February 24, 1886; "The Prairie Waif," *Ogden Herald*, February 26, 1886.

34. "Buffalo Bill and His Play."

35. "Union Opera House! One Night," *Ogden Herald*, February 23, 1886; "Prairie Waif," February 26, 1886.

36. "The Prairie Waif," *Ogden Herald*, February 27, 1886.

37. "Personal," *Salt Lake Herald*, February 27, 1886.

38. "Buffalo Bill," *Salt Lake Herald*, February 27, 1886; "Dramatic and Lyric," *Salt Lake Herald*, February 28, 1886.

39. Untitled, *Salt Lake Herald*, January 9, 1887.

40. "Amusements," *Salt Lake Herald*, February 26, 1886.

41. "Salvini," *Salt Lake Tribune*, February 26, 1886; "Salvini at the Theater," *Salt Lake Tribune*, February 27, 1886.

42. Advertisement, *Salt Lake Tribune*, February 25, 1886; "Salvini."

43. "Dramatic and Lyric."

44. Warren, *Buffalo Bill's America*, 282–83.

45. Griffin, *Four Years in Europe*, xviii; Foote, *Letters from "Buffalo Bill,"* 33.

46. "Victoria and Buffalo Bill," *Deseret News*, May 25, 1887; see also Warren, *Buffalo Bill's America*, 282–340; and Joy Kasson, *Buffalo Bill's Wild West*, 65–92.

47. Cody, *Wild West in England*, 78–79.

48. Warren, *Buffalo Bill's America*, 283–86.

49. Ellis, *Law and Order*, 170; Andreas, *Andreas' History*.

50. Cody to Bierbower, May 21, 1887, CHL. The postmark has Ogden, Utah, but was forwarded by the postal service to Hailey.

51. Warren, *Buffalo Bill's America*, 298.

52. "Anti-Mormonism in Wales," *Deseret News*, October 17, 1888.

53. Madsen, *Emmeline B. Wells*, 246.

54. Edmunds-Tucker Act, 49th Cong., 2nd Sess. (1887), vol. 24, chap. 397, in Sanger, *Statutes at Large*, 635–37.

55. Gordon, *Mormon Question*, 180–81, 211–12; Daynes, *More Wives Than One*, 173–75.

56. Late Corporation of The Church of Jesus Christ of Latter-day Saints v. United States, 136 U.S. 1 (1890).

57. Bennett, *Temples Rising*, 268–69.

58. Cannon and O'Higgins, *Under the Prophet*, 35.

59. W. Woodruff, journal, September 25, 1890, CHL.

60. "Official Declaration," *Deseret Evening News*, September 25, 1890.

61. Nearly a year earlier, the First Presidency used this language in another official declaration to combat the "gross misrepresentations of the doctrine, aims and practices" of the church, particularly as it related to rumors about "blood atonement." That official declaration further denied that the church was or

sought to be a temporal kingdom on the earth. Wilford Woodruff, George Q. Cannon, and Joseph F. Smith, "Official Declaration," December 12, 1889, in J. Clark, *Messages*, 184–87.

62. "Official Declaration."

63. "The Abolition of Polygamy," *Harper's Weekly*, November 1, 1890.

64. Ingraham produced many dime novels in the late nineteenth century; he was also a prominent promoter of Buffalo Bill's Wild West show. Austin and Parshall, *Dime Novel Mormons*, xiv.

65. "In the Grand Canon, Buffalo Bill Describes the Inspiring Scenery," *New York Advertiser*, June 24, 1894, Salsbury Collection, DPL.

66. Burke, *Buffalo Bill*. Here is a list of participants, according to Burke: "Col. W. F. Cody (Buffalo Bill); Col. Frank D. Baldwin, U.S. Army; Col. W. H. MacKinnon, Grenadier Guards, England; Maj. St. John Mildmay, Grenadier Guards; Col. Allison Nailor, Washington DC; Maj. John M. Burke (Arizona John); Col. Prentiss Ingraham, Washington DC; Hon. George P. Everhart, Chicago; Elder Daniel Seigmiller, Utah; Elder Junius Wells, Utah; Robert H. Haslam (Pony Bob); Horton S. Boal, Nebraska; Edward Bradford, Denver; William B. Dowd, New York; and John Hance, Guide of Grand Cañon of the Colorado."

67. Seegmiller, *Legacy of Eternal Worth*, 47–48.

68. Burke, *Buffalo Bill*.

69. Seegmiller, *Legacy of Eternal Worth*, 47–48.

70. Burke, *Buffalo Bill*.

71. "Col. Cody's Hunting Party Disbands," *Chicago Tribune*, December 11, 1892.

72. Junius F. Wells, journal, October 19, 23–25, November 4, 1892, Wells Papers, box 1, folder 15, CHL.

73. Wells, journal, November 10, 1892, CHL; Rust, "V. T. Ranch Hotel," 356; Kimball, *Mary E. Woolley Chamberlain*, 120 (my thanks to David and Grant Barnes for showing me this source from their family history); Burke, *Buffalo Bill*.

74. "Col. Ingraham's Letter, No. 4: In the Saddle with Buffalo Bill," *New York Banner Weekly*, February 25, 1893.

75. "Col. Ingraham's Letter."

76. Wells, journal, November 28, 29, 1892, CHL.

77. "Col. Cody's Hunting Party."

78. "The Buffalo Bill Party," *Salt Lake Daily Tribune*, December 7, 1892.

79. "Hero of the Plains: Buffalo Bill and His Britishers Dash into the City; A Broncho Trip from Arizona: Their Perilous Trip through the Rugged Grand Canyon Country; Looking for a Big Game Preserve," *Salt Lake Herald*, December 7, 1892.

80. "In the Grand Canon"; "Hero of the Plains"; Burke, *Buffalo Bill*.

81. "In the Grand Canon"; "Hero of the Plains."

82. "In the Grand Canon"; "Hero of the Plains."

83. Wells, journal, November 29, 1892, CHL.

84. "Buffalo Bill Party."

85. Winchester, "God Bless the Hands."

86. Kimball, *Mary E. Woolley Chamberlain*, 120–22.

87. "Col. Cody's Hunting Party."

88. "Hero of the Plains."

89. Wells, journal, November 29, December 5–6, 1892, CHL; "Hero of the Plains."

90. "Buffalo Bill Party."

91. George Q. Cannon, journal, December 7, 1892, *Journal of George Q. Cannon*.

92. W. Woodruff, journal, December 7, 1892, CHL.

93. "Took in the City, Buffalo Bill and His Party See the Sights," *Salt Lake Herald*, December 8, 1892.

94. "Wild West of Today."

95. Wells, journal, December 7, 1892, CHL.

96. "Wild West of Today."

97. "Took in the City."

98. Wells, journal, December 8, 1892, CHL.

99. Lyman, *Political Deliverance*, 5, 76–79; Neilson, *Exhibiting Mormonism*, 17, 40–41; Alexander, *Mormonism in Transition*.

100. William F. Cody to Junius F. Wells, December 22, 24, 1892, Wells Papers, box 2, folder 4, CHL.

101. "Buffalo Bill on Utah."

102. "Wild West of Today."

103. "In the Grand Canon."

104. W. Cody to Wells, December 24, 1892, CHL.

105. "Hero of the Plains"; W. Cody to Wells, December 24, 1892, CHL.

106. "Wild West Heroes," *Chicago Daily Inter Ocean*, December 23, 1892, reprinted as "Some Western Heroes," *Galveston Daily News*, January 1, 1893; "In the Grand Canon."

107. "Wild West of Today."

108. "In the Grand Canon."

109. Harrison, "Proclamation 346"; "Wild West of Today."

4. ON THE WORLD'S STAGE

1. "Chicago 1893, World's Fair May to Nov," route schedules, Cody Collection, box 10, folder 2, HMRL.

2. Joy Kasson, *Buffalo Bill's Wild West*, 99.

3. "Buffalo Bill's Wild West," program, 1893, HMRL, 4.

4. Promotional images of the congress highlighted the "Wild Rivalries of Savage, Barbarous, and Civilized Races," where American Indian, Arab, and other ethnic riders trailed the majestic-looking Buffalo Bill. See Joy Kasson, *Buffalo Bill's Wild West*, 54.

5. *The Rough Rider*, 1st ed., Cody Collection, DPL, 1:2.

6. Edwards, *New Spirits*, 6.

7. Rotundo, *American Manhood*, 4–8; see also Gorn, *Manly Art*.

8. "Buffalo Bill's Wild West," official programs, 1893–1903, HMRL.

9. "Buffalo Bill's Wild West," program, 1893, HMRL, 21.

10. "Buffalo Bill's Wild West," program, 1893, HMRL, 23–25, 36–52, 61–63.

11. "Buffalo Bill Wild West," program, 1893, HMRL, 26.

12. Kimmel, *Manhood in America*, 151; "Buffalo Bill's Wild West," program, 1893, HMRL, 21.

13. Richardson, *How the South Won*, 96.

14. Early short films would eventually come to present the same construction of whiteness. See Bernardi, *Birth of Whiteness*.

15. Joy Kasson, *Buffalo Bill's Wild West*, 119.

16. "Buffalo Bill's Wild West," programs, 1897, 1898, HMRL.

17. Fulbright and Stehno, *Oklahoma Rough Rider*, 104.

18. Warren, *Buffalo Bill's America*, 128.

19. Painter, *Standing at Armageddon*, xxi.

20. This included other white men, particularly Europeans, who were viewed as overcivilized, corpulent, or more feminine. Debates and discourse about whiteness and racial gradations among "whites" were common at the turn of the twentieth century, as European immigrants continued to pour into the borders of the United States. See Jacobson, *Whiteness*.

21. *Rough Rider*, 4th ed., Cody Collection, DPL, 3:2.

22. Turner, "Significance of the Frontier," 199–227; Billington, *Frederick Jackson Turner*.

23. Richardson, *How the South Won*, 112–14; Sharp, "Evolution of the West," 232; Drinnon, *Facing West*.

24. Higham and Katerberg, *Conquests and Consequences*, 7.

25. "Notable People at Buffalo Bill's," *Chicago Tribune*, September 10, 1893.

26. Joseph F. Smith, personal photographs, A-Sh, Cody, William Frederick, PH 2016, CHL.

27. W. Woodruff, journal, September 7, 1893, CHL, 32; Cannon, September 7, 1893, *Journal of George Q. Cannon*.

28. Cannon, September 8, 1893, *Journal of George Q. Cannon.*

29. K. Smith, "Appropriating the Secular," 179.

30. Hansen, *Frontier Religion*, 178.

31. W. Woodruff, journal, September 8, 1893, CHL, 33.

32. Walker, *Railroading Religion*, 191; for more on Latter-day Saint efforts to combat negative representations and take ownership of their image, see Grow, "Contesting the LDS Image."

33. Ingraham, *Seventy Years*, 61, 67.

34. Julian Ralph, "A Week with the Mormons," *Harper's Weekly*, April 8, 1893.

35. Ralph, "Week with the Mormons."

36. Ralph, "Week with the Mormons"; Powell, *Arid Lands*, 16. The Latter-day Saint system of irrigation required a high degree of community cooperation and willingness to accede to the established religious authority in the distribution of a resource that was essentially under common ownership for the welfare of the community. John Wesley Powell had admired the Saints' accomplishments, though he was unsure if their system of irrigation could be replicated outside of a cohesive religious community. Such a system would require a firm authority to enact. Rowley, *Bureau of Reclamation*, 56–57.

37. Powell, *Arid Lands*, 19–20.

38. Ralph, "Week with the Mormons."

39. E. A. McDaniel, "Utah World's Fair Commission," *Salt Lake Herald*, March 1, 1893.

40. McDaniel, *World's Columbian Exposition*, 37–38.

41. McDaniel, *World's Columbian Exposition*, 37, 41, 44.

42. E. A. McDaniel, secretary's report, Utah World's Fair Commission, read in legislature, February 1, 1894, in McDaniel, *World's Columbian Exposition*, 79.

43. McDaniel, *World's Columbian Exposition*, 53.

44. Walker, *Railroading Religion*, 237.

45. Worster, *Rivers of Empire*, 77.

46. Neilson, *Exhibiting Mormonism*, 76, 79, 95, 99, 180.

47. Merrill, "Tabernacle Choir," 569.

48. McDaniel, *World's Columbian Exposition*, 41–42, 37–38, 53.

49. Rowley, *Bureau of Reclamation*, 47–48.

50. Wilkerson, *Caste*, 125.

51. Patterson, *Pioneers in the Attic*, 26; Farmer, *On Zion's Mount*, 370–72. Non-Mormons allowed their conception of God to expand to include Mormons as believing in the same God who oversaw the Manifest Destiny of the United States. This thinking allowed Mormons to be considered successful pioneers.

52. Pisani, *Divided West*, 236–37; Rowley, *Bureau of Reclamation*, 77–79.

53. Smythe, *Conquest of Arid America*, 55–56, 55, 52, 56.

54. See Reeve, *Different Color*.

55. Painter, *History of White People*, 235; Jacobson, *Whiteness*.

56. Scholar Ibram X. Kendi discusses the intellectual process of normalization, justification, and rationalization of racist ideas. I have employed his model for generalizing group negativity here. See Kendi, *Stamped from the Beginning*, 43.

57. Heber M. Wells to William McKinley, May 1, 1897, CHL.

58. Nytroe, "Taming the Past," 128.

59. Charles O. Whittemore to the President, July 14, 1897, McKinley Correspondence, CHL.

60. Joseph F. Smith, "Address Given at the Tabernacle on (Sunday) July 25, 1897," *Deseret Semi-Weekly News*, July 26, 1897.

61. Nytroe, "Taming the Past," 132; Painter, *History of White People*, 264.

62. West, *Last Indian War*, 319.

63. Speaking to this moment, which equated true Americans with pioneers, the historian Frank Van Nuys has written, "The importance of being white pioneers, or at least possessing a direct link to white pioneer antecedents, needs to be understood as a vital frame of reference for immigration and Americanization in Western states. . . . Race factored mightily in constructing an American identity in the West." Van Nuys, *Race, Immigrants, and Citizenship*, 3, 9, 11.

64. R. White, *Republic*, 589–92.

65. Taylor, *Racial Frontier*, 19; R. White, *Republic*, 861.

66. Peterson and Cannon, *Awkward State of Utah*, 2, 19.

67. Pioneer celebrations depicted a history worthy of commendation. Latter-day Saint celebrations demonstrated the industriousness, diligence, and efficiency of their forebears in becoming an archetypal American success story. Haws, "Mormons at Mid-Century," 202–5.

68. Bonner, "Buffalo Bill Cody," 434.

69. Beck, *Beckoning Frontiers*, 202–5.

70. Beck, *Beckoning Frontiers*, x, liv, 202–3.

71. Beck, *Beckoning Frontiers*, 205.

72. Charles H. Morrill to Charles E. Perkins, November 4, 1899, Chicago, Burlington, and Quincy Railroad Company Records, Newberry Library.

73. Pisani, *Divided West*, 73.

74. "A Cody Enterprise," *Rough Rider*, 1st ed., season of 1899, Wojtowicz Collection, HMRL, 1:12.

75. Graham, "Mormon Migration," 6.

76. A. MacKinnon, *Public Waters*, 30.

77. "Letter from State Engineer," *Rough Rider*, 1st ed., season of 1899, Wojtowicz Collection, HMRL, 1:12.

78. Beck, *Beckoning Frontiers*, 215.

79. "'Buffalo Bill' to Raise Horses." Estimates of Cody's holdings vary. In a later newspaper article, Cody claimed that through the Shoshone Irrigation Company "we got a concession from the State for 300,000 acres, went to building a canal and got settlers." "Colonel William F. Cody: Buffalo Bill," *Dallas Morning News*, July 20, 1901.

80. Morrill to Perkins, November 4, 1899, Newberry Library; Wasden, *From Beaver to Oil*, 163.

81. Wasden, *From Beaver to Oil*, 164.

82. Worster, *Rivers of Empire*, 131; Pisani, *Divided West*, 105; Porter, "Hydraulic West," 335; "The Cody Colony," *Salt Lake Tribune*, March 5, 1898.

83. Powell, *Arid Lands*, 21.

84. W. Cody to J. Cody Goodman, May 20, 1901, in Foote, *Letters from "Buffalo Bill,"* 67.

85. "Of Women," *Baltimore Sun*, April 3, 1898.

86. Cody to Jones, April 9, 1898, AHC.

87. Inman and Cody, *Great Salt Lake Trail*, 111.

88. Inman and Cody, *Great Salt Lake Trail*, 141–42.

89. Inman and Cody, *Great Salt Lake Trail*, 132.

5. NEGOTIATING OPPORTUNITIES

1. Most of the men in the regiment came from the western territories of New Mexico, Arizona, Oklahoma, and Indian Territory, but the occupations of the men do not appear to match up to the public image. While cowboys made up the single highest occupation, with 160 registered, they constituted only approximately 15 percent of the total regiment. Furthermore, only 6 hunters are recorded among all the Rough Riders, while miners constituted the second-highest occupation with 87, approximately 8 percent; ranchers were 4 percent and cattlemen 1 percent. As for Roosevelt's Rough Riders who later performed in the Wild West show, there were 6 cowboys (24 percent), 3 ranchers (12 percent), 2 cattlemen (8 percent), and no miners or hunters. The statistics used come from Buffalo Bill Wild West route books for the 1899 through 1902 seasons, HMRL; and Virgil Carrington Jones's book *Roosevelt's Rough Riders*.

2. Roosevelt, *Rough Riders*, 15–16.

3. "Buffalo Bill's Wild West," programs, 1898, 1899, HMRL.

4. "Breaking Wild Horses: Buffalo Bill's 'Bronco Busters' Prepare New Stock for the Coming Season," *New York Times*, April 17, 1902.

5. Beck, *Beckoning Frontiers*, 222.

6. *Rough Rider*, 2nd ed., season of 1900, HMRL, 2:14.

7. "Cody Enterprise," HMRL, 1:12.

8. "Cody Enterprise," HMRL, 1:12.

9. "Letter from State Engineer," HMRL, 1:12.

10. A. H. Whitaker to George T. Beck, July 29, 1899, Beck Papers, box 2, folder 2, AHC.

11. *Homes in the Big Horn Basin*, Shoshone Irrigation Company, brochure, Decade Subject File, New Lines, Wyoming, 1896–1901, Chicago, Burlington, and Quincy Railroad Company Records, box 166, folder 1223, Newberry Library.

12. Bonner, "Buffalo Bill Cody," 437; "Cody's Irrigation Scheme," *Salt Lake Tribune*, December 31, 1896; Beck, *Beckoning Frontiers*, 222.

13. "Cody's Irrigation Scheme"; Morrill to Perkins, November 22, 1899, Newberry Library.

14. William F. Cody to George B. Harris, March 31, 1896, July 31, 1896, October 6, 1896, Chicago, Burlington, and Quincy Railroad Company Records, box 144, folder 2098, Newberry Library; Thomas E. Calvert, Lincoln, Nebraska, to George W. Holdrege, General Manager, Omaha, Nebraska, September 4, 1896, Decade Subject File, New Lines, Wyoming, 1896–1901, Chicago, Burlington, and Quincy Railroad Company Records, box 166, folder 1223, Newberry Library.

15. Warren, *Buffalo Bill's America*, 489.

16. William F. Cody to George T. Beck, March 9, 1899, March 10, 1899, Beck Papers, box 2, folder 1, AHC.

17. Nate Salsbury to George T. Beck, April 5, 1899, Beck Papers, box 2, folder 1, AHC.

18. W. Cody to Beck, April 23, 1899, AHC.

19. Morrill to Perkins, November 4 and 22, 1899, Newberry Library.

20. Arrington, "Utah and the Depression," 6; Arrington, *Great Basin Kingdom*, 383; Alexander, *Mormonism in Transition*, 197.

21. Quoted in Graham, "Mormon Migration," xi.

22. Arrington, *Great Basin Kingdom*, 400–403.

23. Larson, *History of Wyoming*, 295.

24. Abraham O. Woodruff, journal, July 6, 1899, Woodruff Papers, box 1, folder 2, BYU, 94.

25. Charles Kingston to Abraham O. Woodruff, June 12, 1899, Woodruff Papers, box 5, folder 11, BYU.

26. A. Woodruff, journal, July 17–27, 1899, July 25, 1899, BYU.

27. A. Woodruff, journal, July 27, 1899, July 30, 1899, BYU.

28. A. Woodruff, journal, August 24–25, 1899, September 25, 1899, November 9, 1899, January 12, 1900, BYU.

29. Charles Kingston to George T. Beck, October 17, 1899, Beck Papers, box 2, folder 2, AHC.

30. Curtis L. Hinkle, State Board of Land Commissioners, to Abraham O. Woodruff, December 27, 1899, Woodruff Papers, box 5, folder 8, BYU.

31. Kingston to A. Woodruff, January 17, 1900, BYU.

32. Cody's overture to Kingston is apparently no longer extant. It is referenced in Charles Kingston to William F. Cody, December 29, 1899, Woodruff Papers, box 5, folder 11, BYU.

33. Kingston to Cody, December 29, 1899, BYU.

34. Kingston to A. Woodruff, January 19, 1900, BYU.

35. Charles Kingston to DeForest Richards, February 1, 1900, Woodruff Papers, box 5, folder 11, BYU.

36. Kingston to Richards, December 30, 1899, enclosure in Kingston to A. Woodruff, January 3, 1900, BYU.

37. Abraham Woodruff to DeForest Richards, March 30, 1900, Woodruff Papers, Letterbook, BYU.

38. Kingston to Richards, February 1, 1900, BYU.

39. William F. Cody to Michael R. Russell, December 27, 1899, Cody Collection, box 13, folder 39, HMRL.

40. George T. Beck to the Board of Directors of the Shoshone Irrigation Company, March 9, 1900, Beck Papers, box 20, folder 9, AHC.

41. Wood to Snow, December 27, 1898, CHL; Richardson to Snow, March 9, 1900, CHL; Wallace to Snow, May 8, 1900, CHL.

42. "'Buffalo Bill' to Raise Horses."

43. Charles F. Manderson to Charles E. Perkins, March 8, 1900, Chicago, Burlington, and Quincy Railroad Company Records, Newberry Library.

44. Larson, *History of Wyoming*, 108.

45. Kingston to Richards, December 30, 1899, enclosure in Kingston to A. Woodruff, January 3, 1900, BYU.

46. DeForest Richards to Charles Kingston, January 2, 1900, enclosure in Kingston to A. Woodruff, January 3, 1900, BYU; see also DeForest Richards to Abraham O. Woodruff, January 2, 1900, Woodruff Papers, box 5, folder 19, BYU.

47. Kingston to A. Woodruff, January 17, 1900, BYU.

48. A. Woodruff, journal, January 12, 16, 22, 1900, BYU.

49. A. Woodruff, journal, January 5, 1900, BYU, 171; A. Woodruff to Richards, March 30, 1900, Woodruff Papers, Letterbook, BYU.

50. George T. Beck, "Report to Directors," January 14, 1900, Beck Papers, box 20, folder 9, AHC.

51. Beck to Kingston, January 1900, enclosure no longer extant, referenced in Kingston to A. Woodruff, January 19, 1900, BYU.

52. Kingston to A. Woodruff, January 19, 1900, BYU.

53. "'Buffalo Bill' to Raise Horses"; "City and Neighborhood," *Salt Lake Tribune*, January 15, 1900.

54. "Big Horn Basin Colonization: Officials of the State of Wyoming Make a Social and Friendly Call upon the First Presidency and Express Pleasure at the Prospects," *Deseret Evening News*, February 5, 1900; A. Woodruff, journal, February 5, 1900, BYU.

55. "Big Horn Basin Colonization"; A. Woodruff, journal, February 5, 1900, BYU.

56. An article in the *Deseret Evening News* reporting on this trip outlined the growth of the Latter-day Saint contingent. The article stated, "At Ogden they were joined by Elders George H. Taggart, Wm. G. Simmons, John J. Simmons and Chas. A. Welch of Morgan City, and John Croft of Enterprise, Morgan county, Utah. At Pocatello, the party was further increased by Elder B. L. Tippets and W. B. Graham of Bennington, Bishop W. P. Larson of Thomas Fork, and S. P. Sorenson and John Stevens of Montpelier, Bear Lake county, Idaho." "Exploring the Big Horn Basin."

57. A. Woodruff, journal, February 6–8, 1900, BYU; "Exploring the Big Horn Basin."

58. A. Woodruff, journal, February 8, 1900, BYU; "Exploring the Big Horn Basin."

59. C. Welch, *Big Horn Basin*, 56.

60. A. Woodruff, journal, February 8, 1900, BYU; "Exploring the Big Horn Basin."

61. Inman and Cody, *Great Salt Lake Trail*, 131.

62. C. Welch, *Big Horn Basin*, 58; Fillerup, *Sidon*, 10.

63. C. Welch, *Big Horn Basin*, 58–60; A. Woodruff, journal, February 6–8, 1900, BYU.

64. A. Welch, *Frederick Arza Welch*, 12; C. Welch, *Big Horn Basin*, 58.

65. A. Welch, *Frederick Arza Welch*, 12.

66. "Exploring the Big Horn Basin."

67. A. Woodruff, journal, February 12–14, 1900, BYU.

68. "Exploring the Big Horn Basin."

69. "The Visiting Committee of Land Locators," *Cody Enterprise*, February 8, 1900; see also "Cody and Mormons," *Salt Lake Herald*, February 20, 1900.

70. "Mormons to Wyoming," *Omaha World-Herald*, February 25, 1900.

71. "Cody and Mormons."

72. A. Woodruff, journal, February 18–19, 1900, BYU.

73. A. Woodruff, journal, March 3, 1900, BYU; C. Welch, *Big Horn Basin*, 58; Bonner, *Cody's Wyoming Empire*, 189.

74. C. Welch, *Big Horn Basin*, 58.

75. A. Woodruff, journal, March 2, 3, 1900, BYU.

76. Abraham Woodruff to Fenimore Chatterton, March 7, 1900; Abraham Woodruff to W. M. Ryan, March 8, 1900; Abraham Woodruff to Robert G. Fraser, March 26, 1900; Abraham Woodruff to Joseph Tomlinson, March 10, 1900, all in Woodruff Papers, Letterbook, box 1, folder 5, BYU.

77. A. Woodruff to Chatterton, March 7, 1900, BYU.

78. Permit 2111, Records of the Bureau of Reclamation, Shoshone Project, box 912, entry 3, folder 958, NARA; "Brief Early History of Shoshone Project," Irrigation Projects, Sidon Canal, Vertical Files, PCA; C. Welch, *Big Horn Basin*, 56–60.

79. A. Woodruff, journal, March 3, 1900, BYU; C. Welch, *Big Horn Basin*, 58; Bonner, *Cody's Wyoming Empire*, 189.

80. C. Welch, *Big Horn Basin*, 58–60.

81. A. Woodruff to Chatterton, March 10, 7, 1900, BYU; David P. Woodruff to DeForest Richards, April 4, 1900, RG 0001.15, Governor DeForest Richards, Administrative Records, General Correspondence, box 10, folder Win-Wy, WSA.

82. Abraham O. Woodruff to William F. Cody, March 15, 1900, Woodruff Papers, Letterbook, box 1, folder 5, BYU.

83. A. Woodruff to W. Cody, March 15, 1900, BYU.

84. A. Woodruff to Richards, March 15, 1900, BYU.

85. William F. Cody to Abraham O. Woodruff, March 20, 1900, Cody Collection, box 14, folder 1, HMRL.

86. A. Woodruff to W. Cody, March 22, 1900, BYU.

87. William F. Cody to Charles F. Manderson, March 5, 1900, Chicago, Burlington, and Quincy Railroad Company Records, Big Horn Basin, Newberry Library.

88. W. Cody to Manderson, March 5, 1900, Newberry Library.

89. Manderson to Perkins, March 8, 1900, Newberry Library.

90. George W. Holdrege to Charles E. Perkins, February 22, 1900, Chicago, Burlington, and Quincy Railroad Company Records, Big Horn Basin, Newberry Library.

91. Mary Lowe Dickinson, New York City, to Mrs. Thaddeus M. Mahon, Chambersburg PA, October 1899; Sara Melissa Ingersoll to Miss Helen Miller

Gould, November 27, 1899, both in Mormon Miscellaneous Collection, NYPL; Sillito, *B. H. Roberts*.

92. William F. Cody to Charles E. Perkins, April 2, 1900, Chicago, Burlington, and Quincy Railroad Company Records, Big Horn Basin, box 179, folder 2784, Newberry Library.

93. Cody, quoted in "Buffalo Bill, the Cowboy King," *Echo*, December 31, 1902.

6. THE SAINTS SETTLE CODY COUNTRY

1. A. Woodruff, journal, April 6, 1900, March 26, 1900, May 26, 1900, BYU.

2. A. Woodruff, journal, May 5, 12, 14, 1900, BYU.

3. A. Woodruff, journal, May 4, 1900, BYU.

4. C. Welch, *Big Horn Basin*, 65–66.

5. A. Woodruff, journal, April 23–May 28, 1900, BYU; C. Welch, *Big Horn Basin*, 65–66; Charles A. Welch, "Mormons in the Big Horn Basin," *Basin Republican*, January 10, 1908, Churches, Mormon (LDS), Powell, Vertical Files, PCA. Some later colonists took an alternate route from Utah to the Big Horn Basin. The point of divergence was after crossing the Owl Creek Mountains; these later settlers would go to Thermopolis and then down the Bighorn River to the town of Basin and thence to Burlington. From Burlington they would head north to the Shoshone River and ford it to get to the towns of Byron and Cowley.

6. A. Woodruff, journal, May 18, 1900, BYU.

7. Patty S. Mann, interview in Graham, "Mormon Migration," 38.

8. Black, *Mother Stood Tall*, 49.

9. A. Woodruff, journal, May 22–23, 1900, BYU.

10. Biography of Byron Sessions, Sessions Collection, CHL.

11. A. Woodruff, journal, May 28, 1900, BYU.

12. A. Woodruff, journal, May 28, 29, 1900, BYU.

13. Hatch, *Danish Apostle*, 86.

14. DeForest Richards to Abraham O. Woodruff, September 14, 1900, Governor DeForest Richards, Administrative Records, Governor's Letterbook 3, WSA, 281.

15. Charles Kingston to DeForest Richards, August 26, 1901, Governor DeForest Richards, General Correspondence, Ba-Bl, box 5, WSA; DeForest Richards to Charles Kingston, September 10, 1901, Governor DeForest Richards, Administrative Records, Governor's Letterbook, WSA, 438.

16. Richards to A. Woodruff, September 4, 1900, December 29, 1900, BYU.

17. DeForest Richards to William F. Cody, June 21, 1902, Governor DeForest Richards, Administrative Records, Governor's Letterbook, WSA, 451–52; Richards to W. Cody, September 4, 1900, WSA.

18. Richards to W. Cody, September 4, 1900, WSA.

19. Richards to W. Cody, September 4, 1900, June 4, 1902, WSA.

20. William F. Cody, "The Big Horn Basin: An American Eden," *Success*, June 1900, Cody Collection, HMRL.

21. Cody, "Big Horn Basin."

22. Cody, "Big Horn Basin"; "Pioneer's Paradise," *Rough Rider*, 2nd ed., season of 1900, Wojtowicz Collection, HMRL, 2:14.

23. Graham, "Mormon Migration," 49; Fillerup, *Sidon*, 52–62.

24. C. Welch, "Mormons in the Big Horn."

25. A. Welch, *Frederick Arza Welch*, 34.

26. C. Welch, "Mormons in the Big Horn"; "Death of I. S. P. Weeks," *Nebraska State Journal*, September 1, 1908.

27. Larson, *History of Wyoming*, 339; William F. Cody, New York City, to Charles E. Perkins, April 30, 1900; "Resolutions Establishing Toluca Branch in Montana," February 23, 1900, both in Decade Subject File, New Lines, Big Horn Basin, 1900, Chicago, Burlington, and Quincy Railroad Company Records, 33.1890.6, box 161, folder 1187, Newberry Library; Calvert to Holdrege, February 4, 1901, Newberry Library.

28. Calvert to Holdrege, February 4, 1901, Newberry Library.

29. Dearinger, *Filth of Progress*, 137.

30. "McShane's Big Job: A 600-Foot Tunnel in Solid Rock, and Eight Miles of Rock Work," *Cody Enterprise*, September 27, 1900.

31. Jesse W. Crosby to Abraham O. Woodruff, April 10, 1901, Woodruff Papers, box 5, folder 4, BYU.

32. C. Welch, *Big Horn Basin*, 84–85.

33. Crosby to A. Woodruff, April 10, 1901, January 21, 1901, December 23, 1900, October 21, 1900, BYU.

34. Jesse W. Crosby, Bowler, Montana (railroad camp), to Apostle Abraham O. Woodruff, December 23, 1900, Woodruff Papers, box 5, folder 4, BYU.

35. Byron Sessions, ledger book, 1899–1901, History of the Sessions and Call Families, folder 4, CHL, 136.

36. "In the Big Horn Colony, Wyoming: Land under the Canal Has All Been Taken Up by Settlers; Another Canal to Come: Then There Will Be Plenty More Ground; Secret of Success in the Great Colonization," *Deseret Evening News*, September 3, 1900.

37. A. Welch, *Frederick Arza Welch*, 36.

38. Black, *Mother Stood Tall*, 27.

39. George W. Horne, journal, June 20, 21, 26, 28, 1901, Horne Family Collection, box 1, folder 10, CHL.

40. Charles A. Welch to Abraham O. Woodruff, March 6, 1901, Woodruff Papers, box 6, folder 3, BYU.

41. Graham, "Mormon Migration," 68.

42. "The Big Horn Colonies: Wild West Show on the 4th at Cody; Celebration at Byron: Crops Doing Well; Progress on Canal and Railroad Work: Boring for Water; Sawmill Outfit," *Deseret Evening News*, July 13, 1901.

43. Graham, "Mormon Migration," 64.

44. Maxwell, *Last Called Mormon Colonization*, 66.

45. "Large Force of Men to Build Road to Eastern Outlet of Yellowstone Park," *Cody Enterprise*, July 10, 1902.

46. "In the Big Horn Country," *Deseret Evening News*, September 17, 1901.

47. Editorial, *Cody Enterprise*, August 1, 1901.

48. "Observations by Our Greybull Correspondent," *Cody Enterprise*, March 21, 1901; "Republican State Politics," *Cody Enterprise*, May 29, 1902; Cody to Jones, April 9, 1898, AHC; William F. Cody to Francis M. Lyman, October 4, 1903, enclosure included in Francis M. Lyman to Junius F. Wells, October 9, 1903, Wells Papers, box 2, folder 6, CHL.

49. William E. Smythe, "The Secret of Mormon Success," *Harper's Weekly*, February 9, 1901, 164–65.

50. Smythe, "Secret of Mormon Success," 164.

51. Smythe, "Secret of Mormon Success," 165.

52. *Rough Rider*, 2nd ed., season of 1900, HMRL, 2:14.

53. William F. Cody, New York, to Mike Russell, March 14, 1901, Cody Collection, box 14, folder 2, HMRL.

54. William F. Cody, *Ideal Western Lands, Selected by the Famous "Buffalo Bill,"* Shoshone Irrigation Company, Vertical Files, PCA.

55. William F. Cody, Altoona PA, to "My Dear Jim," May 31, 1901, Cody Collection, box 14, folder 2, HMRL.

56. "Reclamation of Big Horn Basin: Col. Cody Talks Encouragingly Concerning Its Development; Many Settlers Are Going In: Most of Them Are 'Mormons,'" *Deseret Evening News*, December 27, 1901.

57. W. Cody to J. Cody Goodman, March 23, 1902, in Foote, *Letters from "Buffalo Bill,"* 49.

58. Fulbright and Stehno, *Oklahoma Rough Rider*, 104.

59. Official Route and Roster of Buffalo Bill's Wild West, season of 1902, Cody Collection, box 10, folder 2, HMRL, 24–26.

60. "Buffalo Bill Outdoors," *New York Times*, May 26, 1902.

61. Advertisement, *Salt Lake Tribune*, August 3, 1902.

62. "Thousands Saw Wild West," *Salt Lake Tribune*, August 14, 1902.

63. "Maj. Burke Arrives," *Salt Lake Tribune*, August 5, 1902.

64. "Wild West Today, Noted Exhibition Gives Afternoon and Evening Performances Following Street Parade," *Salt Lake Tribune*, August 13, 1902.

65. "Thousands Saw Wild West."

66. "Buffalo Bill," *Deseret Evening News*, August 14, 1902.

67. William F. Cody to Junius F. Wells, Western Union telegram from Laramie WY, August 10, 1902, Wells Papers, box 2, folder 1, CHL. My thanks to Brett Dowdle for bringing this telegram to my attention.

68. "Buffalo Bill," *Deseret Evening News*.

69. Anthon Lund, diary, August 14, 1902, in Hatch, *Danish Apostle*, 200.

70. "Buffalo Bill," *Deseret Evening News*.

71. "Cody Submits Plan of Irrigation to Mormons: 'Buffalo Bill' Consults with First Presidency as to Big Horn Colonization Scheme," *Salt Lake Telegram*, August 15, 1902.

72. Bonner, *Cody's Wyoming Empire*, 188–205; W. Cody to A. Woodruff, March 20, 1900, HMRL.

73. "Buffalo Bill," *Deseret Evening News*.

74. "Buffalo Bill," *Deseret Evening News*.

75. "Buffalo Bill," *Deseret Evening News*.

76. "Wild West's Visit: Byron Reid Painfully Wounded by Toy Pistol during Juvenile Performance of Show," *Salt Lake Tribune*, August 21, 1902.

77. Official Route and Roster, HMRL.

78. Invitation to the opening of the Irma, Fall 1902, Cody Collection, box 1, folder 1, DPL; Foote, *Letters from "Buffalo Bill,"* 51.

79. Untitled, *London Penny Illustrated Times*, December 20, 1902.

7. FRIENDS IN THE END

1. Allen, Esplin, and Whittaker, *Men with a Mission*.

2. Foster, *Penny Tracts and Polemics*; Rasmussen, *Mormonism*, 78–103.

3. Francis M. Lyman to John R. Winder, May 12, 1903; Francis M. Lyman to Henry J. Randall, May 15, 1903, both in Francis M. Lyman Letterpress Copybooks, box 1, folder 1, CHL, 890, 891.

4. Lyman to Winder, May 12, 1903, CHL, 890.

5. Lyman to Winder, May 12, 1903, CHL, 890; Francis M. Lyman to Richard and Amy Brown Lyman, May 15, 1903, Francis M. Lyman Letterpress Copybooks, box 1, folder 1, CHL, 895.

6. Lyman to R. and A. Brown Lyman, May 15, 1903, Francis M. Lyman Letterpress Copybooks, box 1, folder 1, CHL, 895; Lyman to Winder, May 12, 1903, CHL, 890.

7. Francis M. Lyman to Junius F. Wells, May 16, 1903, Francis M. Lyman Letterpress Copybooks, box 1, folder 1, CHL, 898.

8. Francis M. Lyman to William F. Cody, October 2, 1903, Francis M. Lyman Letterpress Copybooks, box 1, folder 2, CHL, 68.

9. Cody to Lyman, October 4, 1903, enclosure included in Lyman to Wells, October 9, 1903, CHL.

10. "Praise from 'Buffalo Bill,'" *Deseret Evening News*, July 23, 1904.

11. William F. Cody to Fenimore Chatterton, May 24, 1903, Fenimore Chatterton, General Records, Incoming Correspondence, RG 0001.16, box 2, WSA; William F. Cody to DeForest Richards, March 9, 1903, Governor Deforest Richards, Administrative Records, Richards Correspondence, box 5, General Correspondence, Cl-Cof, 1899–1903, WSA.

12. W. Cody to Chatterton, May 24, 1903, WSA.

13. William F. Cody to Curtis L. Hinkle, March 10, 1902, Cody Collection, box 14, folder 3, HMRL.

14. DeForest Richards to William F. Cody, February 24, 1903, Governor Deforest Richards, Administrative Records, Richards Correspondence, box 5, General Correspondence, Cl-Cof, 1899–1903, WSA.

15. William F. Cody to George W. Holdrege, September 19, 1902, Records of the Bureau of Reclamation, Shoshone Project, box 912, entry 3, folder 958, NARA.

16. W. Cody to Chatterton, May 24, 1903, WSA.

17. Charles A. Welch, "Mormons in Big Horn Basin," *Basin Republican*, January 10, 1908, transcript, Churches, Mormon (LDS), Powell, Vertical Files, PCA. Estimates vary, but the cost appears to have been in the low $100,000 range. Mark Austin, "Gen. Agr. Supt" of the Utah Sugar Company, to Thomas E. Cutler, General Manager, Utah Sugar Company, February 23, 1904, Woodruff Papers, box 5, folder 1, BYU.

18. "In the Big Horn Colonies: Surprising Amount of Work Accomplished on Railroad and Canal Projects; Former Being Completed, Canyon Roads and Homes Will Now Be Built: Fine Crops at Byron," *Deseret Evening News*, August 23, 1901; Cody Town Council, minutes, excerpts, February 13, 1904, Cody, Early Settlers, Vertical Files, PCA; George Austin to Thomas R. Cutler, report, February 23, 1904, Woodruff Papers, box 5, folder 1, BYU.

19. Byron Sessions, talk to the Big Horn Stake, April 1903, Sessions Collection, CHL; "The Typical Mormon Colony," *Deseret Evening News*, December 25, 1909.

20. Idella W. Twombly Sessions, "Life Story," Sessions Collection, CHL.

21. "Byron, Wyoming: Room for Homeseekers; Opportunities in Big Horn Country: Local Improvements," *Deseret Evening News*, January 24, 1903.

22. Austin to Cutler, February 23, 1904, BYU.

23. Austin to Cutler, report, February 23, 1904, BYU.

24. Ettie Lythgoe, "My Wyoming," 1908, in Big Horn Stake, *Gems to Treasure*, 31.

25. Cody, *Ideal Western Lands*, PCA.

26. William F. Cody, England, to Fenimore Chatterton, Cheyenne WY, May 26, 1903, Fenimore Chatterton, General Records, Incoming Correspondence, box 2, WSA; Bonner, "Buffalo Bill Cody," 438–39, 447.

27. Warren, *Buffalo Bill's America*, 490.

28. A. MacKinnon, *Public Waters*, 114.

29. W. Cody to Richards, August 29, 1902, WSA.

30. Fenimore Chatterton, Cheyenne WY, to Charles D. Walcott, February 10, 1904; William F. Cody and Ethan Allen Hitchcock, indenture, February 13, 1904, both in Records of the Bureau of Reclamation, Shoshone Project, box 912, entry 3, folder 958, NARA.

31. W. Cody and Hitchcock, indenture, February 13, 1904, NARA.

32. Bob Landgren, comp., excerpts from Cody Town Council minutes, Vertical Files, Cody, Early Settlers, Vertical Files, PCA, 5.

33. Warren, *Buffalo Bill's America*, 489.

34. "Uncle Sam's Immense Irrigation Scheme Near Mormon Settlements in the Big Horn," *Deseret Evening News*, December 31, 1904.

35. "Uncle Sam's Immense Irrigation."

36. Charles A. Welch, Cowley WY, to Fenimore Chatterton, Cheyenne WY, February 5, 1904, Fenimore Chatterton, General Records, Incoming Correspondence, box 2, WSA.

37. Bonner, "Buffalo Bill Cody," 447.

38. H. N. Savage, Supervising Engineer, Cody WY, to Frederick H. Newell, Chief Engineer, USGS, Washington DC, April 16, 1905, Records of the Bureau of Reclamation, Shoshone Project, box 912, entry 3, folder 958, NARA.

39. H. N. Savage to unnamed hydrographer of the Geological Survey, Washington DC, telegram, April 17, 1905, Records of the Bureau of Reclamation, Shoshone Project, box 912, entry 3, folder 958, NARA.

40. Savage to Newell, April 16, 1905, NARA.

41. Assignment of Water Right Applications, nos. 1191 and 5329, Records of the Bureau of Reclamation, Shoshone Project, box 912, entry 3, folder 958, NARA.

42. William F. Cody to Theodore Roosevelt, March 10, 1905, Records of the Bureau of Reclamation, Shoshone Project, box 912, entry 3, folder 958, NARA.

43. William F. Cody, Milan, Italy, to Frederick Haynes Newell, Reclamation Bureau, Washington DC, May 4, 1906, Records of the Bureau of Reclamation, Shoshone Project, box 912, entry 3, folder 958, NARA.

44. William F. Cody, Bausten, Germany, to Theodore Roosevelt, President of the United States, August 16, 1906, Records of the Bureau of Reclamation, Shoshone Project, box 912, entry 3, folder 958, NARA.

45. Unsigned letter to William Loeb, Secretary to Theodore Roosevelt, March 5, 1908, Records of the Bureau of Reclamation, Shoshone 48, Miscellaneous, box 888, NARA.

46. For more on the Reed Smoot hearings, see, for example, Flake, *American Religious Identity*.

47. Hardy, *Solemn Covenant*; Quinn, "LDS Church Authority," 9; Quinn, "Plural Marriage," 4; McDannell, *Sister Saints*, 32.

48. Burchell Hopkin, oral history, October 22, 2001, interviewed by Christy Fleming, Powell WY, Homesteader; Burchell Hopkin and Ruby Hopkin, oral history, October 5, 2005, interviewed by Marjorie A. White, Homesteader.

49. A. Woodruff, journal, August 30, 1900, BYU.

50. Star Valley was a refuge for Latter-day Saints who had left Utah to escape federal pressure on polygamy. Erickson, "Star Valley," 125.

51. Eliza Avery Clark, Autobiography and Recollections, BYU, 34–35.

52. A. Woodruff, journal, November 1, 1900, BYU.

53. Joseph Charles Bentley, "Journal and Notes," November 18–19, 1900, 61, quoted in Hardy, *Solemn Covenant*, 190.

54. Erickson, "Star Valley," 154–55.

55. Clark, Autobiography and Recollections, BYU, 41–42.

56. Erickson, "Star Valley," 154–55.

57. Reed Smoot to Abraham O. Woodruff, January 21, 1904, February 27, 1904, Woodruff Papers, box 4, folder 11, BYU.

58. Smoot to A. Woodruff, February 27, 1904, BYU.

59. Snyder and Snyder, *Post-manifesto Polygamy*, 41; McDannell, *Sister Saints*, 33.

60. Winder, "Theodore Roosevelt," 13.

61. *Buffalo Bill's Mormon Quarrel, or At War with the Danites*, June 24, 1905, Buffalo Bill Stories, Cody Collection, series 7, item 215, HMRL, 2.

62. *Buffalo Bill's Mormon Quarrel*, HMRL, 4.

63. *Buffalo Bill's Mormon Quarrel*, HMRL, 28.

64. *Buffalo Bill's Waif of the Plains, or At Odds with the Danites*, May 2, 1908, Buffalo Bill Stories, Cody Collection, series 7, item 364, HMRL.

65. Warren, *Buffalo Bill's America*, 504–19.

66. William F. Cody to Julia Cody Goodman, June 14, 1905, Cody Collection, HMRL; Friesen, "No Swearing or Drinking."

67. "Famous Wild West Show Coming," *Inter-Mountain Republican*, September 6, 1908; "Buffalo Bill Is Still Good Shot," *Salt Lake Telegram*, September 8,

1908; "Buffalo Bill's Wild West Show Is at Fair Grounds Today with New Features," *Inter-Mountain Republican*, September 9, 1908.

68. "Buffalo Bill Is in Town," *Salt Lake Herald*, September 9, 1908.

69. "Thousands Stung at Wild West Show: Buffalo Bill's Entertainment Not Up to Pace Set in Old Days; Complaints Are Registered: It Was a Case of First Come First Served When It Came to Much Advertised Reserved Seats," *Deseret Evening News*, September 10, 1908.

70. "Twenty Thousand Persons Witness Buffalo Bill's Wild West Show," *Salt Lake Herald*, September 10, 1908.

71. "Large Crowds See Wild West Show: Buffalo Bill, with New Features, Pleases Afternoon and Evening Throngs; Always Something Doing: Debonaire Col. Cody Rides and Shoots as in Former Years," *Inter-Mountain Republican*, September 10, 1908.

72. "Praise for Buffalo Bill: Thousands Saw the Wild West Salt Lake; Comments of the Salt Lake Papers on the Performances Given on Wednesday," *Ogden Standard Examiner*, September 10, 1908.

73. "Twenty Thousand Persons."

74. "Large Crowds."

75. "Buffalo Bill Is in Town."

76. "'Buffalo Bill' Revives Memories of Frontier," *Los Angeles Herald*, October 9, 1910; for more on Cody's work in the early film industry, see Sagala, *Silver Screen*.

77. "Buffalo Bill's Wild West," official program, 1893, HMRL; "The Home of History and Heroism," program, 1901, Cody Collection, DPL, 64.

78. "Buffalo Bill's Farewell Proclamation to the Public!" Cody Collection, box 1, DPL.

79. Warren, *Buffalo Bill's America*, 536–37.

80. "Sells-Floto Circus Here Tomorrow," *Salt Lake Telegram*, June 10, 1914; "Buffalo Bill Sees President Smith," *Salt Lake Telegram*, June 11, 1914.

81. "Sells-Floto Parade a Big Success," *Logan Republican*, June 11, 1914.

82. "Local Art Gallery Attracts Visitors," *Salt Lake Tribune*, June 14, 1914.

83. "Buffalo Bill Sees President."

84. "Buffalo Bill Sees President"; "Special Organ Recital in Honor of Col. W. F. Cody (Buffalo Bill) Tendered by the First Presidency," Salt Lake Tabernacle, June 11, 1914, CHL; Compton, "John J. McClellan," iii, 9.

85. "A Friend in Days of Old," *Ogden Standard*, June 10, 1914.

86. "Sells-Floto Circus," *Salt Lake Herald*, June 18, 1915.

87. William Barrett, "Buffalo Bill Was Baptised by a Sligo Priest," *Catholic Digest*, October 1960, Cody Collection, HMRL; "Buffalo Bill Baptized by Reverend

Christopher V. Walsh," *Denver Catholic Register*, January 11, 1917, 1; Friesen, "No Swearing or Drinking."

CONCLUSION

1. Zac Taylor, "Cody Slated for Church of Jesus Christ of Latter-day Saints Temple," *Cody Enterprise*, October 4, 2021; C. J. Baker, "LDS Church to Build Temple in Cody," *Powell Tribune*, October 5, 2021.

Bibliography

ARCHIVES AND MANUSCRIPT MATERIALS

AHC. American Heritage Center. University of Wyoming, Laramie.

Beck, George T. Papers, 1869–1968. Collection Number 59.

Buffalo Bill Letters to George T. Beck, 1895–1910. Collection Number 09972.

BYU. L. Tom Perry Special Collections. Harold B. Lee Library. Brigham Young University, Provo, Utah.

Clark, Eliza Avery. Autobiography and Recollections. MSS 6211.

Woodruff, Abraham Owen. Papers, 1894–1904. Vault MSS 777.

CHL. Church History Library. Church of Jesus Christ of Latter-day Saints, Salt Lake City.

Alexander, Sara. Scrapbooks, 1863–1924. MS 21200.

Cody, William F. Letters. MS 2837.

History of the Sessions and Call Families, 1896–ca. 1950s. MS 23534.

Horne Family Collection, 1872–1978. MS 9361.

Lyman, Francis M. Letterpress Copybooks, 1901–3. MS 2497.

McKinley William. Correspondence, 1897–1901. MS 8190 22.

Mowry, Sylvester. Letters. MS 23526.

Pratt, Orson. Autobiography and Journals, 1833–47. MS 587.

Rogers, Samuel H. Reminiscences and Diary, 1846. MS 883.

Sessions, Edwin S. Collection, ca. 1900–1940. MS 15588.

Snow, Lorenzo. General Correspondence, 1898–1901. CR 1 170.

Special Organ Recital in Honor of Col. W. F. Cody, 1914. M285.301 S741.

Stout, Hosea. Reminiscences and Journals, 1845–69. MS 8332.

Wells, Junius F. Papers, 1867–1930. MS 1351.

Woodruff, Wilford. Journals and Papers, 1828–98. MS 1352.

Young, Brigham. Journals, 1832–77. Brigham Young Office Files, 1832–78. CR 1234 1.

DPL. Denver Public Library. Western History and Genealogy Repository, Denver, Colorado.

    Cody, William Frederick/Buffalo Bill Collection, 1870–1980 and 1870–1992. WH 72.

    Salsbury, Nate. Papers. M688.

HMRL. Harold McCracken Research Library. Buffalo Bill Center of the West, Cody, Wyoming.

    Beck, George. Letters. MS 157.

    Cody, William F. Collection, 1840–2011. MS 006.

    Mercaldo, Vincent. Collection, 1850–1945. MS 071.

    Rapp, Charles. Collection, 1874–78. MS 017.

    Wojtowicz, James. Collection, 1880–1929. MS 327.

Homesteader. Homesteader Museum, Powell, Wyoming.

    Hopkin, Burchell. Oral History.

    Hopkin, Burchell, and Ruby Hopkin. Oral History.

KHS. Kansas Historical Society, Topeka.

    Railroads History Collection, ca. 1870–1930. MS Coll. 632.

    Records of the Governor's Office. Correspondence Files. Administration of Governor Samuel J. Crawford, 1865–68.

NARA. National Archives and Records Administration, Denver, Colorado.

    Records of the Bureau of Reclamation, Washington DC. RG 115. General Administrative and Project Records, 1902–19. Shoshone 489-1057B. Shoshone Project: Cody and Salsbury Tract Relinquishment of Land and Water Rights.

    ———. Shoshone 48-48-7. Miscellaneous.

Newberry. The Newberry, Chicago.

    Chicago, Burlington, and Quincy Railroad Company Records, 1890. 6.8. Subseries 33 1890 6: New Lines, 1882–1916.

    Gray, John S. Research Papers, 1942–91. Edward E. Ayer Manuscript Collection.

NYPL. New York Public Library. Manuscripts and Archives Division, New York City.

    Mormon Miscellaneous Collection, 1842–1920. MSS Col 2060.

PCA. Park County Archives, Cody, Wyoming.

    Vertical Files.

        Churches. Mormon (LDS). Powell.

        Cody. Early Settlers.

        Irrigation Projects. Sidon Canal.

        Shoshone Irrigation Company.

SRL. Kenneth Spencer Research Library. University of Kansas, Lawrence.

> Gorden, D. R. Pioneer Stories. MS RH P45.

> Hill, W. A. "Rome: The Predecessor of Hays: Founded by 'Buffalo Bill' Cody." Miscellaneous Publications about Hays. Kansas. PH P610.

> Kansas History Scrapbooks. RH MF 154.5. Vol. 2. Kansas Collection.

> Stotts, John O. History and War Record of J. O. Stotts. Sergeant Co. G. 3rd Regt. U.S. Infantry, 1866–68. RH MS P155.

USHS. Utah State Historical Society, Salt Lake City.

> Records of the War Department. Office of the Adjutant General. Misc. Collection. Mowry, 1853–55. MSS A 15.

> Wells, Governor. Correspondence, 1895–1904. Series 235.

> Wells, Heber Manning. Scrapbooks. Political Matters, 1899–1900. MSS A 313-2.

WSA. Wyoming State Archives, Cheyenne.

> Chatterton, Fenimore. General Records. Incoming Correspondence. RG 0001.16.

> Richards, Governor DeForest. Administrative Records. General Correspondence. RG 0001.15.

PUBLISHED WORKS

Abruzzi, William S. *Dam That River! Ecology and Mormon Settlement in the Little Colorado River Basin.* Lanham MD: University Press of America, 1993.

Alexander, Thomas G. *Brigham Young and the Expansion of the Mormon Faith.* Norman: University of Oklahoma Press, 2019.

———. *Mormonism in Transition: A History of the Latter-day Saints, 1890–1930.* Salt Lake City: Kofford Books, 2012.

Allen, James B., Ronald K. Esplin, and David Whittaker. *Men with a Mission, 1837–1841: The Quorum of the Twelve Apostles in the British Isles.* Salt Lake City: Deseret Book, 1992.

Andreas, Alfred T. *Andreas' History of the State of Nebraska, Cheyenne County.* Chicago: Western Historical, 1882.

Arrington, Leonard J. *Great Basin Kingdom: An Economic History of the Latter-day Saints, 1830–1900.* Reprint, Salt Lake City: University of Utah Press, 1993.

———. "Utah and the Depression of the 1890s." *Utah Historical Quarterly* 29, no. 1 (1961): 2–18.

Arthur, Chester A. "First Annual Message." American Presidency Project. December 6, 1881. http://www.presidency.ucsb.edu/ws/?pid=29522.

Austin, Michael, and Ardis E. Parshall, eds. *Dime Novel Mormons.* Salt Lake City: Kofford Books, 2017.

Ayers, Edward L. *The Promise of the New South: Life after Reconstruction*. New York: Oxford University Press, 1992.

Bagley, Will. *Blood of the Prophets: Brigham Young and the Massacre at Mountain Meadows*. Norman: University of Oklahoma Press, 2004.

Bahr, Howard M. *Saints Observed: Studies of Mormon Village Life, 1850–2005*. Salt Lake City: University of Utah Press, 2014.

Bashore, Melvin L. "'The Bloodiest Drama Ever Perpetrated on American Soil': Staging the Mountain Meadows Massacre for Entertainment." *Utah Historical Quarterly* 80, no. 3 (Summer 2012): 258–71.

Basso, Matthew, Laura McCall, and Dee Garceau, eds. *Across the Great Divide: Cultures of Manhood in the American West*. New York: Routledge, 2001.

Baugh, Alexander L. "'We Have a Company of Danites in These Times': The Danites, Joseph Smith, and the 1838 Missouri-Mormon Conflict." *Journal of Mormon History* 45, no. 33 (July 2019): 1–25.

Beadle, John H. *Brigham's Destroying Angel*. New York: Crofutt, 1872.

Beck, George W. T. *Beckoning Frontiers: The Memoir of a Wyoming Entrepreneur*. Edited by Lynn J. Houze and Jeremy M. Johnston. Lincoln: University of Nebraska Press, 2020.

Bederman, Gail. *Manliness and Civilization: A Cultural History of Gender and Race in the United States, 1880–1917*. Chicago: University of Chicago Press, 1995.

Bennett, Richard E. *Temples Rising: A Heritage of Sacrifice*. Salt Lake City: Deseret Book, 2019.

Bernardi, Daniel, ed. *The Birth of Whiteness: Race and the Emergence of U.S. Cinema*. New Brunswick NJ: Rutgers University Press, 1996.

Big Horn Stake of the Church of Jesus Christ of Latter-Day Saints. *Gems to Treasure*. N.p., 1960.

Billington, Ray Allen. *Frederick Jackson Turner: Historian, Teacher, Scholar*. New York: Oxford University Press, 1973.

Black, Rosa Vida. *Mother Stood Tall: Writings and History of Our Mother Eliza Rosetta King Black Lythgoe Wife, Pioneer, Educator, Writer, Friend, Mother of Utah and Cowley, Big Horn County, Wyoming*. N.p., ca. 1971.

Blight, David W. *Race and Reunion: The Civil War in American Memory*. Cambridge MA: Belknap, 2001.

Boisseau, T. J., and Abigail M. Markwyn, eds. *Gendering the Fair: Histories of Women at World's Fairs*. Urbana: University of Illinois Press, 2010.

Bold, Christine. *The Frontier Club: Popular Westerns and Cultural Power, 1880–1924*. New York: Oxford University Press, 2013.

———. *Selling the Wild West: Popular Western Fiction, 1860 to 1960*. Bloomington: Indiana University Press, 1987.

———. "Where Did the Black Rough Riders Go?" *Canadian Review of American Studies* 39, no. 3 (2009): 273–97.

Bonner, Robert E. "Buffalo Bill Cody and Wyoming Water Politics." *Western Historical Quarterly* 33, no. 4 (Winter 2002): 432–51.

———. *William F. Cody's Wyoming Empire: The Buffalo Bill Nobody Knows*. Norman: University of Oklahoma Press, 2007.

Branch, E. Douglas. *The Hunting of the Buffalo*. Lincoln: Bison Books, 1963.

Brimhall, Sandra Dawn. "Sara Alexander: Pioneer Actress and Dancer." *Utah Historical Quarterly* 66, no. 4 (1998): 320–33.

Brooks, Joanna. *Mormonism and White Supremacy: American Religion and the Problem of Racial Innocence*. New York: Oxford University Press, 2020.

Brooks, Juanita. *The Mountain Meadows Massacre*. Norman: University of Oklahoma Press, 1950.

Buchanan, James. "First Annual Message to Congress on the State of the Union." American Presidency Project. December 8, 1857. https://www.presidency.ucsb.edu/node/202407.

Bunker, Gary L., and Davis Bitton. *The Mormon Graphic Image, 1834–1914: Cartoons, Caricatures, and Illustrations*. Salt Lake City: University of Utah Press, 1983.

Burke, John M. *"Buffalo Bill" from Prairie to Palace*. Chicago: Rand McNally, 1893.

Cahill, Luke. "An Indian Campaign and Buffalo Hunting with 'Buffalo Bill.'" *Colorado Magazine* 4, no. 4 (August 1927): 125–35.

Campbell, Eugene E. *Establishing Zion: The Mormon Church in the American West, 1847–1869*. Salt Lake City: Signature Books, 1988.

Cannon, Frank J., and Harvey J. O'Higgins. *Under the Prophet in Utah: The National Menace of a Political Priestcraft*. Boston: Clark, 1911.

Cannon, George Q. *The Journal of George Q. Cannon*. Church Historian's Press. Accessed February 6, 2019. https://www.churchhistorianspress.org/george-q-cannon?lang=eng.

Carter, Sarah. *The Importance of Being Monogamous: Marriage and Nation Building in Western Canada to 1915*. Edmonton: University of Alberta Press, 2008.

Clark, James R., ed. *Messages of the First Presidency of the Church of Jesus Christ of Latter-day Saints, 1833–1964*. Vol. 3. Salt Lake City: Bookcraft, 1966.

Clark, Michael J. "Improbable Ambassadors: Black Soldiers at Fort Douglas, 1896–99." *Utah Historical Quarterly* 46, no. 3 (Summer 1978): 282–301.

Cleveland, Grover. "First Annual Message." American Presidency Project. December 8, 1885. http://www.presidency.ucsb.edu/ws/?pid=29526.

Cody, William F. *The Life of Hon. William F. Cody, Known as Buffalo Bill*. Edited by Frank Christianson. 1879. Reprint, Lincoln: University of Nebraska Press, 2011.

———. *The Wild West in England*. Edited by Frank Christianson. Lincoln: University of Nebraska Press, 2012.

Compiled Laws of Utah. Vol. 1. Salt Lake City: Pembroke, 1888.

Compton, Annie Rosella. "John J. McClellan, Tabernacle Organist." Master's thesis, Brigham Young University, 1951.

Cornwall, Rebecca Foster, and Leonard J. Arrington. "Perpetuation of a Myth: Mormon Danites in Five Western Novels, 1840–1900." *Brigham Young University Studies* 23, no. 2 (Spring 1983): 147–65.

"Danites." Joseph Smith Papers. Accessed January 31, 2018. http://www.josephsmithpapers.org/topic/danites.

Daynes, Kathryn M. *More Wives Than One: Transformation of the Mormon Marriage System, 1840–1910*. Urbana: University of Illinois Press, 2001.

Dearinger, Ryan. *The Filth of Progress: Immigrants, Americans, and the Building of Canals and Railroads in the West*. Oakland: University of California Press, 2016.

Deseret Deserted, or The Last Days of Brigham Young. New York: French, 1858.

Drinnon, Richard. *Facing West: The Metaphysics of Indian-Hating and Empire-Building*. Norman: University of Oklahoma Press, 1997.

Edwards, Rebecca. *New Spirits: Americans in the Gilded Age, 1865–1905*. New York: Oxford University Press, 2006.

Ellis, Mark R. *Law and Order in Buffalo Bill's Country: Legal Culture and Community in the Great Plains, 1867–1910*. Lincoln: University of Nebraska Press, 2009.

Engle, Ron, and Tice L. Miller. *The American Stage: Social and Economic Issues from the Colonial Period to the Present*. New York: Cambridge University Press, 1993.

English, Thomas Dunn. *The Mormons, or Life at Salt Lake City*. New York: French, 1858.

Erickson, Dan. "Star Valley, Wyoming: Polygamous Haven." *Journal of Mormon History* 26, no. 1 (Spring 2000): 123–64.

Etcheson, Nicole. *Bleeding Kansas: Contested Liberty in the Civil War Era*. Lawrence: University Press of Kansas, 2004.

Farmer, Jared. *On Zion's Mount: Mormons, Indians, and the American Landscape*. Cambridge MA: Harvard University Press, 2008.

———. "This Was the Place: The Making and Unmaking of Utah." *Utah Historical Quarterly* 82, no. 3 (Summer 2014): 185–93.

Fillerup, Melvin M. *Sidon: The Canal That Faith Built*. Cody WY: Ptarmigan, 1988.

Flake, Kathleen. *The Politics of American Religious Identity: The Seating of Senator Reed Smoot, Mormon Apostle*. Chapel Hill: University of North Carolina Press, 2004.

Foner, Eric. *Reconstruction: America's Unfinished Revolution, 1863–1877*. New York: Harper and Row, 1988.

———. *A Short History of Reconstruction*. New York: HarperCollins, 1990.

Foote, Stella. *Letters from "Buffalo Bill."* Billings MT: Foote, 1954.

Foster, Craig L. *Penny Tracts and Polemics: A Critical Analysis of Anti-Mormon Pamphleteering in Great Britain, 1837–1860*. Salt Lake City: Kofford Books, 2002.

Friesen, Steve. "'No Swearing or Drinking in My Company since I Got Good': Buffalo Bill Finds God." *Points West*, Winter 2003. https://centerofthewest.org/2018/03/23/points-west-no-swearing-drinking/.

Fryxell, Fritiof M. "The Codys in Le Claire." *Annals of Iowa* 17, no. 1 (July 1929): 3–11.

Fulbright, Jim, and Albert Stehno, eds. *Oklahoma Rough Rider: Billy McGinty's Own Story*. Norman: University of Oklahoma Press, 2008.

Garfield, James A. "Inaugural Address." American Presidency Project. March 4, 1881. http://www.presidency.ucsb.edu/ws/?pid=25823.

Godfrey, Kenneth W., Audrey M. Godfrey, and Jill Mulvay Derr. *Women's Voices: An Untold History of the Latter-day Saints, 1830–1900*. Salt Lake City: Deseret Book, 1982.

Gordon, Sarah Barringer. *The Mormon Question: Polygamy and Constitutional Conflict in Nineteenth-Century America*. Chapel Hill: University of North Carolina Press, 2002.

Gorn, Elliot J. *The Manly Art: Bare-Knuckle Prize Fighting in America*. Ithaca NY: Cornell University Press, 2010.

Graham, D. Kurt. "The Mormon Migration to Wyoming's Big Horn Basin in 1900." Master's thesis, Brigham Young University, 1994.

Gray, John S. "Fact versus Fiction in the Kansas Boyhood of Buffalo Bill." *Kansas History* 8, no. 1 (Spring 1985): 2–20.

Greenberg, Amy S. "'The Way of the Transgressor Is Hard': The Black Hawk and Mormon Wars in the Construction of Illinois Political Culture, 1832–1846." In McBride, Rogers, and Erekson, *Contingent Citizens*, 75–91.

Griffin, Charles Eldridge. *Four Years in Europe with Buffalo Bill*. Edited by Chris Dixon. Lincoln: University of Nebraska Press, 2010.

Grow, Matthew J. "Contesting the LDS Image: The *North American Review* and the Mormons, 1881–1907." *Journal of Mormon History* 32, no. 2 (Summer 2006): 111–36.

Hahn, Steven. *A Nation without Borders: The United States and Its World in an Age of Civil Wars, 1830–1910*. New York: Viking, 2016.

Hall, Roger A. *Performing the American Frontier, 1870–1906*. Cambridge: Cambridge University Press, 2001.

Hansen, Konden Smith. *Frontier Religion: Mormons and America, 1857–1907.* Salt Lake City: University of Utah Press, 2019.

Hardy, B. Carmon. *Solemn Covenant: The Mormon Polygamous Passage.* Urbana: University of Illinois Press, 1992.

Harrison, Benjamin. "Proclamation 346: Granting Amnesty and Pardon for the Offense of Engaging in Polygamous or Plural Marriage to Members of the Church of Latter-Day Saints." American Presidency Project. January 4, 1893. http://www.presidency.ucsb.edu/node/205484.

Hatch, John P., ed. *Danish Apostle: The Diaries of Anthon H. Lund, 1890–1921.* Salt Lake City: Signature Books, 2006.

Haws, J. B. "Mormons at Mid-Century: 'Crushed Politically, Curtailed Economically,' but Winning 'Universal Respect for Their Devotion and Achievements.'" In McBride, Rogers, and Erekson, *Contingent Citizens*, 193–207.

Hayes, Rutherford B. "Fourth Annual Message." American Presidency Project. December 6, 1880. http://www.presidency.ucsb.edu/ws/?pid=29521.

———. "Third Annual Message." American Presidency Project. December 1, 1879. http://www.presidency.ucsb.edu/node/204252.

Higham, Carol L., and William H. Katerberg. *Conquests and Consequences: The American West from Frontier to Region.* Wheeling IL: Davidson, 2009.

Hirota, Hidetaka. *Expelling the Poor: Atlantic Seaboard States and the 19th-Century Origins of American Immigration Policy.* New York: Oxford University Press, 2017.

Hoganson, Kristin L. *Fighting for American Manhood: How Gender Politics Provoked the Spanish-American and Philippine-American Wars.* New Haven CT: Yale University Press, 1998.

Hopkins, Sarah Winnemucca. *Life among the Piutes: Their Wrongs and Claims.* Boston: Cupples, Upham; New York: Putnam's Sons, 1883.

Howe, Eber D. *Mormonism Unvailed.* Painesville OH: Howe, 1834.

Ingraham, Prentiss, ed. *Seventy Years on the Frontier: Alexander Majors' Memoirs of a Lifetime on the Border.* Chicago: Rand, McNally, 1893.

Inman, Henry, and William F. Cody. *The Great Salt Lake Trail.* 1898. Reprint, Minneapolis: Ross and Haines, 1966.

Isenberg, Andrew C. *The Destruction of the Bison: An Environmental History, 1750–1920.* Cambridge: Cambridge University Press, 2000.

Jacobson, Matthew Frye. *Barbarian Virtues: The United States Encounters Foreign Peoples at Home and Abroad, 1876–1917.* New York: Hill and Wang, 2000.

———. *Whiteness of a Different Color: European Immigrants and the Alchemy of Race.* Cambridge MA: Harvard University Press, 1998.

Jenson, Andrew. *Latter-day Saint Biographical Encyclopedia*. 4 vols. Salt Lake City: Deseret News Press, 1901–36.

Jessen, Nathan. *Populism and Imperialism: Politics, Culture, and Foreign Policy in the American West, 1890–1900*. Lawrence: University Press of Kansas, 2017.

Jones, Megan Sanborn. *Performing American Identity in Anti-Mormon Melodrama*. New York: Routledge, 2009.

Jones, Virgil Carrington. *Roosevelt's Rough Riders*. Garden City NY: Doubleday, 1971.

Journal of Discourses. Reported by George F. Gibbs et al. 26 vols. Liverpool: Wells; London: Latter-day Saints' Book Depot, 1886.

Kasson, John F. *Houdini, Tarzan, and the Perfect Man: The White Male Body and the Challenge of Modernity in America*. New York: Hill and Wang, 2001.

Kasson, Joy S. *Buffalo Bill's Wild West: Celebrity, Memory, and Popular History*. New York: Hill and Wang, 2000.

Kendi, Ibram X. *Stamped from the Beginning: The Definitive History of Racist Ideas in America*. New York: Nation Books, 2016.

Kimball, Farel Chamberlain. *Mary E. Woolley Chamberlain: Handmaiden of the Lord*. Self-published, [1981?].

Kimmel, Michael. *Manhood in America: A Cultural History*. New York: Free Press, 1996.

Lamar, Howard R. *The Far Southwest, 1846–1912: A Territorial History*. Rev. ed. Albuquerque: University of New Mexico Press, 2000.

Larson, Taft Alfred. *History of Wyoming*. 2nd ed. Lincoln: University of Nebraska Press, 1990.

Lee, John D. *Mormonism Unveiled, or The Life and Confessions of the Late Mormon Bishop*. St. Louis: Bryan, Brand, 1877.

Lewis, Alfred Henry, ed. *A Compilation of the Messages and Speeches of Theodore Roosevelt, 1901–1905*. New York: Bureau of National Literature and Art, 1906.

Lindsay, John S. *The Mormons and the Theatre, or The History of Theatricals in Utah*. Salt Lake City: Century, 1905.

Lyman, Edward Leo. *Political Deliverance: The Mormon Quest for Utah Statehood*. Urbana: University of Illinois Press, 1986.

MacKinnon, Anne. *Public Waters: Lessons from Wyoming for the American West*. Albuquerque: University of New Mexico Press, 2021.

MacKinnon, William P., ed. *At Sword's Point*. Pt. 1, *A Documentary History of the Utah War to 1858*. Norman OK: Clark, 2008.

Madsen, Carol Cornwall. *Emmeline B. Wells: An Intimate History*. Salt Lake City: University of Utah Press, 2017.

Martin, Jonathan D. "'The Grandest and Most Cosmopolitan Object Teacher': Buffalo Bill's Wild West and the Politics of American Identity." *Radical History Review* 66 (1996): 92–123.

Mason, Patrick Q. *The Mormon Menace: Violence and Anti-Mormonism in the Postbellum South.* New York: Oxford University Press, 2011.

Mattes, Merrill J. *Indians, Infants, and Infantry: Andrew and Elizabeth Burt on the Frontier.* Denver CO: Old West, 1960.

Maxwell, John Gary. *The Last Called Mormon Colonization: Polygamy, Kinship, and Wealth in Wyoming's Bighorn Basin.* Salt Lake City: University of Utah Press, 2022.

McBride, Spencer W., Brent M. Rogers, and Keith A. Erekson, eds. *Contingent Citizens: Shifting Perceptions of Latter-day Saints in American Political Culture.* Ithaca NY: Cornell University Press, 2020.

McDaniel, E. A. *Utah at the World's Columbian Exposition.* Salt Lake City: Salt Lake Lithographing, 1894.

McDannell, Colleen. *Sister Saints: Mormon Women since the End of Polygamy.* New York: Oxford University Press, 2019.

Merrill, Joseph F. "Tabernacle Choir at Chicago Fair." *Millennial Star* 96, no. 36 (September 6, 1934): 568–69.

Meserve, Walter J. "Social Awareness on Stage: Tensions Mounting, 1850–1859." In *The American Stage: Social and Economic Issues from the Colonial Period to the Present,* edited by Ron Engle and Tice L. Miller, 81–100. New York: Cambridge University Press, 1993.

Miller, Joaquin. *First Fam'lies of the Sierras.* Chicago: Jansen, McClurg, 1876.

Moore, John Bassett, ed. *The Works of James Buchanan.* Vol. 10. Philadelphia: Lippincott, 1910.

Neilson, Reid L. *Exhibiting Mormonism: The Latter-day Saints and the 1893 Chicago World's Fair.* New York: Oxford University Press, 2011.

Nelson, Jessica Marie. "Whiteness in Modern Latter-day Saint History and Culture." *Mormon Studies Review* 7 (2020): 29–34.

North, Luther. *Man of the Plains: Recollections of Luther North.* Norman: University of Oklahoma Press, 1961.

Nytroe, Sarah K. "Taming the Past to Conquer the Future: The Pioneer Jubilee of 1897." *Journal of Mormon History* 42, no. 4 (October 2016): 125–46.

Painter, Nell Irvin. *The History of White People.* New York: Norton, 2010.

———. *Standing at Armageddon: The United States, 1877–1919.* New York: Norton, 1987.

Papers Relating to the Foreign Relations of the United States. Washington DC: Government Printing Office, 1879.

Patterson, Sara M. *Pioneers in the Attic: Place and Memory along the Mormon Trail*. New York: Oxford University Press, 2020.

Pearsall, Sarah M. S. *Polygamy: An Early American History*. New Haven CT: Yale University Press, 2019.

Peters, Gerhard, and John T. Woolley. American Presidency Project. Accessed May 10, 2023. https://www.presidency.ucsb.edu.

Peterson, Charles S., and Brian Q. Cannon. *The Awkward State of Utah: Coming of Age in the Nation, 1896–1945*. Salt Lake City: Utah State Historical Society/ University of Utah Press, 2015.

Pisani, Donald J. *To Reclaim a Divided West: Water, Law, and Public Policy, 1848–1902*. Albuquerque: University of New Mexico Press, 1992.

Porter, Charles R. "The Hydraulic West: The History of Irrigation." In *The World of the American West*, edited by Gordon Morris Bakken, 308–53. New York: Routledge, 2011.

Post, Charles Johnson. *The Little War of Private Post: The Spanish-American War Seen Up Close*. Lincoln: University of Nebraska Press, 1999.

Powell, John Wesley. *The Arid Lands*. Edited by Wallace Stegner. Lincoln: University of Nebraska Press, 2004.

Quinn, D. Michael. "LDS Church Authority and New Plural Marriages: 1890–1904." *Dialogue: A Journal of Mormon Thought* 18, no. 1 (Spring 1985): 9–105.

———. "Plural Marriage and Mormon Fundamentalism." *Dialogue: A Journal of Mormon Thought* 31, no. 2 (Summer 1998): 1–68.

Rasmussen, Matthew Lyman. *Mormonism and the Making of a British Zion*. Salt Lake City: University of Utah Press, 2016.

Reddin, Paul. *Wild West Shows*. Urbana: University of Illinois Press, 1999.

Reeve, W. Paul. *Religion of a Different Color: Race and the Mormon Struggle for Whiteness*. New York: Oxford University Press, 2015.

Richardson, Heather Cox. *How the South Won the Civil War: Oligarchy, Democracy, and the Continuing Fight for the Soul of America*. New York: Oxford University Press, 2020.

———. *West from Appomattox: The Reconstruction of America after the Civil War*. New Haven CT: Yale University Press, 2007.

Rogers, Brent M. *Unpopular Sovereignty: Mormons and the Federal Management of Early Utah Territory*. Lincoln: University of Nebraska Press, 2017.

Roosevelt, Theodore. *The Rough Riders*. Reprint, Lincoln: University of Nebraska Press, 1998.

Ross, Michael, and Anne E. Wilson. "Constructing and Appraising Past Selves." In *Memory, Brain, and Belief*, edited by Daniel L. Schacter and Elaine Scarry, 232–33. Cambridge MA: Harvard University Press, 2000.

Rotundo, E. Anthony. *American Manhood: Transformations in Masculinity from the Revolution to the Modern Era*. New York: Basic Books, 1993.

Rowley, William D. *The Bureau of Reclamation: Origin and Growth to 1945*. Vol. 1. Denver CO: Bureau of Reclamation, U.S. Department of the Interior, 2006.

Russell, Don, ed. "Julia Cody Goodman's Memoirs of Buffalo Bill." *Kansas Historical Quarterly* 28, no. 4 (Winter 1962): 442–96.

———. *The Lives and Legends of Buffalo Bill*. Norman: University of Oklahoma Press, 1960.

Rust, Val D. "The V. T. Ranch Hotel and the Dawn of Tourism on the Kaibab Plateau." *Journal of Arizona History* 54, no. 3 (Winter 2013): 355–74.

Rydell, Robert W. *All the World's a Fair: Visions of Empire at American International Expositions, 1876–1916*. Chicago: University of Chicago Press, 1987.

Sagala, Sandra K. *Buffalo Bill on Stage*. Albuquerque: University of New Mexico Press, 2008.

———. *Buffalo Bill on the Silver Screen: The Films of William F. Cody*. Norman: University of Oklahoma Press, 2013.

Sanger, George P., ed. *Statutes at Large*. Boston: Little, Brown, 1863.

Schacter, Daniel L. *Searching for Memory: The Brain, the Mind, and the Past*. New York: Basic Books, 1996.

Schacter, Daniel L., and Elaine Scarry, eds. *Memory, Brain, and Belief*. Cambridge MA: Harvard University Press, 2000.

Seefeldt, Douglas. "Horrible Massacre of Emigrants!! The Mountain Meadows Massacre in Public Discourse." University of Nebraska–Lincoln. Accessed May 10, 2023. http://mountainmeadows.unl.edu.

Seegmiller, Robert E., ed. *Legacy of Eternal Worth: A Biographical History of the Seegmillers of North America*. Provo UT: Creative/BYU Press, 1997.

Sharp, Patrick B. "The Evolution of the West: Darwinist Visions of Race and Progress in Roosevelt and Turner." In *Darwin in Atlantic Cultures: Evolutionary Visions of Race, Gender, and Sexuality*, edited by Jeannette Eileen Jones and Patrick B. Sharp, 225–36. New York: Routledge, 2010.

Sillito, John. *B. H. Roberts: A Life in the Public Arena*. Salt Lake City: Signature Books, 2021.

Smith, Henry Nash. *Virgin Land: The American West as Symbol and Myth*. Cambridge MA: Harvard University Press, 1973.

Smith, Konden Rich. "Appropriating the Secular: Mormonism and the World's Columbian Exposition of 1893." *Journal of Mormon History* 34, no. 4 (Fall 2008): 153–80.

Smythe, William Ellsworth. *The Conquest of Arid America*. New York: Harper and Brothers, 1900.

Snyder, Lu Ann Faylor, and Phillip A. Snyder. *Post-manifesto Polygamy: The 1899–1904 Correspondence of Helen, Owen, and Avery Woodruff*. Logan: Utah State University Press, 2009.

Stenhouse, Fanny. *Exposé of Polygamy in Utah: A Lady's Life among the Mormons*. Edited by Linda Wilcox DeSimone. 1872. Reprint, Logan: Utah State University Press, 2008.

Talbot, Christine. *A Foreign Kingdom: Mormons and Polygamy in American Political Culture, 1852–1890*. Urbana: University of Illinois Press, 2013.

Taves, Ann, and Steven C. Harper. "Joseph Smith's First Vision: New Methods for the Analysis of Experience-Related Texts." *Mormon Studies Review* 3 (2016): 53–84.

Taylor, Quintard. *In Search of the Racial Frontier: African Americans in the American West, 1528–1990*. New York: Norton, 1998.

Turner, Frederick Jackson. "The Significance of the Frontier in American History." In *Annual Report of the American Historical Association for the Year 1893*, 197–228. Washington DC: Government Printing Office, 1894.

Turner, John G. *Brigham Young: Pioneer Prophet*. Cambridge MA: Belknap Press of Harvard University Press, 2012.

Twain, Mark. *Roughing It*. New York: Signet Classic, 1962.

Ulrich, Laurel Thatcher. *A House Full of Females: Plural Marriage and Women's Rights in Early Mormonism, 1835–1870*. New York: Knopf, 2017.

Utah Commission. *The Edmunds Act: Reports of the Commission, Rules, Regulations and Decisions*. Salt Lake City: Tribune, 1883.

Van Nuys, Frank. *Race, Immigrants, and Citizenship, 1890–1930*. Lawrence: University Press of Kansas, 2002.

Walker, David. *Railroading Religion: Mormons, Tourists, and the Corporate Spirit of the West*. Chapel Hill: University of North Carolina, 2019.

Walker, Ronald W., Richard E. Turley Jr., and Glen M. Leonard. *Massacre at Mountain Meadows*. New York: Oxford University Press, 2008.

Warren, Louis S. *Buffalo Bill's America: William Cody and the Wild West Show*. New York: Vintage Books, 2005.

Wasden, David J. *From Beaver to Oil: A Century in the Development of Wyoming's Big Horn Basin*. Cheyenne: Pioneer Printing and Stationery, 1973.

Webb, William E. *Buffalo Land: An Authentic Account of the Discoveries, Adventures and Mishaps of a Scientific and Sporting Party in the Wild West; with Graphic Descriptions of the Country; the Red Man, Savage and Civilized; Hunting the Buffalo, Antelope, Elk, and Wild Turkey; Etc., Etc.* Cincinnati: Hannaford, 1872.

Welch, Arthur H. *Frederick Arza Welch, Laborer in the Lord's Vineyard (1889–1954)*. N.p.: Family History, 1987.

Welch, Charles A. *History of the Big Horn Basin: With Stories of Early Days, Sketches of Pioneers and Writings of the Author*. Salt Lake City: Deseret News Press, 1940.

Wells, Junius F. [Vaux]. "The Echo Canyon War." *Contributor* 3, no. 4 (January 1882): 102–5.

West, Elliott. *The Last Indian War: The Nez Perce Story*. New York: Oxford University Press, 2009.

Wetmore, Helen Cody, and Zane Grey. *Buffalo Bill: Last of the Great Scouts*. Commemorative ed. Lincoln: University of Nebraska Press, 2003.

White, John H., Jr. "Hunting Buffalo from the Train: Buffalo, Iron Horses, and the Path toward Extinction." *Railroad History* 201 (Fall–Winter 2009): 42–49.

White, Richard. *The Republic for Which It Stands: The United States during Reconstruction and the Gilded Age, 1865–1896*. New York: Oxford University Press, 2017.

Wilkerson, Isabel. *Caste: The Origins of Our Discontents*. New York: Random House, 2020.

Winchester, Juti A. "'God Bless the Hands That Made Them Custard Pies': William F. Cody's North Rim Adventure." *Points West*, Winter 2003. https://centerofthewest.org/2017/11/17/points-west-north-rim-adventure/.

Winder, Michael K. "Theodore Roosevelt and the Mormons." *Theodore Roosevelt Association Journal* 31, no. 4 (Fall 2010): 11–19.

Worster, Donald. *Rivers of Empire: Water, Aridity, and the Growth of the American West*. New York: Oxford University Press, 1985.

Young, Ann Eliza. *Wife No. 19, or The Story of a Life in Bondage, Being a Complete Expose of Mormonism, and Revealing the Sorrows, Sacrifices and Sufferings of Women in Polygamy*. Hartford CT: Dustin, Gilman, 1875.

Index

Page numbers in italics refer to illustrations.